THE PHYSICAL FOUNDATIONS OF THE PSYCHE

THE PHYSICAL FOUNDATIONS

OF THE PSYCHE

By **CHARLES M. FAIR**

WESLEYAN UNIVERSITY PRESS

MIDDLETOWN, CONNECTICUT

Copyright © 1963 by Wesleyan University

131
F163p

Library of Congress Catalog Card Number: 63–8861
Manufactured in the United States of America
First Edition

This book is dedicated to K. P. in appreciation of much help and forbearance, and in the hope that it may justify pains so generously taken.

Acknowledgments

THE author wishes to thank the American Academy of Arts and Sciences for grants in support of this work; also Doctors Sprague, Yakovlev, Mountcastle, and Nauta, for information furnished on request; Dr. Lewis Stevenson and Miss Helen Fraser, Albany Medical College librarian, for the use of various reference works; Dr. J. M. Murray and Mr. Anthony Standen for patient moral support; and Dr. Warren McCulloch for much useful evidence and several stimulating glimpses of the intellectual *haut monde* of neurophysiology cum (or post) Von Neumann. Special thanks are due to Eleanor Klare for help in preparing the manuscript.

Author's Note

BECAUSE of the unusual reference system used in this book, I have included, for the reader's convenience, two short bibliographies. The first lists books of single or joint authorship, with title, publisher, and date; it is arranged alphabetically by author. The second covers collections of papers published in book form, these being listed alphabetically by title.

While involving some duplication, the method of referring to the literature by numbered notes has had the advantage of permitting me to enlarge on certain points made in the text and to cite additional supporting evidence without unduly complicating the main line of argument. In turn, this gives the reader the option of avoiding various minutiae if he feels so inclined. For example, a discussion of "answering-effect" mechanisms, with citations from the literature, is given in note 18, Chapter I. Data concerning rhinencephalic seizure-propagation routes and functional subdivisions of the rhinencephalon and hypothalamus are reviewed in note 25, Chapter VII, and notes 22 and 23, Chapter VIII. The journals referred to in these and other notes include many of the usual ones and are not listed separately.

Contents

	Introductory	3
SECTION I.	Motivation, Affect, the Answering-effect Principle; the Neocortical Memory-systems	13
I.	The Autonomic System and the Answering Effect	15
II.	"Type" and "Thing" Memories	25
III.	Thing Memories and Their Two Modes of "Association"	42
IV.	Memory and Cortical Structure	54
V.	The Distribution and Processing of Information in Neocortex	69
SECTION II.	Core Systems and Core-neocortical Relations	95
VI.	The Reticular System and Central Integration	97
VII.	The Limbic System	120
VIII.	*part i*. Limbic-mesencephalic and Limbic-neocortical Relations	138
VIII.	*part ii*. The Interpeduncular System; Neocortex, Rhinencephalon, and Midbrain as a Functional Unit	152
IX.	Conclusion	178
	References and Notes	195
	Bibliography	261
	Indexes	263

THE PHYSICAL FOUNDATIONS OF THE PSYCHE

Introductory

THE innate aims we identify with "instinct" appear to be that only in effect. They are not present to us in the form of clearly conscious, unlearned ideas; nor is a state of instinctive gratification identical with the satisfaction we feel when we succeed in carrying out a rationally conceived plan—though often, of course, the two coincide. Neither our instinctive urges nor the satisfactions they sometimes bring need greatly involve our conscious mental life. They may present mind with troublesome problems in planning and execution; but at the final stage of satisfaction, mind is, in a sense, a mere spectator. In the heat of sexual desire we are not aware of any intention to increase our numbers; nor does sexual gratification depend on the knowledge that we may soon do so. Besides being as often a source of worry as of enjoyment, such awareness is evidently acquired and secondary. Reproduction can, and frequently does, occur without it. Similarly, children manifest fear and a "drive" to protect themselves well in advance of any clear awareness of their mortality or of the precariousness of life in general.

Instinctive gratification, in other words, does not involve any inborn rational-conscious component, or what could be called innate ideas. Whether positive—in the form of sexual or alimentary pleasure—or negative—in the form of rage-discharge or relief from fear—it seems to be chiefly an emotional and vegetative state. We may be perfectly conscious of it, as we often are of the "drives" impelling us toward it. But the state itself is essentially idea-less reward, needing no rational element to be what it is, and successfully eluding most attempts at rational definition.

4 / THE PHYSICAL FOUNDATIONS OF THE PSYCHE

IN contrast to the brief aftermath phase of satisfaction, "drive" states such as sexual desire, hunger, or the urge to flee apparently consist of one or another form of inner (physiological) imbalance, characterized by more or less unequivocal signs. Roughly in proportion to their intensity, such states appear to cause a generalized speeding up of our mental and bodily activity, simultaneously forcing themselves on our attention as a kind of explosive restlessness or discomfort. Add to this the fact that hunger mobilizes the stomach and salivary glands, sexual longing the genitals, and fear the feet, and you have almost the whole list of clues with which "instinct" furnishes the naïve rational-conscious self.

Lacking ready-made models, we are then obliged to grope our way from the stage of appetence to that of gratification. We may be guided to some extent by the particular organs or motor mechanisms which a particular instinctive-affective state readies for action; but exactly what is required to turn intense craving into satisfaction is in no way immediately apparent to us. Instead, in the course of our lives, by experiment or imitation, or a mixture of the two, we build up a repertoire of more or less habitual actions which serve to convert desire (including negative desire, or fear) into pleasure or relief. In this way we discover what it is we crave, or rather, what acts our cravings demand of us in order temporarily to dissolve into some form of satisfaction.

It would appear that emotion plays a large part in impelling us to construct such behavioral schemes,[1] while a primary function of memory is evidently to make habitual those schemes which have proved most effective. We tend to gauge effectiveness in terms of the intensity of relief or gratification to which a particular action leads, rather than in terms of the instinctive purposes which it in fact fulfills. As it happens, gratification (effectiveness as determined by the pleasure principle) may be no index of the practical effectiveness of the behavior producing it. Some sexual practices may deeply delight us while being by their nature unlikely to result in offspring. Some of the attitudes and behavioral devices we use to ward off anxiety may have temporary value, e.g., in maintaining pride and a delusional self-esteem, while being ineffectual or downright dangerous in that, over a longer course, they may produce a degree of (actual) failure and frustration which finally augments anxiety and turns *amour-propre* into a proportionately intense self-dislike. The fundamental criteria of instinctive success or failure are, in other words, subjective, subrational, and (to that degree) fallible guides to future conduct.

Tinbergen[2] has proposed an interesting flow-sheet for instinctive actions generally. He divides them into a preliminary "variable striving" phase and a final "rigid consummatory" phase. For example, the behavior of a bird seeking prey or a place to nest is relatively fluid and individualized, in the sense that it is apparently dependent upon a variety of learned cues and so can be regarded as a resultant of the creature's present, and its related recalled, experiences. By contrast, a bird's behavior during nest-building or the kill tends to be more standardized, from which we infer that it is more innate than learned.

The implication of the foregoing, as well as of Beach's studies of sexual behavior in apes and monkeys,[3] is that the innate components of various actions serving the "purposes" of instinct may exist in the central nervous system of higher forms, ourselves included, like the parts of various mechanisms each of which can be assembled and combined synergistically with others in a number of ways. However, for each or for a given combination, there is apt to be a particular order of assembly which is optimal in that it leads either to the most profound gratification or to the most prompt relief of desire. It is essentially such an order we are striving toward in the trial-and-error organization of an adaptive act.

Beach points out that prepuberal apes and macaques will make rhythmic pelvic movements, mount other animals, masturbate, or put toys to sexual use. At maturity they then have to learn the whole sequence of acts leading up to the final spasmodic movements of intercourse, the latter evidently being unlearned and, earlier in life, unintegrated with the rest of the behavioral apparatus. He adds that this seems to be especially true of males, females either having a slight advantage in the degree of (inherited) organization of the components of sexual behavior, or else organizing those components somewhat more speedily, once maturation has begun. In temporal pattern, and in certain other respects, our own sexual coming of age is not very different, a fact difficult to reconcile with the Freudian doctrine of the Oedipus complex.[4]

According to Tinbergen, and more recently Money,[5] there is evidence for the existence of innate releasing mechanisms (IRM's) in man. These presumably serve to set off our behavioral improvisations in certain directions. The whole sequence of our actions, from the stage of incipient need or desire to that of relief or gratification, is then apt to follow the flow-sheet proposed by Tinbergen. Eating is a rather standardized activity having many motor components which appear to have subcortical (limbic and mesencephalic) representation and to show release following neopallial damage or impairment (for instance by the Klüver-Bucy procedure, in monkeys; or as a result of bilateral lemniscal section in cats). By contrast, to obtain food—or in human society, to earn one's living—may require a maximum of effort and ingenuity. The same is true of the early, or seduction, stage of courtship, vis-à-vis the final "consummatory" phase. In the former, we may show an improvisatory skill approaching brilliance; in the latter, nearing orgasm, we are apt to find ourselves borne along by automatisms, uttering cries and making movements we may have had no idea were latent in us but which, incidentally, seem to be much the same in all men. However thoroughly we may have prepared ourselves to meet them, events which frighten us or make us very angry may reduce us to quite primal forms of behavior, doing so roughly in proportion to the intensity of those emotions.

It would appear that in the course of evolution, the elements comprising the (largely innate) behavioral apparatus of lower forms have become increasingly dissociated in higher. In proportion as that has occurred, memory or conditionability, and emotion or basal motivation, have become increasingly prominent, memory serving primarily as the means by which the dissociated innate components of various instinct-serving actions come to be knit up into functional units. In general, such units—the more efficient and long-established of which we call habits—may be regarded as the end-result of compromises between external and internal necessity; or more precisely, between the "pleasure principle," apparently represented in older more basal parts of the brain, and the "reality principle," perhaps chiefly represented in the mammalian neopallium or its evolutionary precursors.

Ordinarily we distinguish emotions, drives, and motives as subgroups of the class of conative states.* While there are grounds for these distinctions, they may be somewhat misleading. To illustrate: If I have a strong motive for getting something done, I may not be conscious of any underlying emotion so long as the task in hand gives me no serious trouble. Suppose, however, I find it considerably more difficult than I had anticipated. The first result is likely to be a sharp increase in the vigor of my behavior resulting from a corresponding intensification in my "set" or determination. At this stage my motive has turned into something that might better be called a "drive." If I were to check my EEG, heart-rate, and skin color, I might find that this transition had been accompanied by a shift from a focal to a generalized pattern of cortical activation, and by sympathetic signs such as tachycardia and pallor. If asked, I would say I was now "very anxious" to get the job done, perhaps without realizing the literal truth of that phrase.

Having readjusted to the situation and redoubled my efforts, I may then show flushing and other parasympathetic signs indicating "contrecoup" or a more or less symmetrical rise in autonomic activity. Finally, if it begins to look as though I still can't accomplish what I set out to do, and if this failure is apt to entail a serious loss of face, money, or other forms of reward, I will quite probably falter or show other signs of behavioral incoherence, while beginning consciously to feel emotions such as rage, anxiety, or chagrin.

The question is whether the first stage in this sequence is fundamentally different from the final one. Isn't a motive, in fact, a relatively mild state of emotion accompanied by appropriate rational-conscious activity, it being the latter and the mildness of the state itself which prevent us from noticing that at bottom our motives are emotional? When sufficiently intensified, e.g., by

---

* Emotions may be called conative in the sense that they frequently impel us to do something even if, as in bereavement, it be unavailing and less an action than a gesture.

frustration, a motive may become a "drive"—at which point we may become quite aware of the emotional components in our behavior.[6]

Finally a "drive" which fails within a reasonable time to produce gratifying results, or which shows other signs of being hopelessly misdirected, is apt to break down. That is, our behavior is apt to become temporarily confused or paralyzed, at the same time that we begin to feel strong emotion. In this phase we are likely to become conscious of our own feeling-states to the point of preoccupation, not merely because of their intensity as such, but because our thoughts and attention have become disorganized and lost external focus, thus laying us open to this sort of distraction from within. While usually rather different from those which underlay the original motivated state, or those which may have become noticeable when the latter turned into a "drive," these final emotions have, I believe, a kind of logical continuity with their precursors. Stated another way, it seems probable that physiological studies like Lindsley's[7] would disclose that all but the most trifling or rigidly habitual forms of behavior in the higher animals and man are accompanied by signs of distinct feeling-states, even though in many cases a human subject might report no conscious awareness of them.

Characteristically, what we identify as emotions are the feelings we experience in difficult or irretrievable situations. We are apt to be most violently in love when we are least certain that the object of our passion will return it, or during the first hectic uncertain weeks of consummation. Grief and terror typically result from events which extinguish hope or which make any course of action appear futile from the outset. We feel, in short, in proportion as we can *do* nothing. Conversely, if when frustrated we unexpectedly find a course of action, even a relatively useless one, the intensity of our feelings is likely to diminish, as though a quantity of energy formerly trapped in the central nervous system in the form of diffuse excitation had become organized (e.g., into a behavioral plan) and drained off (e.g., via the pyramidal and other effector pathways).

The assumption I have gone on is that a motive may become fossilized as nearly affectless habits, which neurophysiologically take the form described by Gastaut (cf. Section II). On the other hand, as result of obstacles which prevent development of stable "reward" behavior, a motive may intensify to the point that it results in highly diffuse activity at both neocortical and subcortical levels, and in a corresponding increase in the variability of behavior, at times approaching gross functional confusion or other forms of adaptive breakdown. (E.g., variability may give way to functionally useless stereotypes, in consequence of the release of core-mechanisms of the brain from neopallial control.) States of this kind, arising either at the beginning of a behavioral sequence because of uncertainty as to how to proceed, or at the end of one because of frustration (failure to attain a state of "reward"), are emotional by definition. The emotions concerned are chiefly of the "emergency" type—anxiety, edginess, mental pain—which either anticipate or directly arise from "punishment" states, it being understood that "no-reward" equals "punishment" roughly in proportion to the intensity of the original drive.

It is also obvious that at the outset of some form of appetent behavior which has not become purely habitual, emergency emotions are apt to be mixed with feeling-states which are anticipatory of "reward" and so pleasurable. The argument which follows rests on the assumption that motives and emotions fall into these two major groups, whose physiological equivalents are the subcortical "reward" and "punishment" systems investigated by Olds and others, and the parasympathetic and sympathetic branches of the autonomic nervous system.

Granted that motivation-emotion is a kind of *primum mobile*—the element in our natures which impels us to improvise—a primary function of memory is then to preserve information relating to those improvisations which have proved most or least successful (rewarding or punishing). Since in the main it is adaptive for creatures to repeat actions which have proved successful in the basal sense defined above, and not to repeat those which have failed, it follows that our memory functions may be divisible into two major subsystems, the informational contents of one being readily available as determinants of future actions and the informational contents of the other not, except as an assortment of more or less unorganized cues serving to touch off "avoidance."

In essence, avoidance involves suppression (or Freudian repression) of forms of behavior originally associated with fear- or pain-producing experiences, and the substitution of other forms —often relatively primitive ones—serving to avert fear or pain in like circumstances in the present.

Learned avoidance thus analyzes into primary elements or, one might say, causative recollections, whose function is specifically *not* to re-create the behavior which seemingly led to fear or pain in the first instance, but rather to trigger other forms of behavior which the animal has subsequently found more successful in the same situation. Hence the tendency of memories formed in a climate of fear or pain is perhaps to remain relatively fragmentary or unsystematized and (in man, at least) inaccessible to "consciousness"—the function of repression being to make them unavailable as models for future action. Instead they are, as it were, the invisible source of secondary (subsequently elaborated) forms of behavior whose learned components, such as they may be, *do* form well-organized wholes in memory and are, as we say, conscious. This subdivision of memory-functions may, I think, have clear neurophysiological parallels principally involving the neocortical intrinsic and peri-extrinsic (e.g., Brodmann 18–19 and 22) sectors, their subcortical projection sites, and the circular interactions which can be inferred to occur between the neopallium, the secondary and tertiary olfactory systems of Pribram and Kruger,[8] and the midbrain reticular formation.

To conclude, one might regard motivation-emotion and memory as substitute functions which have gained in prominence in higher evolutionary forms in proportion as these have ceased to have an extensive repertoire of innate reactive mechanisms or ready-made habits. In such animals, the latter appear to have survived in increasingly fragmentary or disjunct form (eating automatisms, spinal autonomic and skeletal motor reflexes, etc.), an arrangement making it possible for each to be incorporated into a greater variety of behavioral schemes, and increasing the potential flexibility of behavior accordingly. It then rests with "drives," or the inner impulsion to improvise new modes of behavior, and with memory, or the faculty of retaining information relating to the most and least successful of these, to determine how large and diverse the behavioral repertoire of the individual creature shall be at maturity.

It is clear that this apparatus is not without defects, the chief being that under certain conditions (e.g., in acute emergency states) it may fail to act as a unit. However, as I will try to show later, there is an evident logic in this arrangement, and the logic works in that on the whole—indeed on the evidence—it favors survival. Because what we *call* emotion refers often to the crisis stage in which our motivated actions have failed and when, for good physiological reasons, our behavior and rational thought-processes may become still further disorganized, we incline like our nineteenth-century forebears to regard emotion as a dangerous relic or primal Enemy Within. While there is considerable justification for this view, it is probably, from a biological standpoint, mistaken. We feel in proportion as we are able to improvise in thought or action, with the curious corollary that we *must* do so—must realize our improvisatory potential—if we are not to be overtaken by the consequences of motivation unrealized—namely, emotion as a chronically recurring state in which clear, rational, external objectives are wanting, in which central nervous effector outflow is correspondingly primitivized or deficient, and in which the higher integrative processes attendant upon perception are radically impaired. Persistent "floating" emotions, usually of an emergency type, are an outstanding feature of many psychoneuroses and psychoses, as is a radical impoverishment of the effector, or improvisatory, self. Man appears to be uniquely subject to disorders of this kind; and a number of them have proved notably resistant to explanation in terms of organic causation or to cure by any means. By contrast, the lower we look on the evolutionary scale, the fainter become the signs of what we ordinarily take to be emotion. To our eyes, the ferocity of the crocodile is mechanical.* While cows down-graded in the butting order of the herd may become "neurotic," they show neither the retaliatory brilliance nor the tendency toward total adaptive collapse which men often do in a similar situation.

Although the more emotional human beings are not invariably

---

* Or in a sense, as false as his tears.

the more intelligent, we sense that, among species, those with the largest apparent capacity for diversity and nuance of feeling are likewise the most intelligent. Conversely, species which seem most nearly affectless strike us as those in which "consciousness" is most limited or dim—an intuition which, unlike many, may be correct.

The object of this book is to show how the memory-systems in human neocortex may be organized and the ways in which these may influence and be influenced by activities of the subcortical core. Chapter I has to do with the general principles according to which a given affective or "drive" state comes into being and likewise determines, with varying degrees of probability (depending upon the state concerned) those states which succeed it. Chapters II through V concern memory mechanisms and their possible cytoarchitectural and transactional substrates in the neocortex. Chapters VI through IX, comprising Section II, discuss reticulo-cortical relations, the structure and apparent functions of the rhinencephalon (i.e., the "limbic system" or secondary and tertiary olfactory systems of Pribram and Kruger), and the intersystemic relations which may chiefly be responsible for "central integration." In that section, my object has been to suggest how mid- and forebrain structures function as unit. In the course of the discussion I have cited evidence from comparative morphology which I believe may be important to an understanding of how the "higher" functions of the mammalian brain may have arisen. The fact which seems to emerge is that these functions, for instance in the brain of man, are the result of certain makeshifts or gradual structural-functional transformations whose end-product is a system by no means as physiologically harmonious, or as rational or even "adaptive" in its behavioral results, as one might wish. What I hope this analysis shows, with approximate correctness, is the set of fundamental conditions which make for the appearance of reason, more particularly in man, and which also determine its development and the eventual range of its influence.

SECTION I

Motivation, affect, the answering-effect principle; the neocortical memory-systems

CHAPTER I

The Autonomic System and the Answering Effect

THE fundamental objectives of "instinct" appear to be two—survival of the individual or social group, and survival of the species, the former depending essentially upon food-getting, aggression, and self-defense, and the latter upon reproduction and care of the young. Creature behavior is also divisible into two kinds according to the way in which it arises. The first includes those forms which arise "spontaneously"—i.e., as result of inner need. The second includes those which result from the pressure of external circumstances. The primary difference between them is that the former depend upon rhythmically recurring states such as hunger or sexual desire, whereas the latter depend upon states originating in environmental events (e.g., the appearance of an enemy) which occur on no particular schedule and often with extreme suddenness.*

Because, on the whole, external events are apt to be more diverse and ambiguous than those which arise "spontaneously," the evolutionary development of the exteroceptors and their corresponding forebrain systems has far surpassed that of the interoceptors. A second—and for this discussion a more important—consequence is that the machinery of instinctive-affective response may have gradually differentiated into two major subsystems,

---

* It does not follow, however, that the emergency responses are necessarily less "spontaneous" or more apt to occur only on cue than is behavior concerned in food-getting or sex. "Vacuum" reactions of both types have been reported for instance in starling, ducks, and ptarmigan by Lorenz and others (cf. Tinbergen, *Study of Instinct,* Oxford, 1951).

the first mediating forms of behavior which serve to satisfy inner need, and the second those which serve to avert dangers (including crises of deprivation) originating in the environment.

Behavior of the former type, which includes hunting, mating, sexual fighting, and lower-energy activities such as feeding or searching for a place to sleep, I will class under the head of normal survival activity. Behavior of the latter type, which includes fleeing or fighting off aggressors and alerting or "vigilance" responses to external events novel in kind or context, I will class under the head of emergency activity.

Neuroanatomic and neurophysiological evidence suggests that the central nervous structures corresponding to these two classes of behavior are (in the brain) the "reward" and "punishment" systems disclosed by self-stimulation studies, and (in the body) the parasympathetic and sympathetic branches of the autonomic nervous system. On the principle of parsimony, one would expect these two systems to support or complement one another so far as it is feasible for them to do so, and to be competitive only to the extent that the special functions of each make competition unavoidable. A relation of this kind appears to hold for the two branches of the autonomic system, and may be inferred to exist at the limbic level as well—notably between structures of the secondary and tertiary olfactory systems of Pribram and Kruger (see Section II below). This chapter is concerned with the autonomic system, treated as the instrumentality by which instinctive-affective states of higher nervous origin find expression in the body.

Ingram[1] states that "in the isolated spinal cord many of the autonomic mechanisms are truly capable of autonomous activity. These reflexes resemble somatic reflex circuits in many ways. . . . They appear under normal circumstances to be subject to facilitatory and inhibitory influences from higher areas. . . . There is also good evidence that these spinal circuits may be capable of projecting to higher regions, even as high as the cerebral cortex, over definite afferent pathways by which they may bring the modulating feedback influence of the higher regions into action. Separated from the higher brain, these segmental mechanisms function only for the needs of the moment. They are incapable

... in the broad sense, of maintaining homeostasis and homeokinesis of the body after the influence of the brain has been removed by spinal transection."

Ingram's view of the autonomic as a semi-independent but essentially subordinate system is indirectly borne out by Hoagland's study[2] showing that in the lizard *Anolis carolinensis* tonic immobility can be prolonged but cannot be initiated by epinephrine. It is also apparent that autonomic feedback, both neural and endocrine, may be very important in the maintenance or modification of instinctive-affective states of higher nervous origin. Karamyan, Orbeli, Wang Tai-an and Belekhova, and others in Russia[3] have shown that stimulation of the superior cervical ganglion in animals can produce "global" central nervous effects, including neocortical recruitment, presumably via the nonspecific system; and that extirpation of that ganglion (in pigeons and rabbits) results in profound changes in the electrical activity of the cortex, some evidently irreversible. These changes could not be duplicated by adrenal medullectomy. Marrazzi has shown that epinephrine is one of a group of "cerebral synaptic inhibitors" (which includes GABA, LSD-25, bufotenine, and serotonin) whose action appears to be selective for intrinsic (association) areas, and to result in some release of activity in extrinsic (prime receptor) areas.[4]

That the autonomic system figures not only in the genesis of instinctive-affective states but in their reinforcement (by feedback to higher central nervous levels) is suggested by the fact that sympathectomy, and to a lesser degree parasympathectomy, decrease the apparent fear accompanying establishment of an avoidance response in dogs, and also decrease the extinction time of such responses.[5]

Physiological textbooks commonly stress the homeostatic functions of the vegetative nervous system—reflecting Claude Bernard's dictum that "all the vital processes, varied as they are, have only one object, that of preserving constant the conditions of life in the internal environment."[6] While correct, this view is in a sense misleading.

Motivational-affective states and the behavior in which they eventuate might be regarded as a repertoire of devices by which an organism anticipates and precludes still more serious perturbations of its *milieu intérieur* resulting from external emergencies or from internal crises such as starvation or acute sexual need. As such, behavior and its central nervous states-of-origin represent a type of calculated physiological risk; they upset the smooth vegetative functioning of the organism in the interest ultimately of conserving it, and so of prolonging the life of the individual or ensuring continuation of his species.

From this standpoint, there is an important difference between emergency and normal survival (sexual, alimentary) behavior. Not only is the organism more reliably* forewarned of crises of the latter type, but the forms normal survival behavior must take, particularly in the consummatory phase, in order to be most successful, and the demands these are likely to make upon the organism, are as it were the more predictable. In contrast, external emergencies may be of any magnitude, requiring a maximal outlay of energy and a potentially infinite repertoire of behavioral devices. Since the last requirement cannot in fact be met, most creatures appear to have developed an emergency apparatus which, when activated, has two principal effects. The first is a mobilization of the organism's available energy so swift and massive that fear-states, anticipatory of damage or stress, may themselves be stresses. The second is a tendency to set aside other ongoing processes concerned in the genesis of more specialized highly articulated behavior, in favor of relatively primitive all-purpose mechanisms mediating flight or counterattack.

These differences in normal survival and emergency responses are paralleled by the familiar structural differences between the sympathetic and parasympathetic, and by physiological evidence suggesting that the former system is dominant during fear, and the latter during sexual excitement or rage[7] as well as in more passive reparative states. On the principle stated a few pages ago that the two basal motivational-affective systems "support or complement one another so far as it is feasible for them to do so," I have tentatively concluded that the sympathetic and para-

---

* I.e., interoceptive data corresponding to nascent hunger or desire are unambiguous, whereas exteroceptive data corresponding to some imminent danger are frequently not.

sympathetic systems, and their analogues at higher (midbrain, diencephalic, limbic) levels, stand in an "answering effect" relationship to one another, such that if parts of one be activated, parts of the other will respond and so participate synergically in the state then nascent. In effect, the phenomenon of *contrecoup* exemplifies the same principle, crudely and out of adaptive context. As a corollary, the secondary or supporting system will tend to (but will not necessarily) become the dominant one. That is, over periods of time dependent among other things upon the type and intensity of the primary affective-instinctive state, that state will tend to pass into one of its physiological "opposites."

The foregoing is illustrated by the tendency of inhibitory pain- or fear-states to pass into (predominantly facilitatory) states of rage, and so to give rise to correspondingly violent ragelike actions, one such being flight, another counterattack. To the extent that the emergency (now the "supporting") system remains at a high level of activity, such rebound behavior will be (a) highly energetic and accompanied by sympathetic signs (e.g., one may be "white with rage") and (b) correspondingly crude. Going downstairs in the dark, a man trips on a child's toy and barely saves himself from a bad fall. Rebounding from the spasm of fear caused by this experience, he may demolish the toy as if it had meant to hurt him. Similarly, people often multiply their troubles by kicking the chair on which they've just stubbed a toe.

Conversely, the exhaustion of primary rage or its inhibition from higher nervous levels—for instance in the light of the "reality principle" perhaps chiefly represented in functions of the neopallium—may lead to dominance of the supporting emergency system as if by default, resulting in acute depression or anxiety and, if the latter be sufficiently frequent or protracted, in visceral disorders or organic damage. Sexual excitement may similarly be followed by anxiety or an active depressive state (post-coital melancholy). In this connection it is interesting that in man ejaculation of semen and prostatic fluid appears to be controlled by sympathetic fibers of the hypogastric plexus,[8] orgasm presumably marking the point at which activity of the supporting system has come equal with, or is just about to exceed, that of the "dominant" one—in this case the sexual branch of the pleasure system and its parasympathetic equivalents. The frequently reported tendency of anxious insecure males toward premature ejaculation suggests that conditioning—in particular perhaps of the type which favors a guilty fearlike response to sex as an activity which is "dirty," socially dangerous, etc.—is capable of altering the normal balance of activity between the "pleasure" and its supporting "punishment" system so that during sexual excitement the latter reaches too high and too prompt a peak of activity, thereby cutting short the whole proceeding. Needless to add, concurrent anxiety, whatever its origins in conditioning, may have the same effect.

It does not follow, of course, that any intense motivational-affective state automatically passes into its "opposite." Nor is it true as mentioned above that the emergency system, having evolved as a principal means of dealing with threats arising in the environment, only shows primary activation on presentation of appropriate learned cues*

The concept of the answering effect proposed here is intended merely to suggest the *sequences* in which major subsystems of the CNS tend to be mobilized, for instance during onset of a particular motivational-affective state. An important feature of the answering-effect principle is the economy it appears to effect. The physiological state of rage is much the same, whether it arise directly—e.g. by intensification of pique—or indirectly on the rebound from intense fear. In other words, essentially the same synergy of the subcortical "reward" and "punishment" systems and their autonomic equivalents is involved. All that differs is the temporal order in which the components of the synergy are brought into play.

Viewed in this way, the autonomic manifestations of intense emotion and their relation to homeostasis are more understandable. To give two examples: The bradycardia which some but not all[9] species show at onset of fear might be accounted for as due to diffuse parasympathetic activation during the primary rise in sympathetic activity. The result is then a transitory

---

* See, for instance, the discussion of the orienting reflex, in Chapter II.

vagal depression of the heart rate, followed by sympathetic acceleration as the latter system reaches high or emergency levels of activity. Secondly, as mentioned in the Introductory, the tendency of powerful motives, denied behavioral expression, is to turn into what we usually identify as strong emotion, whose autonomic signs may be mixed to the point of apparent chaos. In the case of a soldier coming under fire for the first time, the fear of death—which would normally rebound into a ragelike fury of escape—may be blocked from the neocortical level by "reality principle" processes, equivalent to his awareness that if he tries to run away, he will be shot by one of his own. The net effect is to reinforce primary fear and its answering effects, and to defer the shift in dominance from the fear-punishment to the ferocity-reward system. The accompanying autonomic signs may then be highly diffuse—e.g., sympathetic sweating, pallor, tachycardia, urination, defecation, etc.

Under such circumstances our overwhelming urge to *do* something—if not to run away, then to fight, suicidal as the latter may prove—results from our intuitive awareness that only action will break this inner deadlock, or the arrest—painful by definition—of our emergency responses in the primary fear-punishment phase. Conversely, the neopallium, as *par excellence* the organ of factual prophecy, seems uniquely capable of producing such deadlocks, not merely in proportion to the lopsidedness of an animal's conditioning (e.g., in favor of emergency responses), but also in proportion to its native intelligence or gross neocortical potential. Thus man, to the degree that he clearly sees what he can *not* hope to change or accomplish, is a creature uniquely emotional and one uniquely prone to disorders of mind and body which are describable in terms of distortions of the answering effect. Similar disorders can be produced experimentally in other mammals, as Maier and others have exhaustively shown;[10] but the capacity for them evidently diminishes as we go down the evolutionary scale and seems to be nonexistent in decerebrate higher forms, including Sprague *et al.*'s bilaterally lemniscal cats, whose disorders are chiefly of the release or deficit type.[11]

That ferocity and sexuality may be represented in parts of the same subsystem—e.g. at the limbic level—is suggested by the fact that the behavioral as well as the autonomic manifestations of anger and passion are quite similar. The biting, scratching, grimacing, and involuntary cries which may occur at the height of lovemaking mimic the signs of fury and give this activity something of the air of mortal combat.[12] Tinbergen mentions that the "threat display" which some birds use to drive off rival males closely resembles their courtship display.[13] A similar dual-purpose behavioral mechanism has been observed in the scorpion (*Scorpio maurus*) by Rosin and Shulov.[14]

So far as it applies to neural processes—rather than, say, to cyclic metabolic changes in uninnervated organisms—the answering effect can be regarded as an outcome of the evolutionary process of differentiation described by Herrick.[15] Briefly, the gradual emergence of nuclei or higher nervous "centers" from primitive neuropil appears to have been accompanied by the emergence of synchronizing or timing mechanisms whose function is to organize the short-term cyclical activity of individual neurons into volley form or as crescendos of activity, the intervals between whose peaks may be on the order of seconds to hours.[16]

Secondly, in consequence of the interconnection between subsystems of the CNS, the local development of such a crescendo tends to be "answered" elsewhere and also presently to cede functional dominance to other subsystems in the manner described above. In effect, inner changes equivalent to the development of physiological need or external changes equivalent to some form of incipient emergency play upon parts of the CNS, each of which can be thought of as a variable oscillator systematically cross-coupled with a number of others. The effect of such inputs is then to establish some form of self-propagating disturbance whose major consequences are either homeostatic adjustments* or overt behavior, a usual subjective concomitant of the latter being what we call a motivated or emotional state.

In mammalian brain such longer-term "cycles" or sequences

---

* E.g., when the initial perturbation is relatively limited and involves few or no conditioned elements.

of peak-activity seem to take shape chiefly at subcortical levels and to appear in more pronounced form, as release phenomena, in consequence of neocortical dysfunction.[17]

A principal function of the neopallium then seems to be not only to elaborate behavior arising out of inner need or external emergency, but also increasingly to influence the genesis of affective-instinctive states proper—that is to say, the course taken by subcortical "answering effects" once initiated by internal or external circumstance.

To the extent that the neocortical memory-systems, described later in this section, give rise to "reality principle" processes, the function of the neopallium is to impose upon basal appetent or avoidance responses forms suitable to the organism's actual situation—suitability implying a degree of anticipation of the probable (external, objective) consequences of behavior. Memory, and the logic of the labile activities or "thought" which arise out of it, accordingly serve as an extrapolating device for predicting the results of action. Developed beyond a certain point, it is clear that neopallial "reality principle" processes might modify or suppress basal instinctive-affective activities to an unadaptive degree. In fact, however, it appears that the neocortex has evolved in such a way that this situation is highly unlikely to arise. On the contrary, the priority of basal instinctive-affective responses is, even in ourselves, only too well established. Not only do their subcortical structures-of-origin tend to be activated roughly simultaneously with those embodying "reality principle" functions; a considerable part of the neocortical apparatus itself participates automatically in these basal primary responses, and may on occasion disastrously reinforce them.

To conclude, I have suggested that behavior may be divisible into two kinds, according to whether it originates in events within or external to the organism. Secondly, I have postulated that the basal apparatus which generates motivational-affective states and accordingly determines the effector outflows giving rise to these two classes of behavior and their corresponding autonomic adjustments is the dual subcortical "reward" and "punishment" system described by Olds, Delgado, and others (cf. Section II). On the answering-effect principle, primary activation of parts of one of these systems will then evoke varying degrees of support from the other, with the corollary that as a result (e.g. of post-inhibitory rebound),[18] functional dominance will tend to pass to the latter.

In this way, physiological states (of motivation or emotion) which are identical except in regard to the temporal order in which the systems concerned are brought into play, are made to serve a variety of adaptive purposes. Or to put it another way, this arrangement has made it unnecessary for a variety of specialized forms of behavior each to have separate subcortical representation of the motivational-affective processes to which it corresponds. In the same way, the partially segmental "homeostatic" functions of the autonomic system have been adapted—and to a degree made *un*-homeostatic—so as to figure in the genesis of motivational-affective states of higher nervous origin,[19] including modification of those states by autonomic-endocrine feedback. Finally, in a given answering-effect pattern, the tendency for the supporting to become the functionally dominant system may be regarded as a mechanism guaranteeing the continual succession of fundamental "drive" states. While highly plastic in respect both of the order and duration of states comprising the day-to-day or moment-to-moment chain, such successions, it is clear, arise out of and in the longer course faithfully reflect more fundamental diurnal physiological rhythms such as those described in lower forms by Welsh.[20] Thus in an environment abnormally stabilized—in which the arhythmic occurrence of various emergencies, for example, is eliminated, and the means to various satisfactions are constantly at hand—creature behavior, our own included, readily becomes routinized. Relieved of the pressures of circumstance, our inner needs and their consequent motivational-emotional states tend to fall into a regular rhythm of recurrence whose ancestral source is the periodicity of metabolic processes generally—a periodicity adapted from the outset to the daily alternation of light and dark.

CHAPTER II

"Type" and "Thing" Memories

ONE thinks of an innate reactive mechanism as possibly consisting of a group of inherited axonal firing-orders which serve to mobilize parts of the effector apparatus when activated by sensory inputs of the required configuration. Memories, while functionally similar, owe their structure as much to experience as to inheritance; and, depending upon where in the central nervous system they are represented, may be more or less fugitive. In living forms we call lower, it is probable that little of the individual's experience is minutely or lastingly recorded since the reserves of neural tissue lying outside the main streams of afferent and efferent traffic are too small to permit such selective recording and undisturbed retention of sense-data.[1] The question is: How are these reserves organized in higher forms?

It has been known for some time that a degree of conditionability survives decortication in mammals. It is also generally agreed that the mammalian neocortex is *par excellence* the seat of detailed recollection. The deficits resulting in higher forms from functional or surgical decortication suggest that the capacity of subcortical structures to form memories or to engender activities equivalent to thought is too small to support minimal adaptive behavior. While apparently correct, the conclusion is paradoxical.

How does it happen, for instance, that the tectum and midbrain reticular formation, which appear to mediate important discriminative and integrative functions in bony fishes, amphibians,[2] and birds,[3] show little or no ability to maintain such functions, e.g., in the split-brain or bilaterally lemniscal cat?[4,5] These structures have not shown regression in higher forms; if anything the contrary.[6] The answer, I suspect, is that with progressive telencephalization in mammals, the patterns of activity of subcortical structures such as the limbic system and midbrain reticular formation have more and more come to depend upon feedback from the neocortex—that is, upon the superior "resolving" power of that system as the element crucial to their own proper functioning. This seems to be the conclusion following from some of Sperry's work[4] and from the findings of Sprague, Chambers, and Stellar.[5]

It does *not* follow, I think, that the relatively primitive memory-functions which can be inferred for various subcortical structures, e.g., the reticular "closure" of Gastaut, have ceased to be important in conditioning; nor that the regulation of behavior in primates and man is necessarily or even largely from the top down. In later chapters, I have proposed a model which pictures conditioning as a vertical process, involving trace-formation at several neuraxial levels; and I have also sought to show how attention and behavior may arise as result of circular interaction between the highly organized sense-receptor and memory systems of the neocortex, and the essentially dual motivational system of the core. A feature of the two-way relationships suggested by this model is that the thalamus and neocortex may exhibit a topographic order according to the parts of the subcortical motivational system to which their various subdivisions most nearly correspond.[7]

The important point, for the discussion in this chapter, is that the circular (subcortico-cortical) interactions which result from subcortical motivational-affective states may be a prime factor in determining what we most clearly and lastingly recall (i.e., record in neocortex). Conversely, experiences which do not evoke a certain minimum of subcortical "support" of the processes of neocortical memory-formation are perhaps not lastingly recorded. As a corollary, to the degree that neocortical "reality principle" processes act, by cortico-subcortical paths discussed below, to remold motivational-affective responses along more rational lines, the functional expansion of the neocortical memory-system itself tends to become more rational. That is, accretions to memory increasingly tend to follow a plan imitative of the relatively objective logic of external events and to constitute an interdigitated system of the kind we call knowledge.

In contrast to knowledge, conditioning consists essentially of memories established (i.e., at several levels, including the neocortical) by motivational-affective states relatively unmodified from above, and upon which "reality principle" processes have as it were only a local and incidental influence. The logic of conditioned responses is primarily that of wishes, negative or positive; and is only that of external events to the degree required by circumstance if such responses are to result in survival or (more properly) in terminal states of "reward." Similarly, the interdigitation of the miscellaneous memories comprising conditioning is less extensive and, in an intellectual sense, less logical. The logic of the unconscious, for example, is somewhat primitive by ordinary (conscious) standards. The logic of much appetent or fearful behavior, while in a sense conscious, is also apt to strike the uninvolved bystander as patently forced. From it arises the vast realm of human thought known as rationalization. The fact that that realm *is* so vast argues a stubborn primacy of the subcortical motivational system, or its common predominance in cortico-subcortical interactions. The fact that we also recognize rationalization as a form of false reason argues that, however intermittently, we can shift the balance of power in favor of the neocortex and thereby achieve a degree of realism or objectivity in our thinking. To the extent that the individual succeeds from day to day in making this shift, his additions to lasting memory will also tend to correspond to his now more "rational" or neocortically controlled motivation. Such additions will accordingly follow a logic more nearly that of external events than of native wishes or "instinct"; and that logic will be more or less consistent for a wide range of things memorized. As described in Chapter V below, it will itself tend to become an item of recall, directly controlling or shaping the activities equivalent to thought and thus exerting an important indirect influence upon subcortical activities equivalent to nascent emotions or wishes.

A prime function of memory, in other words, is to perpetuate improvised—or in a sense accidental—forms of behavior, their "objective" logic included. It makes more or less permanent those compromises between the "pleasure principle" and the "reality principle" which circumstances have forced upon the organism; and is accordingly bifunctional with respect to the processes it entrains. In evolutionary terms, the faculty of memory has developed as an adjunct to certain forms or classes of behavior, in particular those which could least successfully be prefabricated. A case in point is the wasp *Philanthus triangulum*, which has the capacity to memorize landmarks around its nest, the rest of its behavior evidently being innate.[8]

If one regards the system of connections linking the neopallium with subcortical structures—notably of the rhinencephalon and midbrain—as an arrangement favoring a struggle for *de facto* control of the central nervous system, as between neocortex and the subcortical core, it is apparent that the activity we call thought may be most important in enlarging whatever functional advantage the neopallium may have in this struggle.

Conversely, the advantage which subcortical systems have—and it is frequently a crucial one—is that via cortical projection systems discussed below they may determine, from very early on in life, *what* shall be committed to lasting recall, and in what basal groupings. A still more crucial factor is that such memories may be essentially bifunctional, subserving neopallial "reality principle" processes or thought on the one hand, and on the other acting as feedback elements which automatically reinforce subcortical motivational-affective states corresponding to those in which they are originally formed. It is this latter scheme of relationships which I shall explore here, beginning with the suggestion, made by McCulloch, that several types of memory apparatus must be supposed to exist in the central nervous system.

THE three types of memory mechanism proposed by McCulloch are 1) a short-term process dependent e.g. upon reverberatory thalamocortical circuits; 2) a process dependent upon alterations of the nerve-net with use; and 3) a storage process, by which certain of those alterations are preserved for relatively long periods or in some cases for the life of the organism.[9] A feature of the storage system is that it involves "a bottleneck both in putting in information and in taking it out."[10]

The model of neocortical memory-functions I shall propose is, in its essentials, similar to this one. It was, however, arrived at rather differently, and it specifies in somewhat more detail the neural structures and processes which may be involved in these three types of trace-maintenance.

Some years ago I was struck by the following rather common experience, which seemed to shed some light on the processes of recall. I am walking down the street, busy with my thoughts, when I unexpectedly see a friend coming toward me in the crowd. At first my eye tends to slip past him as it has past the innumerable other faces going by. As this occurs, I experience, so to speak, a wave of delayed recognition, and swing my gaze back for a second look. As a result, with a rush of surprise and something like alarm, I think, "Why, that's old So-and-so." Meantime, perhaps, he has been doing a similar "double-take"; we now rush up to one another with exclamations, greetings, expressions of amazement, etc.

There is often in this experience an element of odd momentary confusion or even embarrassment which, on analysis, seems to arise out of the fact of our having, for the first fraction of a second, misclassified someone we may know quite well. It is as though we had seen him as two different people in rapid succession—the first a mere generalized Somebody (man; passerby) and the second the particular man we know him to be. We are embarrassed, perhaps, from an awareness that if he detected it, he might be offended at our mistake—entirely overlooking the fact that he shows signs of having made a similar one himself. Hence, frequently, the overeffusiveness of both parties in this sort of encounter, expressing both relief (from momentary confusion) and apology (for a momentary mistake).

The mistake is not one in the usual sense, but simply, I believe, a consequence of the way our memories are organized. Briefly, we seem to have one apparatus subserving relatively crude, generic recognition, and a second and presumably more selective apparatus which subserves the recognition of familiar particulars. Both derive their content from previous experience, the function of memories of the former type being to "orient" us—that is, to furnish on cue a system of rough inner equivalents of our external *mise-en-scène* without any conscious effort on our part.

In the episode just described, as I walked down the street, I did not have to identify my surroundings by establishing a clear focus of perceptual attention and "casing" them, item by item. In other words, every time I go out I am not obliged consciously to resynthesize my awareness of my milieu. Given a few cues, it is simply *there,* mentally as well as in fact; and fortunately too, since we could hardly afford the time orientation would take otherwise.

This ease of orientation is, however, achieved at the cost of some imprecision in awareness, since the memories upon which it depends may be relatively crude or generalized. Since these may also (for neurophysiological reasons discussed presently) constitute the temporally prior mechanism of recognition, they readily lead us into the sort of momentary error just described.

Conversely, in states of intense anticipation, the memory apparatus upon which specific recognition depends—and which ordinarily tends to be activated, as above, some tens or hundreds of milliseconds later than corresponding parts of the memory apparatus involved in generic recognition—is selectively pre-facilitated. Not only does this close the temporal gap between "generic" and "specific" recognition when the latter occurs; it also makes us liable to errors the reverse of the one just described. When we are keenly expecting or hoping or wishing to see a friend in a crowd, we are apt momentarily to mistake a stranger for him, by a mechanism analogous to Freudian "projection." In effect, we momentarily force the comparison between an item of recall and one of immediate perception. A factor making such errors possible, not to say likely, may be inherent in the mode of organization of our perceptual processes, which is such that all primary perceptions may first reach conscious awareness as it were through a filter consisting of pre-established generalized memories subserving orientation. It is then only by subsequent attentional processes—that is, by making a quick item-by-item resurvey of the person or object just perceived—that we can establish definite match or mismatch between the person (or object), and the corresponding detailed recollection, prefacilitated by the process of anticipation.

To summarize the foregoing, it would appear that recognition of external objects is roughly a two-stage process. The first involves crude generic recognition; and the second, relatively precise or specific recognition. The former tends to be the shorter in latency, and may be inferred to depend upon memories representative not of particularities but of type-objects derived from our past experience by a process of semicontinuous sorting (i.e., of invariances from the flux of miscellaneous sensory detail).

The latter, or specific recognition, is longer in latency, often by a perceptible interval, and depends upon memories representative of particularities. These two kinds of memory I shall call "type" and "thing" memory respectively. I have supposed that the former is represented in prime receptor or neocortical extrinsic areas and the latter in posterior intrinsic sectors (see Chapters IV and V below).

"Type" memories may owe their fluid statistical character to the relatively high rate of transaction in extrinsic sectors, in particular perhaps at levels including and overlying the territory of distribution of the specific afferents.[11] Consisting of invariant or commonly occurring features automatically abstracted from the flux of daily experience, they may be regarded as resultants of the organism's past, rather than as clear-cut representatives of any special part of it. To the extent that the "invariants" of experience are not really that, "type" memories themselves exhibit continuous gradual change,[12] preserving, for instance during sleep, the whole of our apprehended environment, in the shape in which our most recent perceptual experiences have left it.

Two features of "type" memories, involving their possible mode of neocortical representation, deserve mention at this point. One is that the unit "invariances" derived from perception may be further organized into "invariant" groupings, which in turn involve intermodal "association"—e.g., via projections of the pulvinar linking temporal area 22 and parastrate 18. Data from stimulation studies suggest that such groupings of invariants in a given modality may be formed in corresponding peripheral extrinsic areas.[13] If they are, it is probable that corticothalamocortical relays play a far larger part in the process than do transcortical pathways (association and U fibers).[14] The adaptive-psychological function of such groupings is to provide the basis for quick automatic recognition on a panoramic scale. At a glance we recognize one combination of visual sense-data as "countryside," another as "city." The sight "city" (not necessarily one specifically familiar) implies corresponding sounds, and conversely. If I were to be set down blindfolded in a busy thoroughfare, what I heard would conjure up vague visual impressions of cities previously known—i.e., the sounds would pre-facilitate my visual system for sights I'd be likely to see when the blindfold was removed.

Unlike "thing" memories, "type" memories, including their larger groupings, may form or undergo revision more or less continuously, these events not being contingent upon subcortico-cortical inputs which a) exceed a theoretically specifiable normal waking-state intensity range and b) result from core activities equivalent to some form of motivational-affective "state." While the areas of neocortical representation and the potential forms of "type" memory are doubtless determined by the pattern of distribution of specific thalamocortical afferents and by the fine-structural characteristics of that system;[15] and while the rate of "type" memory formation may vary directly with reticulocortical input and the process itself be selective in proportion as perception is restricted by attentional mechanisms—nonetheless, "type" memory formation may still be significantly less intermittent and selective than is that of "thing" memories, the latter being represented, as it were, on the periphery of the neocortical specific system.

Both sorts of memory, however, may mediate learned motivational-affective responses. (In the case of "type" memories, these may involve the "strip" regions discussed in Chapter VIII.) However, a peculiar feature of the motivational core-systems is that at high levels of activity, they may enhance neocortical primary receptor activity (and so "type" memory formation) while in varying degrees disorganizing activity in "peripheral" areas (e.g., the posterior intrinsic; see Section II, *passim*). Thus while old "thing" memories may be reactivated or new ones form during the onset and die-away phase of an intense motivational-affective state, there may also be a period of peak-intensity during which neocortical functions mediated by the "thing" memory apparatus are radically disrupted. In these periods processes such as perceptual discrimination may become largely dependent upon the "type" memory systems.

This second feature of "type" memories—namely, that on occasion they may become the principal determinants of informed behavior—coupled with the fact that they represent statistical rather than highly particularized residues of experience, may account for the tendency toward stimulus generalization which primary fear states or normal survival states such as rage (involving intense supporting action of the emergency system) often seem to entail. A given memory, either "type" or "thing," I have conceived as consisting of a mosaic of probably discontiguous components synchronously or serially activated—each being comparable to a Mountcastle (specific) "vertical column" and/or a nonspecific column of the kind described by the Scheibels.[16] Within each column there are relatively invariant preformed* components (axonal firing-orders) and relatively labile or transient components, which jointly determine its output.

In the case of extrinsic and peri-extrinsic sectors, the invariant components are equivalent to "type" memories; and the labile components, to the details of present perception not yet incorporated into, or it may be not congruent with, existing memory-formations. If sufficiently maintained (e.g., by sensory input over a period of time), such noncongruent components may lead either to the modification of existing "type" memories or to formation of new ones, a process likely by its nature to take longer than activation of already established memories.[17] It is consequently the new or unexpected features of an external situation which cause those surpluses as it were of unchanneled central nervous excitation, often subjectively felt as such, which accompany otherwise indifferent or ambiguous perceptual experiences.

---

* I.e., by earlier inputs or experience.

To the extent that cortico-subcortical outflow becomes diffuse or disorganized as result, some subcortical release and intensification of nonspecific input may then occur. (See Chapter VI, p. 104.) Within limits, in other words, this phenomenon is self-augmenting, tending to result in general cortical desynchronization of varying durations dependent (for otherwise "neutral" stimuli) upon the degree of noncongruence of a given input with pre-existing neocortical memory-formations. Such noncongruence effects may involve "thing" as well as "type" memory-systems,* the fundamental plan of organization of both being quite similar (Chapter V).

The phenomenon just described is sometimes called the "orienting reflex," and Sokolov[18] has proposed a similar explanation for it. That explanation has an obvious and interesting consequence. It predicts that if one were to take two groups of animal young from the same species, or preferably from the same litter, and artificially restrict functional development of "type" and "thing" memory-systems in one group by early sensory deprivation, the animals in this group should later show tendencies toward excitability and rudimentary ill-adapted actions sharply distinguishing them from the controls. This prediction is borne out by the work of Thompson and Melzack with Scotties.[19] Ptarmigan appear to learn the alarm call from the mother, which thereafter serves as an important "releaser" of escape behavior. Krätzig found that young ptarmigan, raised in isolation, did not later show this normal response but "developed an increasing tendency to show frantic flight responses at the least disturbance (e.g., a wasp) or even without any discernible external stimulus."[20] I would interpret these results as in part due to a defect in informed feedback control of reticular "arousal" responses.

No experiment has yet been devised which tells us unequivocally what the neural equivalents of a memory are. However,

---

* For instance, one is sometimes startled and momentarily disoriented on discovering new or previously unnoticed features in a person, object, or idea one had thought perfectly familiar, a part of this reaction being pre-rational and physiologically preparatory to changes in "outlook."

hibernating hamsters can be cooled to the point (40° F) that their brains are electrically silent without loss of memories formed previously, and that fact has been interpreted by Gerard to mean that memory does not depend upon continuously maintained reverberatory circuits, but probably does depend upon some form of preferential path- or engram-formation.[21] The engram theory of memory has been criticized by Pribram[22] among others, on the ground that it would require neural aggregates even larger than those of actual brains to produce the memory-capacity which brains in fact have. This objection may not hold, however, for two reasons. One is that a mathematical approach to the problem, such as Mackay and McCulloch's,[23] suggests that the limiting information capacity of a synapse is sufficiently large to account for the actual memory capacity of human brains having a total neuron population on the order of 5×10^9 to 10^{10}.[24] The second is that, according to the view of memory-structure proposed here, components of any given "type" or "thing" memory may be held in common with, or partially constitute, an indefinite number of others. Thus an engram, the structural equivalent of a memory, is not also a locus but more likely a mosaic of n "modality pure" Mountcastle columns[16] or their intrinsic sector homologues, whose temporal order of activation may be as important to the specificity of the memory concerned as are the number and spatial configuration of the vertical columns which go to make it up. This view may be less at odds with Penfield's data than might appear.[25]

The psychological doctrine of associationism and the neurophysiological notion of the transcortical reflex both seemed to imply that memories were built up by a kind of convergence mechanism, the miscellaneous sense-data or "bits" comprising a given memory-to-be being relayed from primary receptor areas to some focus, for instance in Flechsig's terminal zones. However, if one assumes that close cortical grouping of its components is an essential feature of a given memory, the number of other memories which the same components may go to comprise is thereby automatically limited. Given the number of neurons apparently available for the purpose, it then becomes difficult to see how we can form the number of highly specific memories or engrams which we do. Moreover, stepwise removal of cortex, especially in intrinsic sectors, should theoretically result in an item-by-item reduction of the contents of memory; whereas in fact the deficits resulting from various forms of neocortical damage or ablation follow no such simple plan.[26]

The anatomical studies of Lorente de Nó and Sholl,[27] as well as the work of the Scheibels and Mountcastle (see above), suggest that the fundamental mode of action of neocortex is vertical. Consequently, vertical (e.g., cortico-thalamocortical) interactions may largely determine what local cortical elements are activated, and in what order, under given input conditions.

The essential function of callosal[28] and of the longer association fibers[29] is doubtless to relay patterns of inhibition and facilitation which tend to duplicate a given "firing-order" either at corresponding sites in the opposite hemisphere or (in the case of association fibers) at cortical sites in systems functionally distinct from the one of origin. Mountcastle's work suggests that the principal role of local intragriseal spread, or of intracortical fibers distributing within a radius of roughly .5 to 1 mm from their sites of origin,[30] may be to produce primary circumjacent inhibition, the tendency of which will then be to give rise, by post-inhibitory rebound, to a succession of local "answering effects" whose psychic equivalent is roughly the continuous flow of thought, impression, and motor impulse which occurs in us, even in quite static environments (but not wholly static, as sensory deprivation studies seem to show) and in our least-motivated waking states.

A further and most important mode of intracortical communication is provided by the plexiform layer, one of whose functions, as of dendritic networks generally, may be to favor a degree of fluidity or potential diversity in the patterning of axonal activity of those parts of the cortical neuronal population it most directly affects.

The basic assumptions as to memory which I have made here are: first, that the ultimate components of a memory are represented by the most determinate or strictly conditional functions of nerve, namely the all-or-none discharge; secondly, that particular spatio-temporal patterns of axonal discharge tend to perpetuate themselves by synaptic and possibly molecular structural changes[17] in the neurons concerned; and thirdly, that a given memory tends to be represented in the form of mosaics of vertical columns, with the corollary that each of these columnar components may be held in common with a variety of other memories or go to comprise a number of other such mosaics.

Finally, for reasons discussed at length below (Chapter IV, "Memory and Cortical Structure"), I have tentatively concluded that these relatively invariant axonal firing-orders tend preferentially to form in the lower strata of many neocortical sectors and in certain strata in all sectors.

In the case of "type" memories, this implies that a given sense-perception will activate a mosaic of n "vertical columns" each with its preformed relatively invariant component and its labile or "circumstantial" component. To the degree that these two do not coincide in form and that the circumstantial component (or "new" sensory experience) is reinforced, e.g., by prolonged exposure to the stimulus, some alteration of the invariant component will then tend to occur. In other words, pre-established axonal firing-orders in the n columns comprising the mosaic will undergo some change; and will then retain this new form until further revised by sensory inputs as just described. I have supposed that it is in this way that the "type" memories, comprising our apparatus of automatic generic recognition, are continually updated.

Similarly, because communication between cortical layers within a given column is probably prompt and continuous, and because incoming sense-perceptions are probably relayed from the thalamus according to the previously established thalamic firing-orders to which they most closely correspond,[15] there is, as it were, an automatic and sometimes deceptive memory element in all that we perceive—the more so, perhaps, the older we grow. According to Mountcastle,[16] there may be a latency of no more than 2–4 msec between activation, e.g., at the level of the plexus of the specific afferents, and activation elsewhere in the column. Activation of layers embodying the invariant or "type" memory components of a perception might subsequently serve to falsify perception by setting aside "new" patterns of upper-layer activity in favor of old.* From this arrangement may arise our strong tendency to see the unfamiliar in the light of the known, and with it what might be called an analogical reflex in our use of language. A strange object in the sky becomes, by quick forced comparison, a "flying saucer." Moreover, the briefer or more cursory our examination of some new phenomenon, the more prone we are to such misleading comparisons.†

As suggested earlier, however, the mechanism of the orienting reflex militates against this sort of stereotyping and falsification of primary perception. In proportion as we perceive something radically new with some clarity, it serves to establish at certain levels in n vertical columns neuronal action-patterns whose form shows but little coincidence with pre-established firing-orders at other levels. The result may then be a degree of diffuseness or loss of definition in the output of these columns, both to other cortical areas and to subcortcial structures. The latter may in turn show corresponding release from normal waking neocortical control, one consequence of which is a prompt rise in nonspecific neocortical input, and a further increase in labile cortical activity. Manifested in the EEG as a generalized desynchronization, this condition can be conceived as one favoring the dissolution of old and the formation of new axonal firing-orders, e.g., in the n vertical columns originally concerned. Given constancy of the "new" stimulus over a sufficient interval, this reorganization of "invariant" or memory components will then serve to unify action-patterns within each of the n vertical columns, and so in effect reorganize subcortical output of the group. Neurophysiologically, neocortical control over subcortical structures is perhaps in this way restored and the orienting reflex extinguished. Psychologically, the organism has "adjusted" or reintegrated its responses to a novel situation. (Cf. Whitehorn, "Introductory," Note 1, on the reintegrative functions of the "acute emotional experience.")

---

* I.e., ongoing neocortical activity chiefly arising out of pre-established patterns may on occasion effectually block the entry and further influence of new data.

† And from fear of the disturbing effects of novelty, we often seem deliberately to make them, averting our gaze from the new even as we start "explaining" it.

It is an interesting and as yet poorly understood fact that novel events, even those which can in no rational way be interpreted as threatening, tend to stir up a degree of apprehension in us. In other words, in the sequence just described, it is primarily the subcortical emergency system which is released. The primary response of that system will be proportioned to stimulus-intensity while its release will perhaps be proportioned to stimulus-novelty. The biological rationale of this arrangement appears to be that the organism's safest course is to respond to all unfamiliar sensory experiences as though these were potential dangers.

It is clear also that "reverberatory" processes, or a type of internal reinforcement of primary sense-data proportional to (among other things) the latter's novelty, may serve to maintain the labile or as-yet-not-memorized fractions of a given perception over a period of minutes or hours following presentation of the stimulus. In Scoville and Milner's patients,[31] bilateral removal of the anterior two-thirds of the hippocampus seems to have broken a circuit vital to the maintenance of newly formed sensory-impressions in neocortex (cf. Section II), with the result that these or the memory of particulars-just-perceived die out in five to ten minutes if unreinforced from without. This finding perhaps gives us a measure of the half-life of axonal firing-orders formed, e.g., in the external lamina of extrinsic cortex, when maintenance of these is made dependent upon thalamocortical "reverberatory circuits" alone. In dying out, such transitory action-patterns presumably effect some change in "invariant" firing-orders of extrinsic cortex. This amounts to saying that "type" memory functions, or orientative responses dependent upon generic recognition, may not be seriously impaired in these patients. In this connection, it would be interesting to know if they can orient in a general way to novel environments, or show nearly the same adaptive changes in "type" memory as normals do. If so, this fact would underscore the point made above—namely, that "type" memories are too crude to constitute knowledge or to give rise to recollection in the full sense of the word.

In normal adults, the usual half-life of "traces" (i.e., of sense-perceptions we have no motive for committing to more lasting recall) has been estimated[23] at half a day, which gives us

40 / THE PHYSICAL FOUNDATIONS OF THE PSYCHE

a measure of the relative importance of subcorticocortical, as contrasted to thalamocortical* interaction in the maintenance of newly formed neocortical action-patterns. As proposed in the following chapter, intensification of such subcortical support, equivalent to the onset of some motivational-affective state, may lead to formation of more lasting, detailed "traces" ("thing" memories) in sectors lying outside the primary analyzer apparatus, or Bailey and Von Bonin's konio- and parakoniocortex (see Chapter IV).

To return to McCulloch's three types of memory mentioned on page 28 above, I would qualify his scheme with the suggestion that those "traces" which are maintained by reverberatory circuits are not wholly fugitive. Rather, they may, as they die out, cause some change in the relatively invariant firing-orders in the n columns concerned. Thus McCulloch's second form of memory, dependent upon structural alterations in the nerve-net, tends, especially in koniocortical and adjacent (parakoniocortical) areas, to be continually revised by the more transient action-patterns comprising his first form. The two are, in other words, not separable but should be regarded as forming a functional unit, whose structural equivalents may be distributed in the external and internal laminae of a Mountcastle vertical column, as described in Chapters IV and V below.

"Type" memories, then, are equivalent to McCulloch's second form of memory; they are perhaps chiefly represented in specific projection areas and immediately surrounding cortex (e.g., 18–19 and 22), and may serve to embody the organism's sensory experience as it were cumulatively in the shape of relatively crude and continually revised type-objects. The biological value of the columnar apparatus just described is that it preserves not only a record of the statistical "invariants" of sensory experience (as "type" memories) but also, more transiently, a number of its atypical particulars. It thus exerts a holding action on the continuous flux of our sense-impressions, enforcing a brief

---

* The thalamus is, of course, a subcortical structure, but it is also so involved in activity of the neocortex proper that I have here and elsewhere distinguished it from other subcortical systems.

automatic suspension of judgment as to which of these may be important and which may not. It acts as if on the premise that all may be, leaving it to later experience to determine which are actually so, and to the motivational and "thing" memory apparatus to make more detailed records of certain of those.

CHAPTER III

Thing Memories and Their Two Modes of "Association"

DESPITE functional similarities between orbital and anterior temporal cortex, much evidence suggests that frontal intrinsic sector functions differ in certain fundamental respects from those of posterior intrinsic sectors. The frontal intrinsic system will not be considered in this section.

The distinctive feature of thing memories—in particular, perhaps, those formed in posterior intrinsic areas lying outside the territories of distribution of the pulvinar and *lateralis posterior*[1]—is that their frequency of formation and their rates of change once formed, may be far lower than those of type memories. Moreover, this difference is perhaps not merely a graded one, such that in consequence of sensory inputs, thing memories, like type, form automatically but at a somewhat slower rate, owing, e.g., to the longer latency of the projection-systems concerned and the nature of the synaptic junctions these make in intrinsic cortex.[2] The basic assumption I have made here is that special subcortical conditions, equivalent to a motivational-affective state exceeding a certain threshold intensity,* are required for thing memories to form at all.[3] Rises above this hypothetical threshold of subcortical activity, I have supposed to be manifested in neocortex in the form of rises in nonspecific input above the normal waking resting-state range, the probability of thing memory, or "permanent" engram-formation being a function of the extent and duration of such rises.[3]

The same conditions necessary to the formation of thing

---

* I.e., one or another of those comprising the organism's repertoire.

Thing Memories and Their "Association" / 43

memories may also be necessary to their "retrieval" or later reactivation, with the qualification that the latter process may require considerably less subcortical support than the former. Psychologically, this amounts to saying that we tend lastingly to recall those particularities most closely connected in our experience with our most intensely motivated or emotional states. Conversely, the course of our reminiscence or the promptitude of our (specific) recognition of such particularities is apt to be determined by the type and intensity of motives or emotions prevailing in us at the time.

Thing memories correspond to McCulloch's third, or permanent storage, system; while the subcortical conditions necessary to their formation or their subsequent retrieval constitute the "bottleneck" in putting information into, and taking it out of, that system (see page 28 above).

A basic difference, in other words, between extrinsic and posterior intrinsic cortex, may be that inputs into the latter are subject to a far greater degree of subcortical "gating." The psychological consequence of this arrangement is that we lastingly record only a small, or relatively highly motivated, fraction of the ten or so "photos" per second which our brains are reportedly able to take.[4]

While the memories formed in this way are not necessarily, in a strict logical sense, relevant to their motives of origin, they are at least sufficiently so for this sort of memory apparatus to have proved adaptive, and indeed to have shown a steady enlargement in the course of mammalian evolution. The direct effect of the subcortical gating of posterior intrinsic sector input is to permit the organism to build up a repertoire of "photos" of adaptively important occasions. Since, in addition, this process tends to be restricted or given focus by the mechanism of attention, discussed in later chapters, the result is that the information either recorded in the thing memory system or on later occasions retrieved from it, is on the whole of high probable relevance to the animal's concurrent basal states (of appetence or aversion) and their related behavior.

A most important effect of this restriction of posterior intrinsic sector input is that it favors the "intrinsic" recombinative

44 / THE PHYSICAL FOUNDATIONS OF THE PSYCHE

activities of neocortex described below (p. 84) chiefly because it acts to prevent that erosion of detail* which may be one consequence of the high rates of input into extrinsic sectors and give type memories their generalized character.

Scoville and Milner's finding (Chapter II, note 31) suggests that a subcortical structure crucially responsible for the gating of neocortical inputs in such a way as to favor these results is very probably the hippocampus.

Like type memories, thing memories can be conceived as consisting of relatively invariant axonal firing-orders chiefly represented at certain cortical levels in mosaics of posterior intrinsic sector vertical columns. In posterior intrinsic cortex not receiving fibers of the association nuclei, such columns are presumably of the nonspecific type described by the Scheibels.[5] There is some evidence[6] indicating that these columns individually may be "modality pure," like Mountcastle's (post-central cortex; cat), even though the mosaics they go to comprise may include columns not all representative of the same modality and may constitute thing memories, in this sense, mixed. Finally, that the columns comprising such mosaics may in general be dispersed is suggested by the report that in man large portions of the temporal lobes can be destroyed without loss of particular memories.[7]

A further consequence of the scheme of functional relationships just proposed is that our thing memories tend to be "associated" or to form into constellations not according to factual (structural) features they hold in common, but according to their common motivational-affective states of origin. In other words, as result of the fortuities of experience, the thing memories comprising the organism's repertoire of maximally differentiated CS's (recollections facilitating learned responses) fall into functional groups, according to those parts of the subcortical

---

* The repeated superimposition of sense-data conforming in basic pattern, but not in particulars, with an already established type-memory or group of extrinsic sector firing-orders, I have supposed results in an averaging out of such particulars, what survives being certain essential features or basic prototypes of sensory experience and (in peri-extrinsic cortex) certain of the most commonly experienced spatial and/or temporal groupings of these.

emergency and/or "normal survival" systems to which they happen to correspond.

It is a commonplace of our experience that recollective processes form a spectrum, roughly from least "voluntary" and systematic to most. When we are most active and alert, we strive, and are frequently able, to call to mind those items of fact relevant to what we are doing or thinking. To the degree that we consistently succeed, the sort of recollection involved can be called systematic. The fact that we are capable, even for a relatively small portion of our waking lives, of this type of remembering argues that our thing memories are constellated or associately interconnected, according to two somewhat different plans.

Under the first plan, already discussed, they fall into groups, the only common feature of the recalled facts comprising each being their particular motivational-affective state of origin. Moreover, activation of others of *other* groups occurs as much by a kind of emotional progression as in virtue of any logical connection between the former memories and the latter. Sequences of recollection of this type are relatively *in*voluntary, often occurring during fatigue (as result of the relative subsidence of neocortical activity) or during intense motivational-affective states (in which neocortical activities proper may be more or less set aside in favor of subcortical answering-effect trains and their neocortical consequences). Such trains of "emotional" remembering—especially when the emotions concerned are intense—often serve as the basis of arguments or actions which are neither quite voluntary nor to a disinterested bystander particularly logical. Typically, we sense them as arising out of the primordial non-self or Id (which the core-systems by implication constitute); and to preserve our *amour-propre* as ideally self-determined creatures we frequently devote much energy, then or later, to giving such actions or arguments an appearance of logical consistency (i.e., to rationalizing them). As we do so we may be humiliated by an awareness that that activity is itself not only a waste of time but a further victory of the non-self over the supposedly rational self-determined one. The situation as a whole can perhaps be described as one in which "pleasure principle" processes of the core have effectually taken precedence over (and accordingly diminished the realism of) "reality principle" processes of the outer mantle.

In neurophysiological terms, to repeat, local processes or answering-effect trains at the limbic* and midbrain levels are here exerting a decisive influence upon activities intrinsic to neocortex proper, the latter system in effect ceding functional dominance to the former. These subcortical answering effect trains, describable as higher nervous homologues of Sherrington's successive spinal induction,[8] correspond to the "emotional progression" mentioned above, or roughly to the flux of feeling-states which determines the course of idle reminiscence. We often seem to slip into remembering of this sort at the end of a day, when not yet fatigued quite to the point of drowsiness or incoherence. In this condition, for metabolic reasons, the energy or as it were continuity of intrinsic neocortical activity, and very possibly the continuity and effectiveness of hippocampal "gating" (of nonspecific input) are somewhat diminished[9] and dominance passes by default to the core. The result is then a rambling kind of recollection in which scenes from our past present themselves and fade one into another like images on a movie screen, perhaps eliciting a few momentary thoughts as they do so (i.e., evoking some degree of "intrinsic" neocortical activity, though the latter is not usually sufficient in scope or duration to constitute what we call a *train* of thought or thinking in the full sense).

For reasons given in Chapter IV thing memories have been postulated to correspond to axonal firing-orders represented at the level of V–VI, or the internal lamina. We might then imagine the neocortical activities corresponding to the mental state just described as being largely determined at the level of the internal lamina in the n vertical columns concerned, or as proceeding chiefly from the bottom of the cortex up.

---

* "Limbic system" here is used interchangeably with the term "rhinencephalon" to refer to the structures comprising the secondary and tertiary olfactory systems of Pribram and Kruger (see Introductory, note 8).

The second form of associational recall depends upon structural or, so to speak, objective relational features which serve as the nexus between the first item of recollection or immediate perception, and the other items of recollection then comprising the chain, it being understood that with extension of the chain the nexus determinative of components-to-follow may itself change. This form of recall I have supposed to be characteristic of "intrinsic" processes of neocortex (not to be confused with the special neurological meaning of the term intrinsic), the essential function of the labile activities equivalent to thought being to determine the sequence of logical connectors, which sequence in turn determines the course of remembering. In each instance, the choice of such connectors can be conceived as the outcome of a decisive statistical bias in favor of the activation of *this* pattern as against those others, which bias itself reflects the underlying memory-structures out of which this more labile or transiently patterned activity arises. The foregoing is no more than a restatement of the truism that the individual's recalled past experience—including his recalled *interpretations* of experience—is a fundamental determinant of the content and logical trend of his thought-processes in the present.

The fact that the miscellaneous contents of memory are associatively cross-linked according to a variety of objective relations previously inferred or observed to exist between them is illustrated not merely by many of the techniques of mnemonics (see *infra*, note 10.) but by the structure language itself, upon which many such techniques depend.

Grammar, as is well known, embodies a set of theorems as to relations among things named. The memories corresponding to these theorems can be viewed as statistical constructions which have come into being in consequence of repeated experience, e.g., of the conjunction of certain events or classes of them (A implies B), according to certain classes of relationship evidently existing between them (A precludes B, enhances B; certain parameters of A produce this effect on B, others that, etc.). Repeated experience of circular forms, as embodied in highly different objects or contexts of occurrence, leads to the construct "circularity" which is thereafter one among many abstract structural features serving *qua* memory to interconnect present items of perception or recollection with other items of recall.

For obvious reasons, I have called memories of this type, directive of the sequences of more specific recall, "abstract" memories. By implication—and perhaps also, as I will try to show, in literal fact—they constitute an overlying or "meta-informational" system,[10] and are transitional in stability between thing memories proper of the internal lamina and the maximally labile action-patterns of the outermost layers (i.e., they are type-like memory-formations of the external lamina in posterior intrinsic cortex).

Unlike thing memories which, early in the life of the organism, begin to form largely in consequence of activities occurring elsewhere (i.e., subcortically), abstract memories may subsequently take shape as result of the interaction between thing memory-formations and labile "thought" activities of neocortex proper. They can thus be regarded as the form in which the most successful, or at any rate most frequently repeated, of the latter are perpetuated, so as to act in future as sources of preformed or relatively automatic "thoughts" themselves. They are, one might say, the form in which our most successful or repeatedly confirmed inferences as to the relations existing between real things, people, events, etc. have become frozen. However, their mode of neocortical representation, discussed below, may be such that they exhibit rates of change, or a structural plasticity, which thing memories do not. This distinction corresponds to our subjective experience of ideas, even long-entertained ones, as comparatively fluid or fugitive mental constructions, the most permanent or habitual of which remain subject to further change and whose more transitory, or less thoroughly reinforced, forms are hardly distinguishable from the wholly fugitive constructions we call thought.

In contrast, our recollections of particularities constitute comparatively enduring mental objects acquired more or less willy-nilly under the *duresse* of events and of the motivational-affective states in part arising from and in part producing these. Such memories, more especially when acquired at some early critical period, may retain their emotional "meanings" indefinitely. To

Thing Memories and Their "Association" / 49

the extent, one might add, that they do so and are in this sense incapable of "extinction," one of the basic assumptions of psychoanalysis may be founded upon a neurophysiological misconception.[11] Of themselves, thing memories do not embody rational meanings or what might be termed ideas. They represent merely certain conjunctions of fact (sense-data) constituting more or less complete episodes whose original temporal order of occurrence tends severally to be conserved but which may *not* be conserved for sequences of such episodes. That is, we remember given episodes forward, not backward, in time, but may forget which of several preceded which in our experience.

It is then through intrinsic activities of neocortex, leading to the elaboration of overlying abstract memory-systems, that these basal memories, which originate in activities extrinsic to cortex, come to be interlinked according to a second associational system which confers upon them, or *is,* their various rational meanings. In maturation, the elaboration of this "meta-informational" system is of necessity a late development, preceded, e.g., in the infancy and early formative years of the organism by the gradual adventitious accumulation of thing memories comprising its "conditioning." The former or abstract memory system, I have supposed, mediates neocortical activities which proceed chiefly from the top of the cortex down and correspond to Freud's secondary or "reality principle" processes. The latter (or conditioning) mediates neocortical activities which proceed chiefly from the bottom of cortex up and correspond to Freud's primary or "pleasure principle" processes (however, see page 54).

To the degree that activities from the top down effectually predominate—that is, determine the pattern of intracortical communication via cortico-thalamo-cortical circuits, the plexiform layer and the association fiber systems—the sequence and intensity of subcortical motivational-affective states will tend to be modified or redirected by "reality principle" processes as result of corresponding cortico-subcortical outputs. The behavioral result will then be actions more obedient to the inferred logic of external events than expressive of creature "wishes" (whose chief concession to immediate reality consists in those automatic modifications imposed upon them by previous experience in the shape of "conditioning"). The essential difference, in other words, between conditioned adaptive behavior and behavior which is truly rational is that the latter is apt to have a fluidity or capacity for continuous moment-to-moment change, e.g., in response to external events, which the former does not. Conditioned behavior, by contrast, persists as habit so long as it results in terminal "reward" states; is succeeded by periods of behavioral incoherence or "variability"[12] when it begins consistently to fail; and then—thanks perhaps to episodic (in the sense of being relatively confined both in continuity or duration and in neocortical extent) intrinsic activities of neocortex—becomes reorganized into some more reliably rewarding form. As compared to many of the actions arising directly out of conscious reasoning, it shows a high degree of inertia, or a greater tendency to recur in situations to which it is, in fact, not suited.

The foregoing gives us a clue as to the evolutionary origins of the "meta-informational" or abstract memory system in man. In primitive, relatively limited pallial systems, outer laminar activities perhaps have a minor recombinative function serving to inflect or slightly alter final effector outflows. In allocortex, these recombinative activities are conceivable as resultants of sensory (olfactory) inputs via the tangential layer[13] and of those underlying memory-formations concurrently activated from motivational systems of the core.

With the appearance of nonspecific nonolfactory reptilian cortex, an improvement in this arrangement occurs in that outer laminar cortical activity is now no longer so directly stimulus-bound (dominated by sensory inputs in one modality). In cortex of this type, both memory formation proper, and the labile recombinative activities arising on a given occasion from diverse sensory inputs and from the selective activation of memories already in being, are largely dependent upon a projection system homologous to the nonspecific and extrathalamic (reticulocortical) projection systems in mammals. Since that system appears to project heavily to the tangential layer in reptilian neocortex,[14] it can be inferred that on any given occasion the core-systems to a considerable extent determine the duration and also, probably, the general cortical locale of such recombinative activities. One might further suspect that these are episodic, depending upon some gradation of Whitehorn's "acute emotional episode" (rises above normal waking levels of nonspecific input), to occur at all. They may thus remain more or less strictly dependent upon the same subcortical processes which result in cortical memory-formation.

In mammals a still greater improvement occurs, in that the addition of the specific thalamic projection system, including intrathalamic pathways between various new and old nuclear groups, may make available to generalized eulaminate cortex an influx of precise information largely lacking in premammalian forms.[15] True, core-control remains, in the shape of subcortical gating of that influx (and likewise in the shape of nonspecific projections, e.g., to the plexiform layer of association cortex). However, the accumulation of relatively well-articulated memory-formations resulting in this way, when combined with the semi-continuous neocortical activity maintained in the waking state by tonic (midbrain) nonspecific input, leads to a considerable increase in the patterning of that activity and so in the intrinsic recombinative powers of neocortex. With this there begins what might be called an escaping tendency in that system—a tendency to show surpluses of activity whose trend is irrelevant or even contrary to the motives or fundamental biological purposes of the organism and which increasingly expresses itself, in higher forms, as curiosity.

This tendency presumably increases in proportion as the neopallium gains both in absolute extent and in relative extent vis-à-vis structures of the extrapyramidal system, rhinencephalon and midbrain.[16] Of particular significance is the expansion of areas of generalized eulaminate cortex which has occurred in man.[17] That expansion, dramatically illustrated in the frontispiece of Bailey and Von Bonin's monograph on human isocortex (Chapter II, note 37), has been such as to dwarf the koniose and para-koniocortical receptor apparatus, here postulated to be concerned in the elaboration of type memories of several orders of complexity.

The effect of that expansion has perhaps been to bring into

semicontinuous being a system definable as consequent to the virtual unification of neocortical activities according to the "reality principle," and taking shape, during the life of the individual, as result of the elaboration of overlying abstract memory-systems, representative of those labile intrinsic neocortical activities most accurately imitative of various relations holding between people, objects, events, etc.—and hence most frequently reinforced or reconfirmed by experience. As I will try to show presently, the structural features of generalized eulaminate cortex most important in this connection may be the concentrations of large pyramids commonly found in IIIc and upper V, and the arrangement of the granular layers in relation to these.

In pre-human creatures, similar labile neocortical activities—imitative, so to speak, of the motions of reality—undoubtedly occur and are perhaps also selectively conserved *qua* abstract memories. The crucial factor here may be the neuronal power or gross action-potential of neocortex relative to that of structures of the core.* So long, that is, as the latter account for more than a certain percentage of the total activity of the central nervous system, the neocortex remains a subcortical dependency, its "reality principle" processes following a course largely determined from below and tending therefore to remain episodic and as it were compartmented. Each such process may involve a relatively small part of the cortical apparatus over relatively short intervals, and consequently embody a logic of special cases.

Subcortico-cortical input guarantees that all of the special cases so represented shall in some way concern the organism's fundamental motives, and moreover automatically sets a term to local "intrinsic" cortical activities of whatever kind or extent, by forcing a continual progression of focal activities from one group of sites to another according to a logic somewhat at odds with that of external events and accordingly disruptive of neocortical processes imitative of the latter. It might be added that much of the waking mental life of man follows this same pattern, with "reality principle" processes following feebly in the

---

* A second and perhaps equally important factor being the increasing numbers of short axon cells found in many cortical areas in higher mammalian brains.

Thing Memories and Their "Association" / 53

wake of "thoughts" and recollections, determined by neocortical inputs from the core (i.e., determined by the flux of primal motivational states whose form is more determined by conditioning, or acquired automatisms, represented in neocortex as thing memories, than by neocortical rational-conscious processes, dependent upon abstract memory).

With man, however, the absolute extent of neocortex, and the refinement of its intrinsic activities, e.g., as resulting from the relatively large number of Golgi type II cells found in human neocortex,[18] have perhaps become such that a coalescence of local specialized "reality principle" processes can finally occur. In effect the local abstract memory-systems unite,* giving rise to a mode of apprehending reality-in-general—i.e., by means of sets of recalled relations applicable out of their original context of events, and not merely to *some* other (real or recalled) events, but to an indefinite number of others.

In turn this has led to a situation in which, at least at times, cortico-subcortical outflow, arising from "intrinsic" neocortical activity of the type just described, is capable of altering the sequences and intensity of motivational-affective states, and so of bringing the whole of behavior, creature intentions included, under rational control.

These relations, if I have correctly stated them, may be important in that they enable us, almost for the first time, to see how it is that neocortex may be capable of giving rise to a functional system corresponding to the rational-conscious "I." What I shall try to show is how, neurophysiologically, that system may come into being.

---

* Described later here as a process by which abstract memories representative of invariant relations peculiar to limited clusters of fact are themselves sorted for invariances, the resulting second-order abstract memories constituting a kind of master system interlinking forms of recalled experience of maximal diversity.

CHAPTER IV

Memory and Cortical Structure

THIS chapter considers certain morphological features of neocortex which may be fundamental to the memory-functions discussed previously. For the sake of clarity, I will postpone any extended discussion of the probable influence of core-processes upon those of neocortex, trusting it has been made clear that I do not regard the neocortex and dorsal thalamus as forming a self-contained functional unit whose activities are maintained by relatively undifferentiated "tonic" inputs, like an electrical appliance run on house current. Of the four means of intracortical communication mentioned in Chapter III, it is evident that two—the thalamic reticularis and the plexiform layer—serve as major paths of entry for influences arising in the midbrain or rhinencephalon (and relayed from the latter to the midbrain and thalamic reticularis by pathways discussed in Section II). The earlier description of neocortical "reality principle" processes as proceeding largely from the top of the cortex down, will consequently require qualification, since it is obvious that nonspecific inputs may greatly influence activities of this type. Moreover, there is evidence that such inputs do not invariably contribute to "central integration" if one assume orderly well-differentiated neocortical activities to be essential to the latter.

The discussion here will concern neocortical fine-structure and some of its functional implications. The cytoarchitectural data used, chiefly derive from Lorente de Nó's paper in the 1949 edition of Fulton's *Physiology of the Nervous System*,[1] Bailey and Von Bonin's *Isocortex of Man*,[2] and Sholl's *Organization of the Cerebral Cortex*.[3]

Lorente de Nó has stated that "there is no basis for considering the cortex as composed of several layers with specific primordial functions," and has reportedly criticized earlier attempts in that direction as too dogmatic.[2] I must emphasize that in postulating memory-functions for certain layers, I do not mean to imply any hard and fast segregation of the tendency—very likely characteristic of most neural assemblies—to form enduring axonal firing-patterns. I am merely suggesting that in six-layered cortex the *probability* of the persistence of firing-patterns may, for reasons given below, be maximal at certain levels.

Mountcastle's physiological studies, cited earlier, and Lorente de Nó's work on cortical fine-structure both suggest that the local mode of action of neocortex is primarily vertical; while the earlier discussion here implies that the neocortex acts essentially as a sorter of statistical invariances. This sorting is roughly divisible into two groups of processes. Those of the first, e.g., in extrinsic sectors, give rise to type memories. (The formation of thing memories, the mechanism of which is discussed further, below, also belongs in this category.) Those of the second group depend upon the interaction of labile cortical activity (transient action-patterns of diverse origin) with existing type or thing memory-formations, which interaction gives rise to "elaborated" type memories in periextrinsic sectors, and to "abstract" memories in posterior intrinsic sectors.

The laminar arrangement of these memory-systems I have supposed to depend in part upon the probable transaction rates, or variance of unit activity, likely to be found at any given level in a vertical column during the normal range of waking state conditions. Transaction rates will in turn depend upon the type and concentration of afferents characteristic of a given layer; its connections with other layers in the column; and the type and density of its cellular population.

Other things (e.g., amount and variance of input per unit time) being equal, the transaction rate will for a given layer be high in proportion as its cells are small, densely packed, and include a large percentage of neurons such as Golgi type II or Sholl's stellate S_1 which both collect and distribute impulses within the layer.

Via their apical and basilar dendritic networks, as well as by axosomatic synapses,[4] the larger pyramidal cells, frequently found in layer V or in IIIc, may then serve as a collection, or comprehensive summation, apparatus. One can imagine that cells of this type require a comparatively high degree of convergence of facilitatory inputs (i.e., of excitatory p.s.p.'s) to reach threshold for all-or-none discharge, with the result that their activity may, in general, be the outcome of immediately precurrent activity involving far larger numbers of smaller cells—for instance in layers II, IIIa and b, and IV. In turn, to the degree that a given complex of events in the latter layers both leads to summation in the pyramidal "collecting apparatus," and is itself repeated a sufficient number of times, changes may occur at the synapses concerned thereafter favoring activation of *that* pattern, as against the n others of which the whole assembly is theoretically capable. Moreover, the fact that the larger pyramidal bands may for reasons just stated be the more intermittently acting, may mean that any such firing-order, once established, tends to persist for a longer period in them than in their smaller-celled layers of origin. Hence the "memory" functions postulated for these bands, in which net transaction-rates vis-à-vis II or IV may be relatively low. (See also note 5.)

According to Bailey and Von Bonin,[2] the outstanding features of koniose parakoniose and generalized eulaminate cortex are as follows. In koniocortex, IV tends to be thick and densely packed with "granules." V is in general "slight" "poor in cells," or contains only a "fair number" of medium-sized cells scattered over all levels in the layer (postcentral, striate and supratemporal cortex). VI may be rich in "fairly large" cells (striate), denser than V (postcentral) and contains as elsewhere, numbers of fusiform cells. The layer of large pyramids in IIIc does not appear to be as well developed in these sectors as in others. On the basis of the assumptions made above, I have inferred these to be structural features conducive to the formation of comparatively fluid or fugitive action patterns (type memories) in prime receptor cortex.

The principal features of parakoniocortex are the low density of V (which contains large but usually scattered pyramids: see

2) and the concentration of large pyramids in IIIc. These sectors have been postulated as figuring in the elaboration of type memories, e.g., via projection fibers of *lateralis posterior* and the pulvinar. Such memories, that is, do not arise directly out of sensory inputs, their formation corresponding to the second of the two basic processes described above (p. 55). They are thus exact analogues of the abstract memory-formations of intrinsic (generalized eulaminate) cortex. As will be seen presently, they may play a highly important part in the "partitioning"[6] of primary sense data in extrinsic sectors, this process being fundamental to the mechanism of attention. Apropos of this point, Bailey and Von Bonin remark that "the primary sensory areas do not send messages very far into the surrounding cortex" (i.e., transcortically) "and receive impulses almost exclusively *from* the parasensory areas" [italics mine]. "The parasensory areas on the other hand, receive afferents from several other cortical areas and send their corticocortical efferents much further away." The first of these groups of parakoniocortical efferents may figure in attention* and the second, as described later in this chapter, in the elaboration of thing memories.

Generalized eulaminate cortex, of both frontal and posterior intrinsic sectors, shows a remarkable uniformity in certain of its characteristics at least in the brain examined by these authors. (Since, however, they include a thorough review of the earlier cytoarchitectural literature, it is likely that they would have pointed out any features of the brain studied which were atypical in the light of other evidence.)

Their serial sections disclose a well-developed granular layer IV for most sectors; a roughly graded structure in III (the size of pyramids increasing as one moves from IIIa to IIIc); a concentration, in V, of pyramids roughly comparable in size to those of IIIc (approximately $21 \times 13\,\mu$ to $26 \times 18\,\mu$, by uncorrected measurement); a population of cells in VI somewhat smaller than those in V, and including the usual fusiform cells; and a variable layer II which may show a layer of small pyramids

---

* I.e., in the "partitioning" or selective reinforcement of certain of the action-patterns in koniocortex, corresponding to certain immediate sense-data.

next the plexiform layer (orbital and dorsal frontal cortex) or a "ragged" outer boundary (superior temporal gyrus) or "patchy rarefication" (inferior temporal gyrus, anteriorly). Otherwise II contains a high percentage of granules (approximately 30–40 per cent in *parietalis inferior,* or Brodmann 39).

The foregoing features I have inferred to be particularly conducive to elaboration of the dual memory-system described earlier under the head of thing and abstract memory, the structural points of most importance being the granular layers IV and II, and the hypothetical "collection apparatus" embodied in the large pyramid layers of V and IIIc. It should be pointed out, however, that while the question of the afferent supply of layer IV is fairly well answered for some intrinsic sectors it is not for others. Glees Meyer and Meyer[7] reported termination of unmyelinated fibers of *dorsomedialis* in layers III–IV of orbitofrontal cortex in the rabbit. Nauta and Whitlock[8] found that, in cats, lesions to *dorsomedialis* or *lateralis posterior* produced "dense degeneration in layer IV, spilling over into III" in corresponding frontal and posterior sectors. Unless, as seems probable, layer IV in those temporal regions not reached by the pulvinar, receives collaterals of nonspecific fibers ascending to the plexiform layer,[9] the afferent supply of IV in those regions, and the functional role of IV itself, remain in doubt.

In regard to agranular cortex (e.g., of Brodmann 4 and 6) Bailey and Von Bonin note that "this variant differs from typical isocortex by the tendency of granules to disappear and be replaced by small pyramids. The cells of the agranular cortex are relatively large; the inner granular layer is attenuated and the laminar pattern is blurred. Brodmann states that in embryonic life the agranular cortex shows the same six layers as the rest of the cortex, and that the fourth layer disappears only secondarily. What we know of the cortex of the newborn and the baby . . . supports Brodmann's views."

These features of agranular cortex I have supposed fit it to act as a "collection apparatus" for the resultants of more labile recombinative activities relayed to it from elsewhere, e.g., via *ventralis lateralis.* This means to say that many effector outflows from neocortex tend to be restricted in potential variety by the fact that at exit they may pass through a type of cortex so constructed that in the adult organism, action-patterns relatively resistant change, i.e., memories, may predominate—in contrast to the more uneven laminar distribution of memory-formations and the sharper maxima in variance of unit activity which may be found for instance in columns of posterior intrinsic cortex. Psychologically, this arrangement may correspond to the fact that at maturity it is perhaps a great deal easier to go on changing in one's imaginative or "mental" life than it is to go on variegating one's motor skills. Provided only a change in outlook and an increase of knowledge in new directions are required, a man may make a radical change of *métier* in late youth or early middle life; but he cannot hope to become a concert pianist, say, unless formation of the necessary motor memories is started very early, preferably in the first decade.

Apropos of the memory-functions, in particular postulated here for the internal lamina of most sectors, it is significant that in the area *agranularis gigantopyramidalis,* the concentration of Betz cells is found in layer V. (See note 18, below.)

Bailey and Von Bonin are of the opinion that the numerous subvariants of frontal cortex reported by Economo and others (*op. cit.,* 197, 207) have no detectable significance. While inclined to believe that "a precise cytoarchitectural map of the frontal lobe is impossible," they cite Economo and Ngowyang to the effect that from the central sulcus forward the cortex shows progressive thinning and a general decrease in cell-size inclusive of the large pyramids of III and V. They also consider Betz's description of the third frontal convolution "valid."

In a later chapter I have discussed the possible importance of frontal intrinsic cortex in the organization of temporal sequences of behavior. One implication of that view is that memory-formations of frontal eulaminate cortex may be somewhat more fluid than those of posterior eulaminate. They may be because of the respective sources of frontal and posterior intrinsic sector input, there being no clear cytoarchitectural difference paralleling this inferred functional one. Neurophysiological evidence cited in due course suggests that in general, frontal cortex may show more consistent nonspecific "activation" than other areas. Moreover it is probably significant that *dorsomedialis* is a part of the core system of the dorsal thalamus (Pribram, Chapter VIII, note 30), whereas *lateralis posterior* and the pulvinar belong to the external portion, in company with the specific relay nuclei.*

The fact that frontal intrinsic cortex shades off into agranular areas, certain functions (e.g., speech and writing) having representation in cortex extending roughly across this transitional zone, may mean that frontal eulaminate cortex proper has effector functions related to those of Brodmann 4, 6, and 8, but of a far higher order of fluidity. The latter is perhaps guaranteed by its small-celled structure and well-developed granular layers vis-à-vis 4, 6, and 8; and by its high rate of nonspecific input vis-à-vis posterior eulaminate cortex.

To complete this brief review of cytoarchitectural variants, it is interesting that juxtallocortex (e.g., of Brodmann 36) and allocortex (e.g., prepyriform, of Economo's area HA) exhibit a clumping of cells in layer II. In allocortex these clumps correspond to the two forms of the "islands of Calleja" both of which, by uncorrected measurement, run about .5 mm in diameter (or approximately the same diameter as a Mountcastle vertical column). The large-celled clumps consist mostly of star cells; the small-celled, of pyramids and fusiform cells. Cortex of this type exhibits a third layer "which contains a sparse population of not very large cells; an almost nonexistent IV; and a V containing "densely packed" medium pyramids—e.g., in size somewhere between $21 \times 13\,\mu$ and $39 \times 24\,\mu$ by crude measure, or the sizes which Bailey and Von Bonin call "small" and "large" (*op. cit.*, pp. 84, 86).

Particularly since olfactory afferents reach primordial cortex of this type via the tangential (plexiform) layer; and since Lorente de Nó reports that in mesial cortex approaching the limbic region "layers II and III become progressively thinner and the afferent plexus approaches the plexiform layer," one wonders if this clumping, where it exists, may not serve to prelimit the (relatively stimulus-bound) forms of output from the columns concerned. In other words, insofar as it favors for

---

* For this reason I have throughout referred to the thalamocortical "specific" system as including these association nuclei.

structural reasons certain output patterns over others, or makes only a certain range of output patterns possible, this may be one mode of the cortical representation of innate behavior, the latter presumably being dependent upon relatively predetermined, or in this sense restricted, effector outflows. The fact that similar island formations are found in the septum, closely adjoining the region apparently important in producing hippocampal theta activity,[10,11] is of some interest in this connection.

To consider now, the question of the communication between various levels in a given vertical column, and of the probable rates of transaction (input turnover) which can be inferred for each, it is significant that Lorente de Nó makes a fundamental distinction between the external and internal laminae, or layers I–IV and V–VI respectively. This distinction is based chiefly on two facts. The first is that an important group of specific thalamic afferents (including those from VPL, VPM, LP, and the pulvinar) ascend "myelinated and undivided" through V–VI to end in IV–lower III. The second has to do with cortical output arrangements and is described by him as follows:

"The distribution of the (descending) axonal branches is as systematic as that of the dendrites; again there is a sharp difference between layers I–IV and layers V–VI . . . . It is a remarkable fact that layer IV receives but few collaterals from the axons of the pyramids of layers II and III. . . . Once arrived at layer V, *all* the pyramidal axons give off a great number of more or less horizontal branches, distributed throughout layers V and VI but especially in the upper part of V." [Italics mine.]

In other words, on the input side, the internal lamina is in some degree shielded from direct specific thalamic influence. On the output side, layer IV, which receives the bulk of specific fibers, is shielded from excessive feedback influence from the surrounding layers. Instead the specific inputs further processed, e.g., in the overlying layers are principally distributed to upper V of the internal lamina. As result, the more enduring axonal firing orders which take shape in V–VI via the "collecting apparatus" or large pyramids of V are equivalent to memories which reflect the invariance-sorting or resultant-forming action of the overlying layers. The shielding of IV from feedback embodying the same processed data perhaps acts to preserve the integrity of primary perception, in that it prevents contamination of immediate sense-data by processes whose form reflects the organism's recalled past, or (via the nonspecific system) its concurrent motivational states. Were it not for this arrangement, the elaboration of memory-systems might make for a situation in which the accurate perception of novelties in the present would become all but impossible owing to the too direct intrusion of "interpretive" activities upon those of sense-reception. As it is, enough indirect intrusion of this kind may occur to cause many of us, with advancing "maturity" to become increasingly incapable of apprehending the new, except in terms of forced comparisons with the familiar (see below on the mechanism of "partitioning"). Similarly, indirect intrusion of concurrent motivational-affective states may make for distortion of perceptual processes, in particular when the former are intense and nonspecific input is at correspondingly high levels. However, as we shall see, these distortions or deficits may chiefly appear in areas concerned in the final processing of sensory information, i.e., the posterior intrinsic sectors, and be accompanied by enhancement of extrinsic sector activity, equivalent to a measurable increase in perceptual acuity.[12]

Lorente de Nó reports that V–VI are the source of "powerful association tracts,"* these distributing mainly to II, III, and VI elsewhere. Callosal tracts appear to arise largely among the short pyramids of Vc–VIa. Finally he states that nonspecific afferents distribute principally to layers VI and I. From the standpoint of this discussion, the upper granular layer (II) and the plexiform layer are of special interest in that the latter "contains . . . the terminal bushels of pyramids and spindles of *all* the lower strata" [italics mine], while layer II contains few if any small pyramids with basilar dendrites "long enough to reach the zone of distribution of the specific afferents."

These arrangements imply first of all that the diversity of

---

* According to Von Bonin, the principal sources of association tracts are layers III and V (cf. Vol. 1, *The Nervous System,* Ciba, 1953, p. 73).

traffic passing through layer I, and consequently the diversity (variance) of unit activity or of realized action-patterns in II may frequently exceed those in IV–lower III, or be maximal for the neocortex, considered vertically. As postulated above, the cellular structure of II is also in favor of that conclusion. Moreover the relative shortness of the dendritic processes reaching the plexiform layer from II may guarantee a higher percentage of unit axonal activity in II (as compared to that resulting from the same source, in lower layers) because of the factor electrotonic loss, here presumably minimal. Finally, the fact that activity in II only indirectly reflects that resulting in IV–lower III from thalamic input (since unlike III, few or none of its basilar dendrites make connections with the plexus of specific afferents), means that that activity is not merely or predominantly the outcome of any one set of cortical events. Rather it can be inferred to be a resultant of virtually *all* forms of concurrent cortical activity, including that of the underlying "receptor" layers, that arising from both immediate and remote basal cortical memory-formations, and that arising in the still more remote motivational systems of the core. It is this great convergence of influences which I have supposed has made for the maximally labile activities, or "thought" functions of the outermost laminae.

The prediction from this conclusion and from the postulated memory-functions, or tendency to maximally invariant activity, of the internal lamina, is that neocortex must in general show a gradient in the variance of its unit activity, or more broadly in its energy uptake, such that either or both tend to be greatest for the outermost laminae and minimal for V–VI. The fall in the gradient should be sharper from IV through VI than from I to IV, and certain exceptions might be expected—e.g., in the case of the Betz cell layer of precentral cortex. This prediction appears to be borne out by a recent report by Vladimirov et al., on the laminar distribution of ATP and phosphocreatine in the "motor," "visual," "auditory," and "sensory" cortex of the rat.[13] Without exception, maximal concentrations of these substances were found in II. In two cases (auditory and sensory cortex) phosphocreatine concentrations showed increases from V to VI, though these were slight as compared to the fall in concentration between layers II and V.[14] In all cases the sharpest fall in ATP concentration occurred between layers II and IV.

The graded increase in size of the pyramids often found in layer III (e.g., from IIIb to IIIc), suggests that memories may form in two stages. The first perhaps involves the convergence in III, of concurrent sensory inputs via the plexus of specific afferents, and of the maximally diverse action-patterns of II arising from sources just described. The larger pyramids found in lower III then serve to "collect" the most frequently repeated of these resultants and to relay them elsewhere, notably to the similar pyramidal "collecting" apparatus of underlying layer V. The result is then second-stage formation of "basal" memories in the internal lamina.

To the degree that the modulatory influence of specific thalamic inputs falls upon the basilar dendrites of the pyramids of lower III, whose "firing-orders" are, in the mature organism, to some extent pre-established by the prior trend of its experience, it may be correct to say, as above, that our "direct" perceptions are preassorted, or reach "consciousness" as it were through a screen of type memories. This view is not in accord with earlier psychological notions to the effect that sense-data first reach "consciousness" unedited, and are then identified by reference to some form of mental filing system (see, for instance, Freud on this; note 15). The latter view may be quite incorrect and may have arisen in part from a failure to distinguish the two basic forms of—or better, stages in—perceptual recognition described here—the first or generic being of short latency and dependent upon type memories; and the second or specific being often of perceptibly longer latency, and dependent upon thing memories. If critical flicker frequencies are any index of minimum perceptible intervals generally this latency difference may be on the order of 60 to 100 msec—the latter being the time Craik has estimated it may take us to form a "photo" of ongoing external events (Chapter III, note 4). That perceptual recognition may really occur in these two stages is suggested by certain amnesias in which the subject can still generically identify his surroundings but is seemingly unable to name or otherwise "place" certain people, objects, etc., once specifically known to him. Like the phenomenon of stimulus generalization this one argues that the disorganization of neocortical activities by high levels of nonspecific input is frequently selective for intrinsic cortex, including those posterior sectors which seem to be essential to thing memory-formation.

Type memories, then, may show two degrees of fluidity, and in their mode of neocortical representation may be exactly analogous to the basal "thing" and overlying "abstract" memory-formations of posterior intrinsic sectors. Their respective orders of formation may however differ in that basal type memories may largely derive from a further sorting of the invariances embodied in overlying type memories. By contrast, in intrinsic sectors, in which the average rate of input can perhaps be inferred to be less, abstract (or overlying) memory-formations may arise not merely or even mainly from inputs corresponding to immediate sensory experience, but may take shape as result of the continuous waking-state activity of neocortex and of concurrent activities in motivational systems of the core.

The latter act, e.g., via the nonspecific system, to give a certain direction to neocortical activities, in effect via the facilitation of various groups of memories—these standing in the same relation to a given motivational-affective state as do conditioned stimuli to the particular basal "intentions" they subserve (as "releasers" of appropriate behavior). In other words, from fairly early on in the life of the organism, abstract memories begin to form as result of activities proceeding from the bottom of the cortex up* (for instance during activation of a conditioned response. In this connection, note the laminar distribution of nonspecific fibers cited above.) They may thus represent invariances sorted not from inputs proper, but chiefly from the pre-established contents of memory (i.e., basal thing memory-formations); and it is just in the respect that it presumably favors this process over formation of abstract (e.g., layer III) memories in response to moment-to-moment sensory inputs, that the absence of fibers of the specific relay and association nuclei, e.g., in parts of the temporal lobe, may be highly significant.[16]

---

* I.e., by reversal of the two-stage sorting process just described, in the case of type memories.

Abstract memories, therefore, represent the final stage in the elaboration of "intrinsic" activities of neocortex, taking shape as a system relatively late in the life of the organism, the more so the greater its cortical potential. In proportion as they are well developed, or do form a system, they then mediate cortical processes proceeding from the top down which serve to activate basal thing memories in spatio-temporal patterns different from those mediated by neocortical inputs from the core. The consequence of this abstract memory function, in turn, is to modify core-processes via cortico-rhinencephalic and cortico-mesencephalic outflows, it being in this way the basal thing memories cease to be a mere passive reinforcement system vis-à-vis the core. In other words, abstract memories represent the form in which labile activities of the outer laminae cumulatively organize themselves, by interaction with the factual data represented at the level of the internal lamina. Out of this progressive elaboration of abstract memory-systems grow "reality principle" processes —that is to say, central nervous activities imitative of relations obtaining in the world of external fact.* Since invariances corresponding to these relations have been statistically sorted out, chiefly from the miscellaneous data embodied in thing memory, the abstract memory formations which result will the more accurately embody actual "laws" the larger the total of thing memories available as raw material. Partly for this reason, the capacity to "adapt" or behave intelligently is apt to be directly proportioned to the absolute extent of neocortex, though this probably holds more between species than within them since in the latter case, more especially in "higher" forms, the accidents of individual experience may on occasion far outweigh the effect of inherited variations in cortical structure.[17]

In contrast to abstract memories, overlying type memories in extrinsic cortex are subject to continuous relatively direct inputs from the periphery whose only significant preassortment has perhaps occurred in the thalamus.† In cortex of this type, the

---

* These being in fact among the most invariant aspects of our experience, and consequently among those most apt to survive the several-stage sorting process described here.

† See Chapter II, note 15. I understand that Dr. Arnold, in her study

order of memory-formation is perhaps irreversible, or permanently from the top down, maximally invariant residues of sensory influx taking shape as favored firing-patterns at the level of V–VI. The comparative fluidity of type memories then depends essentially upon two factors; the high probable input turnover in koniocortex during waking, and the absence in this cortex of well-developed large-celled bands in IIIc or V (Bailey and Von Bonin).

To conclude, it would appear that the processes leading to memory formation may be much the same in all parts of neocortex; and moreover that the major structural variants found in the latter may have a clear relation to these and so functional properties clearly related to their cytoarchitecture.

The basic assumptions made here are first, that the tendency of any given neural assembly to form "memories" is equivalent to its tendency to form enduring axonal firing-patterns (e.g., in consequence of the repetition of certain patterned inputs, and of synaptic changes within the assembly thereafter favoring activation of those patterns over the n others comprising its combinative potential). Secondly, I have assumed that that tendency may vary directly as the mean cell sizes, and inversely as the packing density and the probable amount and diversity of input traffic per unit time, characteristic of a given assembly.

An analysis of the fine-structure of neocortex suggests that, on these grounds, the probable variance of unit activity may be expected to differ significantly at different cortical depths, and may accordingly enable us to distinguish layers which are "memory-forming" in this relative sense. The model proposed is, in other words, probabilistic, assigning *tendencies* rather than primordial functions, to certain layers.[18] The experimental prediction which follows is obvious—namely, that multiple implanted electrode studies of unit activity at various cortical depths should,

---

Emotion and Personality (2 vols., Columbia, 1960), has postulated a laminar distribution of memory-functions in the lateral geniculate. It seems entirely possible that if it exists, this arrangement might be repeated, with modifications, in neocortex. However, see Chapter V, note 32.

on analysis of variance (preferably of data covering long periods of continuous recording, to allow for large local variance of variance),* show maxima and minima closely corresponding to those found for the laminar distribution of ATP and phosphocreatine by Vladimirov et al.[13]

* In processing such data, the Mean Square Successive Difference statistic developed by Von Neumann might be of use. See Leiderman and Shapiro, *Science,* 138, Oct. 12, 1962, pp. 141–142.

CHAPTER V

The Distribution and Processing of Information in Neocortex

IF one regard the neocortex as a mosaic of "vertically oriented . . . overlapping cylindroids" (Chapter IV, note 9), communication between cylindroids may largely be mediated by four types of fiber system. These include the plexiform layer, the so-called reverberatory thalamocortical circuits,[1] commissural and callosal fibers connecting homologous areas in the two hemispheres,* and long association fibers connecting various areas within each hemisphere. (See note 4, below.)

To these one might add cortico-subcortical projections such as those arising in neocortical "strip" regions and in frontal and temporal intrinsic sectors, many of which appear to reach the mid-brain via rhinencephalic structures such as the septum, amygdala, and hippocampus. Projections of this type can be conceived as modulating neocortical activity generally, to the degree that they exert a roundabout influence upon output of the midbrain to neocortex. However, evidence from split-brain studies suggests that little significant structuring or informational content is imposed upon rostral output of the midbrain reticular formation in this way,[2] those nonspecific inputs which *are* clearly structured possibly becoming so at the level of the thalamic reticularis, in consequence of neocortical feedback to that system.

---

* However, some callosal fibers arising in frontal and parietal cortex reportedly have extensive diffuse contralateral distribution. Cf. R. Ironside et al., *Brain*, Vol. 84, Part ii, 1961, pp. 212–230. These authors point out that the callosum is a recent mammalian addition, lacking in monotremes and "most" marsupials; and describe callosal fibers as arising "infragranularly" and distributing "supragranularly."

The relatively late development, in maturation, of abstract memory-systems—whose psychological parallel is the relatively late emergence of systematic rational thought and of its effects, such as they are, upon behavior and basal motivation—is due essentially to the fact that these memory-systems are derivatives of basal intrinsic sector thing-memory formations. As compared to the development of type-memory systems, formation of thing memories is more intermittent and gradual, this difference perhaps being reflected in the fact that intrinsic cortex is reportedly the last to become myelinated.[3] Bailey and Von Bonin remark that it is just these intrinsic cortical sectors "which develop intimate connections with each other by means of long fiber tracts" and quote Flechsig to the effect that "no long association system is known which connects two primordial zones that are to be regarded as sensory centers."[4]

There seems to be some question as to how vital a role these long fiber systems play—e.g., in the elaboration of memories. According to Pribram, "models of cerebral organization have heretofore been based to a large extent on clinical neurological data and have been formulated with the 'reflex' as prototype. Such models state that input is organized in the extrinsic 'sensory,' elaborated in the intrinsic 'associative,' and from there relayed to the extrinsic 'motor' sectors. I have already pointed out that the afferent-efferent overlap in the extrinsic system makes such notions of cerebral organization suspect. A series of neuropsychological studies by Lashley, Sperry, Chow, Evarts, and Wade in which the extrinsic sectors were surgically cross-hatched, circumsected, or isolated by large resections of their surround, with little apparent effect on behavior, has cast further doubt on the usefulness of such a 'transcortical' model. Additional difficulties are posed by the negative electrophysiological and anatomical findings whenever direct connections are sought between the extrinsic and intrinsic sectors. . . .

"Each investigator has had a slightly different approach to the functions of the intrinsic sectors, but the viewpoints share the proposition that the intrinsic sectors do not function independently of the extrinsic. The common difficulty has been the conceptualization of their interdependence."

Pribram believes that "the hierarchical relationship between intrinsic and extrinsic systems can be attributed to convergence of the *output* of the two systems at a subcortical locus rather than to a specific input from ... extrinsic cortex to ... intrinsic."[5]

This convergence-of-output hypothesis is attractive, particularly since pathways making for such convergence clearly exist.* The question which Pribram does not take up here is that of the informational supply of the intrinsic systems. The question is urgent if only because of the considerable extent of generalized eulaminate cortex in human brain (Bailey and Von Bonin, *op. cit.*, 4, frontispiece; cf. also their serial sections).

It is evident that if information reaching intrinsic cortex derives mainly from extrinsic receptor areas, it probably does not do so either by intragriseal spread or via intracortical pathways of the white matter (Flechsig; see also page 36 above). However, neither dicing of extrinsic cortex on a 1 mm grid (Sperry), nor circumsection of the area, nor ablations of immediately surrounding cortex, would preclude either the essentially vertical transactions involved in local sense-reception, or relay of the resulting outflows from extrinsic to intrinsic sectors via the thalamus. So long as *some* extrinsic and some posterior intrinsic sectors and their respective thalamic fiber systems remained intact, formation of thing memories might be expected to continue, as might discriminatory processes dependent upon activation of pre-established thing memories by present sensory inputs over the same pathways (thalamus→extrinsic→ thalamus→intrinsic).

The question arises as to whether lemniscal, trigeminothalamic, or spinothalamic inputs do not automatically distribute via intrathalamic pathways from relay to association nuclei, with the result that intrinsic sectors are not wholly dependent upon extrinsic-thalamic playback for their supply of sensory information. Studies of humans with "massive" bilateral occipital damage sug-

---

* However, it is worth noting that the neocortical "strip" regions 2s, 19s, and 22s arise in areas described here as periextrinsic, and that the two corticopontine bundles (Arnold's and Türck's) reportedly originate in Brodmann areas 4 and 6 and in the inferior and middle temporal gyri respectively (in the macaque; Fulton, *Physiol. of the Nerv. Sys.* p. 327).

gest that at least in the case of the visual system, such direct intrathalamic distribution of incoming sense-data may not occur to any appreciable extent.[6]

Tentatively, then, one might conclude that intrinsic sectors rely upon the extrinsic receptor apparatus as their prime source of information, the pathways principally concerned passing from the latter to the former via the thalamus. Attentional processes, leading to the "partitioning" of primary sense-data, might be conceived as resulting from the same sequence of events run in reverse—that is, by cortico-thalamo-cortical playback from intrinsic and periextrinsic to extrinsic sectors (frequently if not always reinforced by nonspecific inputs exhibiting the "labile" topographic organization described by Jasper.[7] Sense-data concurrently represented in extrinsic cortex may then be subjected to selective facilitation of *these* action-patterns, and selective inhibition of those others—the foci of perceptual attention being in this way established.*

Thus the processes leading to "specific recognition" may in turn cause modulation-by-feedback of extrinsic sector activities so as to produce, in effect, a singling out of those presently perceived details whose probable significance is greatest in the light of the organism's recalled history. Only part of that significance will have been established via prior labile neocortical activity and the prior formation of abstract memories — that is, by the "intrinsic" or "reality principle" processes of neocortex described in Chapter IV, and below. An additional and perhaps major part of that significance will have been established in the shape of innate or partially "conditioned" responses of systems of the core, to which the basal (layer V–VI) memory-formations of the neocortex stand in the relation of a contributory system

---

* McCulloch (*op. cit.*, Ch. II above) has noted the tendency of recollection always to run forward in time, or in something like the original order of the recalled events. It is this feature which doubtless gives conditioned stimuli their capacity to establish an anticipatory behavioral "set." Hence partitioning is perhaps always in some degree extrapolative. Moreover, these extrapolations appear to occur in peripheral receptor systems, perhaps as result of central outflows—witness the "predictive" retinal responses which Hernández-Peón obtained in human subjects. (See L. Sutro, *Biological Prototypes and Synthetic Systems*, New York, Plenum Press, 1962, p. 77.)

whose outflows, e.g., via tempororhinencephalic or strip-region-septal pathways, act automatically to reinforce certain corresponding activities at subcortical levels.

Therefore to the extent that the motivational-affective and the rational-conscious "meanings" of a given present sensory event do not coincide, the two sets of processes mediating partitioning of sense-data in extrinsic cortex may not have coinciding effects. Which set of effects predominates—or which sense-data the organism finally "attends" to—may then be decided by the outcome of the functional competition between neocortex and core-structures for control of the thalamus.

All of these events, it need not be repeated, are sequels to primary perception itself.[8] Even in the case of keen anticipation, in which both certain intrinsic sector thing memories and certain focal activities of the core may be prefacilitated, the effect may be to diminish, but will not be to abolish, the temporal lag between generic and specific recognition of a given group of sense-data. This does *not* mean to say that by the time the events equivalent to a clear conscious recognition of some familiar particularity have occurred, a parallel motivational or affective response (including autonomic and reticulo-spinal motor components) may not already be well under way.[8]

A recent study by Morillo of the response-latency of various neocortical sectors in cats following thalamic stimulation is of interest in this connection.[9] This study showed that, with roughly the same parameters of stimulation, most responses in striate cortex were elicited within 5 msec and none later than 10 msec following stimulation of the lateral geniculate; in contrast, stimulation of *lateralis posterior* produced some "early activated units" in suprasylvian gyrus, but "a considerable contingent" with latencies up to 30 msec. In the case of *centralis lateralis*, the latency of response in suprasylvian gyrus was between 10 and 45 msec, no units being activated in under 5 msec (i.e., "early").

Latency variability was least and also least frequently observed, in units activated from LGD. In the association system (LP-suprasylvian) "a little less than 50 percent of activated units show marked latency variability"—i.e., up to 20 msec. Variable latency was characteristic of "the majority of activated units" in the nonspecific system (CL–suprasylvian), the range of variation for some units being as high as 49 msec. CL stimulation may potentiate spikes evoked from LP or conversely, at optimal intervals of approximately 6 msec. However, Morillo did not find single cortical units which could be fired by separate stimulation of both of these nuclei—the suggestion being that convergence of fibers of nonspecific and association nuclei upon the same neurons may not in general occur in association cortex. This finding is in accord with Lorente de Nó's report that nonspecific fibers distribute principally to layers I and VI, and Nauta and Whitlock's that fibers of *lateralis posterior* distribute to IV–lower III (preceding chapter, notes 1 and 8). Finally, Morillo reports that he found some evidence of the convergence of fibers of LGD and LP on the same neurons in cat striate, adding however that "the number of experiments carried out is too small to permit a definite statement on the matter."

These data suggest that the lag between generic and specific recognition may in part be due to the longer latency of thalamocortical transmission via the association, as compared to the specific relay, nuclei; while nonspecific thalamic inputs, e.g., originating in the core, may show latencies greater than either of these, taking up to nine times longer to reach neocortex than do inputs from the specific relay nuclei.* Tentatively then (see note 8) one might conclude that the sequence of neocortical events resulting for instance from distance receptor inputs is on any occasion much the same.

IN a later chapter on reticulocortical relations I have suggested that, during waking, neocortical nonspecific input is roughly divisible into two ranges of intensity. In the lower, or normal waking-state range, it is on the whole supportive of, and subject to modulatory control by, "intrinsic" activities of neo-

---

* A recent study by Allison (*EEG clin. Neurophysiol.* 14, 1962, 331–343) of EEG responses to somatic stimulation (median nerve, left wrist) in human subjects appears to conform to the scheme of relative latencies of "specific" "association" and "nonspecific" thalamocortical responses shown by Morillo's data. (See also Allison *et al.*, *EEG clin. Neurophysiol.*, 14, 1962, 697–713.)

cortex. In the higher range, corresponding to motivational-affective states of more than a certain intensity, nonspecific input may cease merely to support and begin in varying degrees to disrupt "intrinsic" neocortical activities, the result being a reversal of the previous order of functional dominance, or some* transfer of central control from the neopallium to structures of the core. The remainder of this chapter will be concerned largely with those neocortical processes in which the nonspecific system plays a subsidiary and largely supportive role.

Perhaps the cardinal fact of neocortical organization is that all of the pathways of intracortical communication listed above have overlapping distribution, with the result that information received in extrinsic sectors, may be relayed to the same peri-extrinsic or intrinsic sites by several routes, the question then being how the processing of primary sense-data is furthered by this redundancy or multiple convergence mechanism.

Lorente de Nó (Chapter IV, note 1) points out that "the interareal association fibers have a distribution similar to many of the collaterals of descending axons. This indicates that when a cortical cell discharges into its axon, it must modify the activity of the cells in the area in which it is located in a way similar to that in which activity of the cells of other cortical areas, or even of subcortical centers, is modified." Similarly, cortico-thalamo-cortical conduction from extrinsic to intrinsic sectors presumably serves to repeat in the latter, action patterns existent in the former; or conversely, in the case of the thalamic relays from intrinsic to extrinsic sectors mediating "partitioning."[10] The plexiform layer can, on anatomic grounds, be supposed to relay modulatory influences from a given column, these outputs serving to facilitate in other columns (initially, at the level of layer II), patterns of activity in some degree reflecting those of the column of origin. The reduplicative functions of commissural and callosal fibers seem sufficiently well established not to require special comment.[11] In view of these arrangements, it is a question

---

* The word "some" here is intended to suggest that this transfer exhibits many gradations, as does, for example, the primitivization of behavior during fear or rage.

whether the mode-specificity of vertical columns, e.g., in temporal intrinsic cortex, is conserved, as Pribram has suggested; or if it is, how it comes to be so.[12]

Considering the system of relays by which a given sensory input may result in type and corresponding thing memory-formations, one might suppose that via these relays, a chain of most probable sites (of future focal activity) is established in extrinsic, periextrinsic and posterior intrinsic sectors, such that later repetition of that input will tend to have roughly the same neocortical consequences, in roughly the original order. Beginning at the thalamus, one can infer that the routing of sense-data by the specific relay nuclei is to a considerable extent predetermined by the topographic arrangement of thalamic input and output fibers. Thus incoming sense-data are automatically fractionated according to modality and submodality (e.g., of tactile sensation) in the thalamus; and from there relayed to an anatomically predetermined (and relatively small) number of mode-specific vertical columns in extrinsic cortex. These paths of entry of sensory information, including their termini, will for a given input be probable to the point of near certainty.

In contrast, the cortical territories which may ultimately be reached by subsequent relay of the same input are much larger. Thus, for an input to which no pre-established action-patterns— e.g., in periextrinsic or intrinsic sectors—correspond, there is perhaps a far lower probability, than in the case of thalamic-extrinsic sector inputs, that *any particular* assembly of vertical columns in outlying neocortex will be preferentially activated. In periextrinsic cortex, such as area 19, there appear to be restrictions on the modality of data received; but beyond that the particular vertical columns which come to figure in the "elaboration" of primary visual data may largely be determined by conditions prevailing in the area on first receipt of the data. Other things being equal—that is, if the sense-datum corresponds to no pre-existing action-pattern, and if the receiving area be considered a *tabula rasa* (in respect of pre-established action-patterns), the columns which come to embody that datum as a "memory" will be those which on its first receipt are in an optimal phase of the "excitability cycle" (Lindsley, 13), or those showing post-inhibitory rebound as result of just prior activity in adjoining colums.

In this sense, one might say that there exists a spectrum of indeterminacy with respect to the loci and total number of neocortical events likely to follow upon receipt of a given sensory input, the more so the younger the organism or the less "saturated" its memory-apparatus as a whole. Those in extrinsic sectors will be most determinate; those in periextrinsic, somewhat less so; and those in intrinsic sectors such as Brodmann 21, perhaps least of all. In the latter, for the one thing, there appear to be the least restrictions on the diversity (modality) of input. For another, those parts of temporal cortex lying outside the area of distribution of the pulvinar may be presumed to be reached chiefly by fibers of the thalamic reticularis (Papez, 14) whose mode of topographic projection seems maximally "labile" (Jasper, 7) and which moreover may serve to establish a potentially wider range of excitability conditions than does the more phasically acting and focally organized specific system. In consequence, the potential variety of conditions upon which a given input may impinge, may, for several reasons, be maximal, e.g., in temporal or frontal intrinsic cortex. (The relation of this fact, if it is one, to the behavioral role of frontal intrinsic sectors, is discussed in Section II.)

Neurophysiologically the above amounts to saying that elaborated type memories have more probable general (areal) loci of representation than do thing memories. Stimulating in peristriate cortex we are reasonably certain of evoking visual, rather than tactile or auditory effects. Once, however, the combining of primary sense-data has gone as far as it may do in temporal association cortex, there may—to judge from Penfield's data—be no telling from subject to subject what sort of combination will be found where.

Livingston has remarked that the neocortex may to some degree localize its own functions.[15] I would qualify his remark with the suggestion that this may be increasingly the case as one moves from koniose into parakoniose and generalized eulaminate cortex —the localizations which occur in the last being most adventitious of all, in that they result from a convergence of internal and external circumstance* which is potentially maximal for neocortex as a whole. The expansion of areas of generalized eulaminate cortex in higher mammals has, in effect lengthened, and may also have steepened, the probability gradient (i.e., the gradient in determinacy or predictability of neocortical events) which may be inferred to exist between events of extrinsic, periextrinsic and intrinsic sectors, pursuant to primary sense-reception.

The foregoing may be summed up by saying that from the specific relay nuclei to extrinsic cortex, the number of pathways available is maximally restricted in respect to random choice, a given input being fractionated according to modality and submodality so as to impinge finally upon a comparatively small number of mode-specific vertical columns. Only within this small assembly will prevailing excitability conditions perhaps determine which columns shall show preferential activation and so in future become "most probable" sites of focal activity on receipt of the same input.

In contrast, this same input, upon cortico-thalamo-cortical relay may be distributed to far larger neocortical territories, according to a topographic scheme which is perhaps less strict in the case of the association nuclei, and least strict of all in the case of the nonspecific. This arrangement implies that the number of vertical columns in periextrinsic or intrinsic sectors which *may* be activated, and come in future to form the most probable route of "irradiation" of the input, is also greater.[16] The range of choice (as to which columns shall figure in irradiation) is further extended by the fact that the nonspecific system appears to exert a differential influence upon intrinsic cortex. As suggested in later chapters that influence may be such as to make intrinsic sector activity inherently more variable, both tonically (i.e., in the magnitude and areal distribution of excitability maxima and minima) and phasically (i.e., in the distribution of facilitatory and inhibitory foci within given vertical columns in a given area). The net effect is to make the formation of thing memories condi-

---

* External circumstance as represented by somatosensory and distance receptor inputs; internal as represented by core-activities and involving pathways (e.g. limbic-hypothalamic system→midbrain RF→neocortex) discussed in Section II.

tional upon a variety of concurrent central nervous events whose influence upon extrinsic sector activities (and so upon type memory-formation) may be comparatively limited.[17] The result is that the "locus" of a thing memory, or the cortical distribution of the vertical columns which come to comprise it, may not be as predictable as, say, the loci of parietal representation of "deep" skin sensation.

The several-stage distribution of thalamic sensory inputs just described thus serves to introduce an increasing element of chance or multiple causation, into the processing of primary sense data, in that those data, upon relay from extrinsic to periextrinsic and intrinsic sectors, tend to impinge upon an ever greater variety of other processes then under way in neocortex. Some of these may be "thought" activities only remotely related to present sensory inputs or their corresponding immediate external occasions; others will have originated in the core-systems, and may be the equivalent either of prior motivational-affective states, or of conditioned or unconditioned motivational-affective responses to present inputs (manifested in neocortex as nonspecific input changes probably of somewhat longer latency than the extrinsic sector events to which they correspond).

As result, where a thing memory now forms, following upon extrinsic-intrinsic sector relay, may to a considerable extent depend upon where other thing memories have formed previously, more particularly those whose motivational-affective states of origin were similar. Memories constellated in this way I have conceived as forming links in a common reverberatory closed circuit running from parts of temporal cortex to rhinencephalic sites (e.g., in the amygdala, septum or hippocampus); thence to certain parts of the midbrain reticular formation; and thence back to neocortex via certain structures and pathways of the thalamic nonspecific system.

This means that if subcortical projections from the temporal lobe as a whole are topographically arranged, such that some temporal areas distribute only or principally to certain rhinencephalic structures, one should be able to find areal groupings of thing memories according to their motivational-affective type, or some segregation of emotional representation in temporal cortex. Such a segregation has been reported by Denis Williams but his study appears to be contradicted by others.[18]

Alternatively one might suppose that with the possible exception of temporopolar cortex, subcortical projections from various parts of the temporal lobe, to the amygdala, septum, etc., are relatively diffuse or overlapping, the preferential route taken by a given temporal lobe outflow being determined at the next synapse; that is to say, by ongoing activities and prevailing excitability-levels in the total of subcortical receptor-systems concerned.

It is evident that neocortical activities are in two senses redundant. In the first, just considered, they are so in that the same sense-data tend to be relayed to a succession of cortical sites, or to have potentially multiple representation as memories. They are redundant, secondly, in that this distribution of inputs, is mediated by several sets of pathways—notably cortico-thalamo-cortical projections, the long association fiber systems, and the plexiform layer—many of whose areas of termination overlap. This means that relay of activity from n vertical columns at site A to n' columns at site B involves a convergence mechanism, such that if all of these relay systems are in optimal condition, all n' columns at B will tend to be activated and to reduplicate action patterns relayed from A. Very probably here $n' < n$, though these relative magnitudes will presumably depend upon prevailing excitability conditions in B.

This arrangement has two functional implications which are of the first importance. One stems from the fact that "optimal" conditions in the several relay systems just mentioned are differently determined—those in the specific thalamic relay system perhaps largely depending upon external (peripheral sensory) input conditions; those in the nonspecific system resulting both from collateral sensory inputs and concurrent core activities equivalent to some existing motivational-affective state; those in the association fiber systems reflecting a diversity of neocortical activities (e.g., other than those arising at extrinsic site A); and those in the plexiform layer reflecting *both* the activity of underlying cortex and remoter activities of the core.

The second implication is that *all* neocortical activity—"spontaneous" resting-state processes as well as sense-reception—involves redundant distribution, e.g., of action-patterns actuated at A to sites B, C, etc., the degree of reduplication of these at B, C, etc. depending upon the degree of convergence of inputs to B, C, etc. over the several sets of pathways concerned. Such convergence, since it represents both core and "intrinsic" neocortical processes, tends to be maximal to the extent that a condition describable as functional unanimity, exists between the neopallial and core-systems.*

In the case of sense-reception, the foregoing principle can be illustrated as follows. Presentation of a stimulus which is "expected"—that is, with which the organism is familiar, and the memories corresponding to which have been prefacilitated by presentation of appropriate cues or by an existing motivational-affective state, or both—results in specific recognition of low or minimal latency. In effect, maximally prompt relay of primary sense-data to outlying neocortical territories occurs in this situation because conjoint action of the neopallial and core systems selectively activates most or all of the paths of intracortical communication described above, thus favoring maximal convergence of inputs, e.g., upon certain already facilitated intrinsic sector vertical columns.

The reverse of this situation is one in which the organism's motivational-affective state does not correspond to the stimulus (was not the basal state-of-origin of the corresponding thing memory); and in which its "intrinsic" neocortical activities may be following a course correspondingly unrelated to the sensory input. The result is that specific recognition may be greatly delayed or may not occur at all, because of insufficient convergence of inputs via the several pathways into, and between, the intrinsic sectors concerned. The psychological parallel of these occurrences is that we may recognize a perfectly familiar person, object, etc.,

---

* I.e., if the trend of "thought" and of basal "intention" is the same. In man this seems often not to be the case, and in proportion as it is not, we tend to feel "distracted." That is, the freedom and efficiency of our conscious mental processes is apt to be reduced and the effort of thinking increased by concurrent unrelated feeling-states.

belatedly or not at all when we are mentally preoccupied, which amounts to saying, when our basic motivational state is inappropriate.

The fact that interareal relay of patterned neocortical activity may not occur merely in response to sensory inputs nor run in only two major directions (extrinsic→thalamus→periextrinsic→thalamus→intrinsic, during specific recognition, and in the reverse order during partitioning) may equally mean that during waking states, the processing of all available information (i.e., both recalled and just received) is continuous, like the activity of the cortex itself, and involves a diversity of widely scattered vertical columns in a variety of temporal orders.

Just as sensory inputs may result, by the convergence mechanism just described, in the establishment of new or the reactivation of old, thing memories, so the resting-state output of n vertical columns at intrinsic sector site A may produce convergences leading to activation of n' columns at site B, B, and A not necessarily being closely adjacent. Subsequent playback from B to A may then find a subtotal of the original n columns in a subthreshold state of excitability, and an additional number of columns now excitable (e.g., as result of the mechanism described on page 36 above). Generally, in other words, such exchanges between two arbitrarily chosen cortical areas will consist not merely in reverberatory interaction between fixed sites in each, but will rather take the form of progressions of focal activity in each.

It is from such semicontinuous intracortical communication, and the local progressions of activity consequent upon it, that the (layer III) abstract memory-systems may arise. Such memories may take shape either as result of the repeated concurrence in experience of otherwise unrelated sense-data or as result of those waking resting-state cortical interchanges by means of which, in effect, diverse recalled sensory information is "compared."* In intrinsic cortex, such information is in general representative of factual clusters or recorded episodes, the corresponding thing

---

* See Chapter IV, note 18, regarding the neuroanatomic correlates of this process.

memories forming similar sequential clusters or "most probable" routes of spread of neocortical activity.

Such comparisons I have visualized as being accomplished by the superimposition of action-patterns characteristic of a given vertical column (characteristic = most invariant = therefore action-patterns chiefly of V–VI) upon others by diverse relays. The most precise and frequently repeated partial congruences between these inputs and the "characteristic" action-patterns of the receptor column may then come to be represented there as relatively labile compromise action-patterns represented at the level of layer III, or in the large-pyramidal apparatus closest to those parts of the column in which transaction-rates, reflecting such inputs, are likely to be highest (see Chapter IV). One reason congruences of this kind are more often partial than one-to-one may be that data in several modalities may be cross-compared, the axonal firing-orders corresponding to the mode of representation of data in each possibly being quite different. Another is that our experiences proper seldom exactly repeat themselves, either in temporal form or in their component particulars.

Abstract memories, then, may act during sense-reception to conserve information as to the further structural or relational features common to groups of primary sense-data whose *prime* common feature is simply the fact of their close spatio-temporal concurrence (i.e., as "experience"). The latter feature, together with the structure of the component data, is conserved in basal memory-formations—the conservation of structural detail being greater in thing (posterior intrinsic) than in elaborated type (parakoniocortical, and possibly circumjacent generalized eulaminate) memory-formations.

Abstract memory-formations may equally arise during "rumination," or in consequence of intracortical communication when external sensory inputs are at a low level of intensity and/or variance, and attentional processes such as partitioning negligible. The comparison mechanism involved is essentially the same, and the resulting layer III action-patterns in effect embody partial formal similarities among thing memories representative of a wide variety of episodes or informational "bits." The so-called "scanning" function of resting-state alpha activity (Walter, 19) may in fact, be vehicular for the formation of abstract from basal thing memories.

It is important to note that as basal thing memories when reactivated tend to "return" recalled episodes severally, in their original order of occurrence, the formation of abstract memories, especially early in the life of the organism, will largely follow upon this process, or be incidental to sequences of intracortical communication determined at the level of layers V–VI and (even more) by core-inputs corresponding to the respective motivational-affective states of origin of the basal memories concerned.

With the later elaboration of abstract memories, this situation may begin to change; in psychological terms, insight and logical mental operations may cease to be incidental to the largely core-determined flux of mood and recollection, and instead come to have a momentum or continuity of functional existence in some degree both independent and determinative of these. For as layer III abstract memories become sufficient in number and distribution they may, in consequence of the higher metabolic and neural transaction rates of the outer laminae, come effectually to determine the action-patterns or information relayed by multiple pathways from column to column.* Moreover, in the process, abstract memories may themselves be "compared" or interact in such a way that a class of them, representative of structural features most widely found among abstract memories proper, gradually comes into existence. Abstract memories of the latter sort correspond psychologically to generalizations from generalizations, that is from certain structural or other relational features themselves abstracted from a variety of perhaps otherwise quite dissimilar concrete occasions (memories and/or immediate experience).

Since for abstract memories of this kind to come into existence presupposes the establishment of an extensive system of abstract memories of a lower order of generality, they represent a final stage in the development of neocortical information-processing

---

* It is this process which the earlier description of "reality principle" activities as proceeding from the top of the cortex down was meant to suggest, the bulk of the information leaving a given column doing so, probably, from the bottom.

activities—a stage increasingly deferred in the life of the individual, the greater his inherited neocortical potential (i.e., the "higher" his species). Neurophysiologically, such abstract memories may be defined as those which show maximal convergences of input from and divergences of output to, other vertical columns; and which, moreover, chiefly exhibit "congruences" with action-patterns established at the level of layer III in those columns.

It seems not unlikely that words are auditory and (in the literate) visual thing memories whose corresponding abstract memories come to show such extensive convergences and divergences. It is just because words *are* thing memories, often established early in the life of the individual and so with profound if not always conscious motivational-affective meanings (subcortical consequences when reactivated), that the logical operations mediated by words and their corresponding abstract memory-formations are apt to be faulty. To think in words (in other words) involves both the conscious "reality principle" process of thinking proper and more or less inevitably, "pleasure principle" processes, arising from simultaneous neocortical outflows to the core, and manifested in neocortex by changes in the pattern of nonspecific inputs. Psychologically, a word—or for that matter any thing memory—tends to entrain two sorts of neocortical event. One consists in a chain of evoked changes in subcortical activity and in nonspecific input which are experienced as a flux of mood and its accompanying trains of "subjective" association—the latter being, like dreams, in general expressive of basal fears or wishes.

In contrast, the same thing memory also serves to initiate trains of intracortical communication, or "intrinsic" neocortical activities which are mediated in large part via the abstract memory systems and (in proportion to the development of these) amount to a succession of logical transformations of the recalled data concerned. In effect, the other thing memories which the first may "call to mind" in this way will be those not necessarily emotionally related to it, but those which in some sense form its rational context, and whose activation thus depends upon some type of formal-logical nexus.

It follows then that to the extent that "intrinsic" neocortical processes, involving all layers, are chiefly determined by focal activity in the external lamina, cortico-subcortical outflows may tend to diverge from the form optimal for producing onset of focal core-activity or for the maintenance of trains of such activity.* The consequence of this, in turn, will be to reduce the competition of the core for control of neocortical activity proper. In this situation neocortical feedback to the thalamic reticularis may exert a decisive patterning action upon nonspecific inputs from this source, the net effect being further to favor *de facto* dominance of "secondary" over "primary" processes, or of the "reality principle" over the "pleasure principle."

In turn this amounts to saying that the more abstract we make our mental operations, the more accurate the resulting imitations of reality are apt to be; or more precisely, the freer these will become of the constraints and distortions frequently imposed upon them by the subcortical systems embodying our creature wishes. There are thus, perhaps, good neurophysiological reasons for the fact that the use of words—e.g., in metaphysics and political ideology—has repeatedly failed to produce tenable or objective systems of thought. Whereas when grammar was formalized and stripped of its related thing memories (i.e., when the *names* of components of relational schemes were omitted), thought exhibited an enormous gain in power and objective validity—as is shown by the unparalleled insights into natural phenomena which have resulted from the use of mathematics in physics, or, more broadly, from the application of pure reason to pure fact.[20]

In the light of the foregoing, Flechsig's observation as to the distribution of the long association fiber systems becomes es-

---

* Hence the unique importance of secondary abstract memories, or those which chiefly activate others. The cortico-subcortical outflows which then result in effect cut across, and may have little relation to, the motivational-affective constellations of thing memories discussed earlier, with the result that core-processes are not systematically forwarded or reinforced. It is perhaps for this reason that the cultivation of detachment and objectivity in thought tends to discourage the build-up of intense passions or emotion and to produce instead that "animated moderation" or "union of spirit with reasonableness" Bagehot mentions in *Physics and Politics*.

pecially significant, since in intrinsic cortex these systems, together with thalamocortical fibers and the plexiform layer, provide the interareal redundancy or multiple convergence mechanism necessary to the functional evolution of neocortical "reality principle" processes just described. In contrast those intrinsic sectors lying closer to or adjoining parakoniocortical and koniose sectors may embody what I have called elaborated type memories. Here the rate of transaction due to specific thalamic inputs may be somewhat higher, and the proportion of redundancy or multiple interareal comparison processes, (such as those in part mediated by the long association fiber tracts), somewhat less. The result is that the memories there represented (e.g., in Brodman 19; cf. note 21) tend to be mode-specific and to exhibit a higher rate of change as determined by the flux of day to day sensory experience. Memories of this sort may provide us, at maturity, with perceptual *Gestalten* such as figure-ground[22]—which is figure and which ground in a given perceptual field depending in part upon the mechanism of partitioning. The psychological phenomenon of "closure," a corollary of the Prägnanz principle[23] exemplifies our tendency to assort sense-data according to the type-memory schemata to which they show the nearest fit.* Interestingly also, the account given here of the way in which neocortical memory-systems come into being appears to be in accord with a basic supposition of Gestalt psychology which was that "[memory] traces undergo progressive changes according to the same principles of organization which govern perception" (*op. cit.*, note 23, p. 141).

As stated earlier, the abstract memory-formations of layer III in generalized eulaminate cortex are in several ways analogous to primary (layer III) type memories of extrinsic sectors. While the informational sources of the former are somewhat different (i.e., consist more of formerly "recorded" than of presently received, sense-data) abstract and primary type memories exhibit a comparable fluidity whose psychological equivalents are the fluidity of present perception and of many of our "ideas," or moment-to-moment conscious mental constructions.

---

* Including a tendency to extrapolate or "complete the picture" either spatially, as here, or temporally, given cues of another sort.

A morphological point relevant in this connection is that both in koniose and parakoniose sectors, layer V exhibits some rarefication of the large pyramidal layer found in V elsewhere; while in parakoniose sectors, in contrast to koniose, the development of large pyramids in IIIc is pronounced (see pages 56–57 above). These features suggest that basal (layer V–VI) memory-formations are less well developed in these sectors, and that parakoniocortex may have a special "collecting" function, mediated by its layer III memory apparatus (and analogous to that of layer III abstract memories elsewhere). To judge from the connections, which Bailey and Von Bonin have described as existing between this and other cortex (page 57 above), parakoniocortex may play an important role in partitioning in particular perhaps, that involving "elaborated type" memories, or the attentional foci established as sequels to generic recognition.

The fact that both layer III and layer V in extrinsic (koniocortical) sectors do not show the concentrations of large pyramids found at these levels in other sectors might be construed as a factor precluding the rigidification of primary perception as result of the development of extensive persistent extrinsic sector memory-formations.

THIS concludes the account of the way in which the several memory-systems proposed earlier may come into being in the neocortex. The latter, to paraphrase Lorente de Nó, may be regarded as an assemblage of internuncial chains parallel to one another and perpendicular to the pial surface. Whether in fact it is subdivided, in all sectors, into "modality pure" functional units on the size-order of a Mountcastle vertical column remains to be seen.

The object of the above has primarily been to show in what way the laminar distribution of major cell-types and of afferent and efferent fiber systems may determine the mode of functioning of vertical neuronal chains, thereby giving rise to areal functional differences in the neopallium which are systematically related to the disposition of the principal isocortical variants as described by Bailey and Von Bonin.

Secondly I have tried to convey some idea of the way in which various parts of the neocortex may interact, so as to subject both immediate and recalled sense-data to a several-stage sorting or "comparison" process; and of how the invariances, thus sorted out, themselves come to form memories of several orders of generality. Finally, I have suggested how it is that the latter make possible or in a sense *are* the rational conscious self.

It is not necessary to point out the deficiencies in this account. Since we do not yet know how even the simplest "bit" of information is represented in neural nets, the notion of the neural representation of an abstract concept such as circularity presents at the moment no unique difficulties. It seems highly probable, and indeed has been suggested[24] that the dentritic apparatus—more particularly perhaps of the plexiform layer—plays a major part in those "labile" neocortical activities possibly corresponding to thought. That memories are residues of such fugitive neural events, taking the form of more or less enduring axonal "firing-orders" is plausible but unproven. Granted these uncertainties, the hypothesis outlined here has the advantage that it yields certain predictions.

If, as result of subcortical "gating," a given sensory input becomes a thing memory, the prediction is that a later repetition of that input will result in its neocortical "irradiation" over certain most probable routes. Under carefully controlled experimental conditions it should therefore be possible to find the *foci* of cortical activity which lie along and partially comprise them.*

At maturity of the organism, or when thing memory-systems have fully taken shape, the variance of unit activity at the level of the internal lamina in Flechsig's "terminal zones" (cf. Bailey and Von Bonin, *op. cit.*, note 4, p. 77) might be thought to be minimal for neocortex as a whole. However, the elaboration of overlying abstract memory-systems can be inferred greatly to increase the probable diversity of local intrinsic cortical re-

---

* As mentioned earlier, however, the fluctuation of physiological baseline states requires that very large statistical samples be taken and that a number of physiological variables be correlated with electrocortical events recorded on any given occasion.

sponses, e.g., to inputs relayed via the thalamus from extrinsic sectors. Like "thought" itself, abstract memories (which are its residues) can be conceived as anti-entropic, in that they act to prevent the "freezing" of intrinsic sector activity into certain set patterns established at the level of V–VI. In a somewhat different way, as will be seen later, core-intervention in the shape of nonspecific inputs may have similar effects, differential for extrinsic and intrinsic sectors, in that it intensifies and decreases the latency of primary sense-reception in the former, while both accelerating and partially disorganizing labile "thought" activities in the latter.

In effect, the foregoing predicts that with considerable allowance for short-term variations—e.g., due to core-quiescence or changes in the rate of gross sensory input—maxima in the variance of unit activity* should be found at the level of the external lamina in parts of frontal and temporal intrinsic cortex. Moreover, in these sectors, the difference between the variance of unit activity in the external and internal laminae should also be maximal for neocortex and have clear parallels in the laminar distribution of ATP and phosphocreatine.

In addition to subserving the functions described above, the redundancy in distribution of primary sense-data throughout neocortex may also serve the purpose suggested by information theory[25]—namely, the minimization of error due to the unreliability of individual components of the network. For "unreliability" in neural nets, read local excitability changes, e.g., consequent to activities not directly related to inputs then being processed.

The foregoing theory of neocortical memory-functions involves two fundamental assumptions, the first concerning the mode of distribution of incoming sensory information, and the second concerning the role of large-celled bands in conserving certain of that information as preferential action-patterns.†

---

* Or more particularly, perhaps, in the variance of variance. This amounts to saying that under controlled input conditions, changes in the variance of unit activity in extrinsic cortex in an experimental animal will be more predictable than those in intrinsic sectors.

† Chapter IV, note 5.

If in fact information is relayed from a relatively small number of extrinsic sector sites to a much larger number of intrinsic sector sites by the pathways discussed here, the question is then how a later economy in the distribution of the same information is brought about. Studies of the electrocortical events accompanying habituation suggest that once a given sense datum becomes a thing memory, the latter does not have multiple or grossly redundant representation. In Section II, I have advanced the view that subcortico-cortical inputs, in particular those arising in the midbrain reticular formation, may have two types of effect upon neocortical processes. In the rising phase, or at onset of an intense motivational-affective state and increasingly as the latter reaches its peak, nonspecific input may be profoundly de-differentiative of previously established patterned activity in neocortex, more particularly in those sectors in which competition from the specific thalamocortical system (nuclei of the external portion of the dorsal thalamus, as defined by Pribram) is minimal. One function of the nonspecific system may thus be periodically to wipe out all but the most thoroughly established, or maximally probable routes by which incoming sense-data are "irradiated." In the descending, or facilitatory aftermath phase of nonspecific activation, the way is then cleared for the establishment of new routes of this type, the majority of which, like their predecessors, will also prove ephemeral. That is, the thing memories which are an end-result of irradiation, together with the action-patterns formed at intermediate (e.g., periextrinsic) sites, will for the most part, soon be superseded as just described, becoming thereafter of low, though not zero, probability. Such memories, though "forgotten" or functionally negligible, can nonetheless be reinstated more readily than new ones can be formed.

As the organism reaches maturity, the development of its neocortical memory-systems means in effect that for any given sensory input or group of them there exists a large number of potential routes of neocortical irradiation—the routes actually taken depending upon the degree of "congruence" of the input with the pre-established patterns which comprise or determine them, and the probability of these routes (essentially a function of prior use or reinforcement). If this interpretation is close to the truth, much of the information which passes by cortico-thalamo-cortical relay and other overlapping pathways, from extrinsic to posterior intrinsic sectors, is of the generalized kind represented in type memories.* This means in turn that our particularized memories are to a considerable extent constructed of type-objects, it being the configuration of these which determines the particularity of the corresponding item of recall. One advantage of the mechanism of attention is that it enables us to change the scale upon which we perceive and commit external facts to memory. However far we carry the small-scale analysis of sensory experience, it does not consist, so to speak, of true particularities, nor do the wholes comprised of these bits and pieces, however elaborately synthesized. In this sense the unknowability of the *Ding an sich* may be built into the central nervous system.

The functional advantage of the divergent distribution of information in the neocortex is that, in proportion to the degree of prior development of the neocortical memory-systems described here, it enables inputs to be quite sensitively assorted according to their spatio-temporal configuration. Similar redundancy or multiple comparison mechanisms evidently exist on the periphery or at way-stations en route to the neopallium. Examples are the possibly commissural functions of tufted cells in the bulb,[26] the increasingly large cell-populations involved in the relay of impulses from the cochlea to auditory koniocortex,[27] and the reported distribution of ipsilateral and contralateral optic fibers to alternate layers of the (six-layered) lateral geniculate in the monkey.[28] To what degree sensory data converging on mitral cells of the bulb or ganglion cells of the retina, or that data cross-compared via tufted cells in the bulb, intralaminarly in the lateral geniculate, or at various levels in the auditory pathway, are conserved locally as typelike memory-formations, remains a question. As suggested earlier (Chapter IV, note 5), I suspect that such conservation may occur and that extrinsic cortex represents a central elaboration of this sort of memory-function. Since, however, the existence of "nonlearning" neurons appears to have been

---

* I.e., as stated earlier, much of the information relayed extrinsic→intrinsic consists of type-memory data.

demonstrated,[29] it is possible that the peripheral sorting of inputs results in action-patterns which are wholly transitory, no matter how often repeated. It is also possible that the several receptors differ in this respect, a phylogenetically old system such as the bulb incorporating memory-functions which the "direct line" systems of the foveola[30] and inner hair cells do not. Coming into prominence later in the course of brain evolution and the telencephalization of function, these latter systems may largely act as non-learning transmitters.

In regard to the distribution of incoming information in neocortex, the role of the second somatosensory and motor cortices Sm II and Ms II[31] is as yet obscure. Certain of the evidence concerning these suggests that they may be more intimately related to the core motivational systems than are the primary motor and somatosensory areas (cf. Nakahama, *op. cit.*, note 31). Finally, it appears that in some primary cortical receiving areas—contrary to Mountcastle—mixing of data in two or more modalities may occur (cf. Glees, *op. cit.*, note 28, p. 252; see also Nakahama, *op. cit.*, note 31, pp. 201–202).

The crucial feature of this theory of memory-functions, whether central or peripheral, is the assumption that large-celled bands may have properties which peculiarly fit them to conserve, as "firing-orders" of varying degrees of "permanence," certain of the more frequently repeated action-patterns which take shape in smaller-celled assemblies presynaptic to them.* The reasons for this assumption are stated in Chapter IV, note 5. If investigation prove it tenable, it should take us a long way toward understanding how neural nets selectively retain a fraction of their inputs, and assort and process subsequent inputs in the light of information thus incorporated as "memories" or structural changes in the net. In this chapter I have attempted to suggest how the large-celled bands found in layers IIIc and V of much generalized eulaminate cortex may act as sieves by which, in effect, the more invariant action-patterns realized in the column as a whole are sifted out, surviving in those bands as preferential

---

* In connection with this point, see note 32, in which recent data of Hubel and Wiesel on the *modus operandi* of cat striate cortex are analyzed in some detail.

94 / THE PHYSICAL FOUNDATIONS OF THE PSYCHE

firing-orders guaranteed by changes in the postsynaptic membrane of the cells concerned.

IN their monograph on the human isocortex, Bailey and Von Bonin wrote: "In spite of the variations we have just described, one fundamental pattern is readily identifiable throughout the isocortex. . . . It is so constant, however, since the appearance of the cortex in the monotremes that it is difficult to escape the conclusion that it has some fundamental significance." I have here undertaken to define that significance in its essentials, with what success only experiment will tell.

SECTION II
Core systems and core-neocortical relations

CHAPTER VI

The Reticular System* and Central Integration

THOUGH it goes back at least as far as Descartes and has been questioned by (among others) Lashley, W. R. Hess, and Livingson,[1] the notion of centers or "seats" of central nervous activity is still very much alive in neurophysiology. In the case of structures such as the hypothalamus, it has proved quite apt—possibly because here application of the concept followed upon the results of experiment. In the case of "central integration," the reverse seems to have occurred. Many investigators appear to have assumed from the outset that we shall one day find some key organ or neural structure in the body, in which the activities of all the rest are knit up into the functional wholes underlying attention, coherent behavior and the appropriate affective and vegetative changes normally associated with these.

Following the early lead of Penfield and his associates[2] and the publication in 1949 of the work of Moruzzi and Magoun on the ascending reticular activating system,[3] many neurophysiologists have come to believe that the reticular system, roughly from the bulbar to the midbrain level, may be the structure in which such final integrations take place (see, e.g., S. Kety[4]). However, certain recent evidence suggests that this conclusion may have been premature, and must now be qualified if it is to hold at all.

A central integrating system of the kind just mentioned should presumably meet the following requirements. First, it

---

* See Bishop's "interlinked system" defined below.

should show maximal convergence of inputs, both from lower (e.g., spinal) levels, and from structures of the brain proper, it being in this way that the central integrating system comes to be maximally informed as to prevailing states and activities of the organism.

Second, it should show maximal divergence of outputs, it being in this way that the central integrating system exerts an influence upon ongoing activities in the remainder of the nervous system, commensurate with its own uniquely "informed" state.

Third, it should show cytoarchitectural and other features indicative of its unique ability to act as a "meta-informational"[5] system—i.e., one uniquely capable of the processing of information as defined below. "Other features" would include a demonstrable capability for highly precise, differentiated activity which, upon relay to appropriate outlying systems, might be expected to give rise to co-ordinated functioning of the organism as a whole.

Our present knowledge of the reticular formation suggests that it meets the first two of these requirements but not the third.

Anatomic studies such as the Scheibels'[6] and physiological studies such as that of Amassian and Waller[7] indicate great convergence of reticular inputs via spinal collaterals. French's report of cortico-septal-mesencephalic,[8] Wada's of cortico-mesencephalic,[9] and McLean's[10] of limbic-mesencephalic pathways suggest a similar convergence of inputs into the RF from forebrain structures. It is also clear that reticular outputs (e.g., to spinal levels, Ward[11]; Kuypers *et al.*[12]), to the hypothalamus and limbic system via Schütz's dorsal longitudinal fasciculus and the system of the mammillary peduncle (Nauta[13]), to the subthalamus and thalamus via Forel's tract (Scheibels[6]; Nauta, *ibid.*) and thence to the neopallium via the nonspecific projection system (Papez[14]; Purpura[15]) are widely distributed in the CNS.

Other points deserving mention in this connection are the following: that mesencephalic lesions in animals and man have been found to impair "consciousness," producing chronic drowsiness or somnolence;[16] that lesions of the interpeduncular nucleus, part of the "ancient motor system" described by Papez,[17] have been shown to interfere with the "skeletal" (motor) aspect of avoidance in rats (Thompson[18]); that "extreme" reward and punishment responses can be evoked by stimulation in ventral and dorsomedial areas of rat tegmentum respectively (Olds[19]); that at least one form of "motivation," is seemingly impaired in rats by medial forebrain bundle lesions anterior or posterior to the far-lateral hypothalamus (Morgane[20]); that the effects of lateral temporal lobe stimulation, and the "global changes" resulting from stimulation in the amygdaloid area in man (Feindel[21]; Adey[22]) have been inferred by Penfield and others to depend upon projections from these structures to the "centrencephalic gray matter" (Feindel, *op. cit.*).

It remains now to consider the third point mentioned above—namely, the respects in which the reticular formation may not be adapted to the final processing of information, postulated here as necessary to the function of central integration.

By "processing" is meant essentially the following: the assorting of immediate sense data according to modality; the preservation of certain clearcut features (e.g., topographic or spatio-temporal ordering; nuances of pattern and intensity) of these data; the selective formation of precisely articulated and potentially enduring memories from them; and the organization of sense data both immediate and recalled in such a way that, along with innate or marginally modifiable components in the behavioral apparatus, they give rise to "functional wholes" or co-ordinated and appropriate effector outflows.

Neither cytoarchitectural nor physiologic evidence appears to support the view that in mammals the reticular formation may have a unique capability for the processing of information as just defined; if anything, the contrary. Other systems may, in this respect, be demonstrably superior to it. In contrast to the fine-structure of neocortex, as described by Cajal, Lorente de No[23] and Sholl,[24] that of the RF appears to be quite primitive (cf. Pribram[25]; Bishop[26]). The anatomic work of the Scheibels[6] suggests that divergence and consequent overlapping of signals introduced into the RF by spinal collaterals, is quite probably great, from which it might be concluded that reticular transmission of signals involves a high loss of information, as compared to the transmission of similar signals to neocortical "analyzer" areas via the specific system. This conclusion seems to be borne out by physiological studies such as that of Amassian and Waller.[7] Using an implanted electrode technique, they studied reticular responses to peripheral stimulation in the cat. The following is an excerpt from their report:

"Some reticular neurons have enormous receptive fields. They can be activated by movement of a few hairs on any limb, trunk, and whiskers, and by auditory stimulation. Hindpaw and auditory stimuli activated reticular neurons more readily in the lateral than the medial midbrain. *This was the only evidence of a somatotopic organization obtained* [italics mine]. Reticular neurons with a wide receptive field which respond similarly to different afferent sources may be related to generalized functions of the reticular formation. However, those which respond with different temporal patterns of discharge to stimulation of (different) afferent sources may be related to local behavioral responses" (Amassian and Waller, *op. cit.*, pp. 104–105).

By contrast, many of the features of information-processing mentioned above appear, in mammals, to depend upon the neocortex. It is well known that conditioning can occur in decorticate preparations, or in animals reversibly "decorticated" by topical applications of aqueous KCl (Bureš[27]). The significant point is that learning capacity seems to be drastically reduced by these procedures (Gastaut[28]). In quite important respects, "central integration" in these animals has evidently broken down. The conclusion suggested by such findings must presumably have anatomic corollaries—e.g., one would expect to find evidence that the neocortex projects to spinal levels in such a way that its influence upon sensory inputs or motor outputs at those levels could be supposed equal to or greater than, that of the reticular formation. Here are some recent data bearing on that point.

In the cat, both anatomic and physiological evidence indicates that neocortical influence upon the gracile and cuneate nuclei may be exerted directly via pyramidal outflow, rather than indirectly via the reticular formation (Moruzzi *et al.*).[29] This finding has been confirmed by Jabbur and Towe[30] who qualify it with the observation that excitatory influence of the motor cortex upon these nuclei appears to be direct, whereas inhibitory influence may be indirect and involve pyramidal tract projections to the RF.

Kuypers *et al.* made lesions in the medulla at the level of the hypoglossal nucleus in rhesus monkeys which "interrupted all the longitudinal bundles throughout the medullary tegmentum, leaving the pyramidal tract and its immediate vicinity intact." Using the Nauta-Gygax technique, they distinguished two long-fiber systems distributed to the lower cord. One terminates "primarily in the basal parts of the posterior horn and in the zona intermedia" (the spinal homologue of the lateral tegmentum); the other "primarily in the medial and dorsomedial parts of the anterior horn and the adjacent parts of the zona intermedia." While "the most medial motor cell groups of the anterior horn might receive some long descending fibers" they also point out that "extremely few of these long descending fibers terminate in the motoneuronal cell groups of the anterior horn or the nucleus proprius of the posterior horn. . . . This distribution of the subcortical fibers to propriospinal neurons contrasts sharply with that of the cortical fibers which are distributed to sensory, motor, and propriospinal cell groups. As a consequence, while the cortical influence on the motor neurons and sensory cells in the posterior horn is direct, the influence of the subcortical centers on these groups must be exerted primarily through propriospinal internuncial neurons." These findings will be discussed further below.

Sprague has mentioned an area below the superior colliculi (in cats) which he considers to be "extremely important in the integration of visual and tactual information," adding that it has "a sizable contribution from the spinal lemniscus" and should probably be classified as tegmentum.[31] The important question is whether the "integrations" which can be inferred from experiment to occur in this or other areas of the midbrain RF, are of an order of complexity and delicacy to warrant regarding the RF as the "seat" of central integration as defined above. At present, the answer to this question seems to be no. For example, Sperry's[32] and, more recently, Meikle's[33] studies of split-brain cats indicate that transfer of supra-threshold brightness, but not of pattern-discrimination,* can occur at the collicular level. This finding argues that, in one respect at least, "processing" of information at the midbrain level, e.g., in areas such as that mentioned by Sprague, is primitive as compared to the processing of similar information, apparently accomplished in unoperated animals, via the neocortical specific system.

Additional evidence pointing to the same conclusion is reported by Sprague, Chambers, and Stellar.[34] In a recent paper they detail the behavioral changes which occurred in cats following unilateral and bilateral lemniscal section. The bilaterally operated animals showed "a marked sensory deficit, characterized mainly by sensory inattention and poor localization in the tactile, proprioceptive, auditory, gustatory, and nociceptive modalities, where direct pathways are interrupted. Similar defects appear in vision and olfaction where no known direct or primary paths are interrupted. . . . These cats are characterized by a lack of affect, showing little or no defensive and aggressive reaction to noxious and aversive situations and no response to pleasurable stimulation. . . . [They] are mute, lack facial expression and show minimal autonomic responses." In addition, these animals show an "incessant sterotyped wandering, sniffing and visual searching, as though hallucinating" as well as oral and pouncing automatisms.

The authors conclude that "without a patterned afferent input to the forebrain via the lemnisci, the remaining portions of the central nervous system, which include a virtually intact reticular formation, seem incapable of elaborating a large part of the animal's repertoire of adaptive behavior."

In contrast, they report that one animal with extensive medially placed reticular lesions, after partial recovery from somnolence (one month), "was hyperexcitable" showing "well-localized affective reactions (hissing, batting, clawing, growling, piloerection, pupillary dilatation) in response to painful stimuli or to any sudden visual, auditory, vibratory or tactile stimulus, even though mild in intensity. Because its threshold for emotional response was so low, this cat was also highly distractible [and]

---

* Very crude patterns perhaps excepted.

possibly because of this and the accompanying hypokinesia . . . performed poorly in formal learning tests." (Another animal with a more laterally placed reticular lesion was asymptomatic.)

Jasper,[35] Purpura,[36] and others have pointed out the importance of the inhibitory component in reticular "activation." The behavior of the mesencephalic cat reported by Sprague *et al.* may then involve two principal factors: diminution of the gross supportive action normally provided by reticular inputs to the forebrain, and diminution of the inhibitory restraint also imposed by those inputs upon forebrain responses, e.g., to sensory excitation. The former results in an animal abnormally drowsy and sluggish when not stimulated (i.e., one whose spontaneous forebrain activity is below normal waking levels); while the latter results in one which, when even mildly stimulated, tends to pass abruptly into a state of excessive (inadaptive) excitation.

The conclusion which Sprague *et al.*, have drawn from the behavior of their lemniscal animals appears to be supported by other anatomic and physiological evidence reviewed here. It would seem that in mammals, or at least in the cat, the RF does not fulfill the third condition postulated above as necessary to "central integration," in that neither it nor the collicular apparatus can supply the neocortex with sufficient information to compensate for interruption of specific inputs; nor, when the neocortex is so deprived, can the RF give rise to the "functional wholes underlying attention, coherent behavior, and the appropriate affective and vegetative changes normally associated with these."*

EXPLICITLY or by implication, much neurophysiological discussion involves a model of intersystemic relations which is roughly as follows. Given are neural systems A and B, having outputs to and inputs from other neuraxial levels, and two-way connections with each other. The output of A to B is viewed as consisting of a tonic or gross regulative, and a phasic or informational component. The function of the former is to maintain ex-

---

* This portion of Chapter VI was originally written as a separate paper for entry in the A. E. Bennett Contest of 1961.

citability of the receptor system (here B) at levels sufficiently high to permit adequate reception of the phasic output of A; and also to prevent excitability in B from rising to levels so high that ongoing activities in that system might effectually preclude imposition of the phasic component of A's output. Hence the tonic output of a given system includes both facilitatory and inhibitory components often, though not always, mediated from different parts of that system,* and whose relative magnitudes are, so to speak, proprioceptively adjusted in response to feedback from the receptor system conveying, among other things, information as to prevailing excitability levels in the latter. In this sense, the tonic output of a given system can be regarded as a carrier or potentiator of its phasic influence over those to which it projects.

Phasic outputs, e.g., from A to B, may be regarded as in general tending to duplicate certain action-patterns of A at functionally corresponding sites in B. While one-to-one duplications perhaps seldom occur, the net effect of this arrangement is to produce a degree of functional unanimity in the final outflows of A and B to lower neuraxial levels. As result for instance of metabolic changes of short-term local and longer-term systemic origin, such orders of functional dominance (e.g., A over B) tend to show both short-term reversal, e.g., on a scale of msec, seconds or minutes, and longer-term reversals on a scale of hours, as illustrated by diurnal sleep-waking cycles or (during sleep) by the sporadic alternance of telencephalic and rhombencephalic stages (Jouvet[37]).

In any given system, the relative prominence of its tonic and phasic output-components will probably depend upon its fine-structure and its input and output arrangements. The more diffuse its inputs and undifferentiated its cytoarchitecture, the larger will be the tonic component of its outputs and the smaller the proportion of information carried by these. Conversely, the more

---

* In Chapter I, note 18, evidence is cited showing that inhibitory and facilitatory effects obtained from the anterior lobe vermis of the cerebellum are frequency specific. Glees (*Experimental Neurology*, p. 195) reports that ipsilateral and contralateral stimulation of the anterior lobe facilitates muscle-spindle discharge, whereas stimulation of the vermis, presumably at the same parameters, evokes inhibition.

highly organized a system is cytoarchitecturally and the more discrete and systematically arranged are its inputs, the larger will be the phasic component of its output so that, in the extreme, the tonic component of its output will be indistinguishable from the sum total of its informational output per unit time (i.e., it will exert its tonic controlling influence exactly in proportion to the extent that its "intrinsic" activities have become highly organized as described in the case of neocortex, in the previous two chapters). As a corollary, such a phasically acting system may to a greater degree than those more primitively constructed, depend upon tonic inputs from elsewhere, since the very discreteness of its "intrinsic" activities may prevent it from likewise being the generator of its own activities.* In all essential respects, this description fits the neocortex whose activities do indeed seem to depend upon maintenance of adequate general excitability levels by tonic inputs from the reticular "activating" system, and whose controlling influence upon other systems, including the RF, appears to be directly proportioned to its capacity to act in a highly organized fashion.

The structural diffuseness of more primitive neural systems will in the extreme, perhaps dispose them to mass-action, or to a mode of activity describable as self-maintaining in the sense that they may display a maximum of output for a minimum of input, as compared to systems of the neopallial type. In effect, this description fits the reticular formation from the *zona intermedia* of the spine to the level of the mesencephalic tegmentum.

The central nervous system can be regarded as composed of discrete subsystems arrayed more or less in order of decreasing

---

* The work of Burns with cortical slabs isolated except for their vascular supply affords evidence in support of this view so far as neocortex is concerned. Cf. B. D. Burns, *J. Physiol.*, 111 (1950), 50–68; *ibid.*, 112 (1951) 156–157; and Burns *et al.*, *J. Neurophysiol.*, 1957, 20, 200–210. However, the question is far from settled. Batsel (Report No. 380 *U.S. Army Med. Res. Lab.* Fort Knox, Ky., April 1959) found that in dogs, after isolation of the cerebrum and extirpation of the midbrain, return of a waking EEG occurs chronically. In connection with similar studies, it has been suggested that denervation sensitization may occur, increasing the tendency of isolated cortex toward humorally mediated activation (Villa blanca, *Science*, Oct. 5, 1962, 138, 44–45), though not, in this case, involving the midbrain RF.

phylogenetic age, from caudal to rostralmost levels of the neuraxis. (An obvious exception is the pons, which in mammals, appears caudal to much older structures.) Many of these are reciprocally connected and in addition show convergence of their outputs at lower levels, with recurrent connections from these. E.g., outputs over pathways from A and B may reach C, caudal to both, a part of the resulting output of C passing spinalward and a part being relayed back to A and B. If C also receives ascending impulses, e.g., from the spinal system, it is clear that feedback from C to A and B will inform the latter systems as to excitability conditions and ongoing phasic activity at a number of neuraxial levels. Moreover feedback from some of these will include a second wave of effects consequent upon changes in endocrine output and in particular involving target structures such as the hypothalamus.[38]

Finally, to the degree that the phylogenetically newer systems added to the neuraxis are more differentiated in structure and more phasically acting than their evolutionary predecessors, they will stand to these in the functionally paradoxical relation of systems which are dependencies in respect of the gross or basal maintenance of their activity, but which nonetheless tend to become functionally dominant when their tonic inputs from older supporting systems, are kept within the required upper and lower limits. These, essentially, appear to be the relations existing between the midbrain RF and the neopallium; or between the former and the primary, secondary and tertiary olfactory systems of Pribram and Kruger.

In this connection, it is important to recall two facts. The first, pointed out by Sperry, is that the CNS as a whole must be regarded primarily as an effector apparatus. The second is that in the course of telencephalization, or the rostralward migration of "centers" of conditioning, effector functions of the more primitive structures on the neuraxis have not disappeared, but rather, co-exist with those of the newer. This arrangement is adaptive in two respects; first, in that it provides the organism early in life with a behavioral apparatus more or less ready made, pending functional development of "higher" nervous activities which may eventually take control; and second, in that the learning of behavior is itself thereby simplified, since what is learned is not a behavioral scheme *in toto* but a set of more or less elaborate modifications which are imposed upon a pre-existing repertoire.*

The foregoing means that in the case of a system such as the midbrain RF, we must make a clear distinction between its rostrally and caudally directed outputs since the character of these may greatly differ. For instance, in human brain, the rostral output of the midbrain RF corresponds to its phylogenetically recent function of providing tonic "support" of rhinencephalic and neocortical activity. In contrast, its outputs to the spinal level perhaps more nearly reflect its former functional supremacy, and so show a more pronounced phasic component. Present evidence suggests that this distinction has some basis in fact.

Ward[39] reports an earlier study by Sprague and Chambers showing that stimulation of the medial RF in cats produced a postural pattern of ipsilateral flexion and contralateral extension, the lateral RF yielding "a pattern opposite in direction." Similar patterns, including "beautifully organized movements," are also obtainable in unanesthetized higher mammals (e.g., the monkey). Ward's conclusion is that "this primitive motor system is capable of complex activity which may be somewhat less stereotyped than was once thought."

In addition, the RF "in higher forms . . . is directly responsible for postural reflexes and righting reactions, and plays a critical role in phasic movement and in the maintenance of muscle tone." Reticular stimulation may evoke rhythmic movements, these being antagonized by anticholinergic drugs. Tremor may be produced by lesions in the ventral tegmentum dorsal to the central part of the *substantia nigra,* unilateral lesions producing tremor contralaterally. Ward concludes that this last may not be a denervation phenomenon but may rather result from the fact that some reticular synapses are cholinergic and some adrenergic.[40] The point is of interest here, since self-stimulation studies show that the dual motivational-affective system discussed earlier,

---

* This applies as much to reticulomotor superimposed upon spinal motor patterns, as to pyramidal outflows superimposed upon reticulomotor. Cf. J. Paillard, *Handbook of Physiology, Neurophysiol.* Vol. III, p. 1686.

has representation in the midbrain RF;* and since the "pleasure" system, like the parasympathetic, may be mainly cholinergic, whereas the "punishment" system, like most of the sympathetic, may be adrenergic.[40] As will be seen shortly, these relations may have certain parallels at the level of the rostral midbrain and thalamic reticularis.

It is well known that a system of rapidly conducting reticulo-spinal fibers exists. Moreover the neuronal apparatus upon which these caudally directed reticular outputs impinge is evidently, from the account of Kuypers *et al.*,[12] such that reticular priming of the motor systems may both precede and outlast pyramidal outflows (cf. French[41] re the work of Lloyd and of Kleyntjens *et al.*).

Consequently, the reticular formation provides, at the spinal level, the preparatory and relatively long-lasting motor "set" upon which the more sharply phasic outputs of the pyramidal system are superimposed—a phenomenon having certain parallels in the more rostral central nervous events equivalent to the evocation of phasic "thought" processes by a basal motivational-affective "set" or mood. In both cases there tends to be a functional consistency between the core-state and its more phasic higher-level sequels, and in both (though possibly to different degrees in each) the latter or phasic, activity may subsequently alter the trend of the former.

The multiple feedback circuits in the model described on page 103 above are illustrated in the case of neocortical vis-à-vis reticular effector outflows by the pathways mentioned by Jung and Hassler.[42] These include outflows from area 4 and the "psychomotor" level (e.g., via Türck's and Arnold's bundles, and temporo-amygdalar pathways) to the midbrain pons and cerebellum; and thence, e.g., as follows: neocerebellum→N. *ventro-oralis posterior thalami*→area 4; or, midbrain→*globus pallidus*→VL→ area 4; or again, amygdala→putamen→GP, etc. By recurrent pathways of this sort, a degree of reconciliation or functional unanimity is established among systems which, in proportion to their phylogenetic age-differences, may severally have quite different output characteristics.

---

* See Chapter VII, below.

In summary, a new system will be one whose phasic and tonic output components closely coincide. Such excitability changes as it effects elsewhere will be integral to the information it relays and will not long precede or outlast the patterned activity equivalent to the latter. For older systems, the converse of these statements holds. In the spinal apparatus, as described by Kuypers *et al.*, we see an arrangement well suited to these output differences, e.g., between the neocortex and reticular formation.

The distribution of medullary tegmental fibers to spinal interneurons, while not precluding phasic actions of reticular origin, also serves to duplicate tonic functions of the more rostral RF, at the spinal level. These in turn are responsible for those relatively prompt and lasting excitability changes—equivalent to various forms of motor "set"—which the pyramidal system, by virtue of its structure, is apparently incapable of producing.[41] However, the fact that pyramidal connections with spinal motoneurons are more direct perhaps implies that neocortical motor outputs, when forthcoming (and also with due allowance for the resultant-producing feedback arrangements discussed above), tend to take precedence over motor outputs of reticular origin.

Thus the characteristic modes of functioning of old and new neural subsystems are reconciled—at more rostral levels, so as to produce simultaneous or temporally overlapping outputs having the necessary minimum of functional consistency with one another; and in the final effector paths, in such a way as to take maximum advantage of the output characteristics peculiar to each.

Two factors can be conceived as essential to telencephalization, or the rostral migration of the "centers" of behavior control in mammals. One is the qualified dominance guaranteed neocortical motor outputs by the directness of spinal pyramidal connections (Kuypers *et al.*). The other is the degree to which, by reason of its subcortical connections, "intrinsic" activities of the neopallium are furthered by tonic supporting inputs from the core and at the same time shielded from phasic inputs from the same source, since the latter, roughly in proportion to the phylogenetic age-difference between the systems concerned, might have the effect of primitivizing neocortical processes proper. If systems A and B, in the model, are of greatly differing phylogenetic age, the phasic output of B, the older, will be apt to exhibit far less diversity or precise articulation than will A's phasic output to B. Great biological inefficiency might thus result if A came under phasic control of B for much of the time, since this would amount to a situation in which "old" functions were being reduplicated in "new" structures, at the expense of the further potential of the latter.

More specifically, had the CNS evolved in such a way that phasic components of rostrally directed reticular outputs were as pronounced as those of caudally directed (e.g., reticulospinal) outputs, the result might have been to preclude that delicacy of function which is the biological *raison d'être* of the neocortex. The latter's activities, in other words, might largely have reflected the necessarily cruder processing of information occurring in the core, and so in effect have remained largely instinct-bound.

Instead, as I have tried to show, the distribution of inputs, both by layers and sectors in neocortex and the trend of its activities are such that in higher mammalian forms, the neocortex increasingly tends to elude core-control and *pari passu* to initiate and control behavior rather than merely inflecting behavior initiated elsewhere.

Herrick[43] notes that "during phylogenetic development of cortex, ascending and descending pallial projection fibers are added to the pre-existing systems of the underlying stem. They do not entirely supplant them, for even in mammals where cortical projection systems are highly developed, the subpallial parts of the hemisphere retain their own diencephalic connections." In the dorsal thalamus, the nuclei of the midline and intralaminar groups are generally regarded as rostral extensions of the reticular system. For reasons given by Papez and others (Chapter V, note 14), the reticular nucleus of the ventral thalamus should probably be included with these.

Bishop[44] states that "a chain of structures extending from the spinal cord level through the various levels to the cerebral cortex has been recognized in as primitive a form as *Amblystoma*, where Herrick designated one region of the alba as the precursor of the reticular formation. These other levels include the reticular formation of the medulla, and certain nuclei and paths of the thalamus and corpus striatum. An analogous region of the cord is the dorsomedial grey, possibly including the *substantia gelatinosa* and ascending tracts. . . . In the mammalian cortex the outer plexiform layer is of special interest as a component of this system. It comprises a synaptic field in which small and unmyelinated fibers make contact with apical dendrites of cortical pyramid cells at some distance from their cell bodies in a primitive arrangement such as occurs in the amphibian. As in all other levels of the primitive system, these synapses connect both the adjacent regions of the cortex with each other and distant levels of the brainstem with the cortex, to form a terminal member of a linked system extending throughout the length of the neuraxis."

According to Jasper,[45] "It has been shown that cortical activation is of two forms, one of rapid onset and brief duration, and another of slow onset and prolonged duration. The former has been called the phasic activation system and the latter the tonic. . . . It now seems clear that the tonic activation system lies in the basal diencephalon and midbrain, and has many properties distinct from the thalamic system. The phasic type of rapid but short duration arousal seems to be characteristic of the thalamic system. The tonic activation system of the brainstem is particularly sensitive to epinephrine and it may well be that the tonic phase of activation from this area is largely due to the humoral aspect." (Apropos of this point, see the cross-perfusion studies of Purpura, suggesting humoral tonic activation of the cortex from the brainstem.[46])

From the work of the Scheibels[47] it would appear that effects of the tonic nonspecific system may be mediated neurally as well as humorally—e.g., via fibers of the "ventral component" to the hypothalamic *zona incerta,* some of which may reach the septum and *corpus striatum,* and may also reach N. *reticularis* and *ventralis anterior* via collaterals.

Jasper reports that blocking of recruitment responses obtained from stimulation of the intralaminar group can be produced by simultaneous stimulation of the midbrain RF at higher frequencies. According to Monnier and Tissot (Lindsley[48]) there may be "a dual mesencephalic reticular system for arousal and alerting, one of short latency and one of very long latency," a similar dual system existing in the thalamic reticularis. A recent study by Schlag et al.[49] shows that electrocoagulation of a region "corresponding approximately to the posterior commissure and pretectum" abolished the lasting EEG arousal formerly obtainable by 60 to 300/sec stimulation of *centralis lateralis, centralis medialis, paracentralis, reuniens,* or *rhomboidens.* This effect was selective for lasting arousal evoked from the thalamic reticularis, since such arousal could still be elicited by *d*-amphetamine, or by electrical stimulation of peripheral nerve or of the midbrain RF; or could arise "spontaneously." The fact that through these lesions "the desynchronizing action of the thalamic stimulation was lost or strikingly reduced" argues that in the course of its normal phasic action, the thalamic reticularis may enlist varying degrees of tonic midbrain support, via projections, e.g., to the pretectal area lesioned in this study or (as these authors put it) by "backward action from diencephalic structures to the lower brain stem." It would be interesting to know if this diencephalic system is cholinergic.* A study by Steiner and Himwich[50] suggests that it may be. In rabbits transected cephalad to the midbrain they obtained short (15–20 sec.) alerting reactions by intracarotid injections of acetycholine chloride—this in contrast to amphetamine alerting which is lost following transection cephalad to the anterior border on the pons. However, the literature on this point is somewhat contradictory (see for instance Van Meter and Ayala, *EEG clin. Neurophysiol.,* 1961, 13, 382–384).

Sharpless and Jasper[45] found that in habituation (i.e., the loss of generalized neocortical responses similar in form and probably in origin to the "tonic" orienting reflex; see Chapter II, note 18), the tonic system dropped out first, the phasic system requiring "many more repetitions of a given stimulus and [recovering] more readily without reinforcement." In addition, Jasper points out that the tonic system does not appear to be

---

* Apropos of the finding of Monnier and Romanowski (Chapter IX, note 9) that in the rabbit acetylcholine produces neocortical desynchronization which is blocked by atropine.

Reticular System and Central Integration / 113

topographically organized, and in contrast to the phasic system, is involved in "the intense excitement of an animal with attack or fear responses." The work of Schlag *et al.*, however, suggests the possibility that the phasic system via its midbrain projections may under certain conditions evoke more widespread rostral midbrain output or mobilization of the tonic system (see a recent paper by Hassler, reporting the effects of stimulation of various thalamic and pallidal sites in waking humans).[51]

A degree of functional competition can be inferred to exist between the tonic and phasic systems from the fact that recruitment responses can be blocked as described in the preceding paragraph but one. It is interesting also, as it may bear upon the question of why the neopallium tends to exhibit "handedness" that activity of one nonspecific nucleus can be inhibited by stimulation of the same nucleus contralaterally. Where handedness of language representation is concerned, the apparent lack of commissural fibers connecting the first and third temporal gyri, reported by Bailey and Von Bonin, and the probable dependence of parts of temporal cortex on inputs of the thalamic reticularis, may likewise be quite important. Finally, the phasic nonspecific system can, according to Jasper, be inferred to interact with the specific thalamocortical system as a result (a) of collaterals to nuclei of the thalamic reticularis from the principal sensory pathways, (b) of intrathalamic connections from intralaminar to specific relay nuclei (but not, apparently, the other way around) and (c) of overlapping projections "in almost all areas of the cerebral cortex. Corticofugal projections provide a fourth means of interaction between specific and unspecific systems."[45]

THE foregoing might be interpreted as follows. The anatomical points cited from Herrick and Bishop may mean, in effect, that as new thalamocortical fiber systems were added to the existing diencephalic apparatus, and as the neocortex itself expanded, the two rostralmost extensions of Bishop's "linked system extending throughout the length of the neuraxis"—namely, the thalamic reticularis and the plexiform layer—became anatomically and functionally so enmeshed in the neocortical specific system as to constitute to a quite considerable extent a functional dependency of that system. Thus, whereas highly organized caudally directed phasic outputs of the RF have clearly survived in higher mammalian forms (cf. Ward), the RF may also have evolved in such a way that a decisive separation has taken place between the structures-of-origin of its *rostrally* directed outputs. Tonic reticular outputs, e.g., to the neopallium, evidently arise in the midbrain proper; while corresponding phasic reticular outputs appear to arise in the thalamic reticularis and may thus largely owe their character as such to interaction with the neocortical specific system (e.g., as described by Jasper). It is perhaps as result of this separation of phasic and tonic reticular functions at the forebrain level, that the neocortex has come to be "shielded" in a way which permits development of "intrinsic" neocortical activities during the life of the individual (see above, Chapter IV and V). In fact this shielding is only partial, in that it clearly does not preclude tonic reticular inputs frequently disruptive of "intrinsic" neocortical activities.*

A second point is that the thalamic reticularis may chiefly represent a rostral extension of the core trophotropic "pleasure" (normal survival) system discussed in Chapter I, whereas the nonspecific system of the midbrain proper may chiefly represent the ergotropic or emergency system (see note 48). It is interesting in this connection that the phasic nonspecific system of Jasper may be cholinergic and the tonic system adrenergic (Steiner and Himwich).

The reader will recall that I postulated the two major motivational-affective systems to act synergically, so that pleasure states ranging from sleepiness or satiety to ferocity or extreme anger enlist graded amounts of dynamogenic support; or conversely that "punishment" states enlist varying degrees of sup-

---

* More precisely, high levels of nonspecific input appear to have different effects upon extrinsic and posterior and frontal intrinsic cortex, this crude topographic differentiation having differential effects upon processes equivalent to reasoning, relevant recall, and direct perception, discussed *passim* here.

port from the pleasure system. When such "answering effects" are large in amplitude, the result may be a secondary state of rage proportioned in intensity to the state of fear which touched it off. When they are small and chronically so—that is, when massive primary fearlike inhibition is indefinitely protracted and rarely or barely relieved by facilitatory *contrecoup*—the result in man may be agitated or involutional depression or, in the extreme, catatonia (as noted earlier, a condition with interesting resemblances to tonic immobility).

The paradox is that such states may frequently depend upon neocortico-subcortical feedback from sectors (e.g., the posterior intrinsic) which, as I have tried to show later here, are more closely related by phylogeny and present function to "reward" systems of the core. However, the fact that basal memory-systems of the neocortex may subserve motivational-affective responses of *any* type to a degree determined in part simply by the accidents of experience has this consequence: that in man, "conditioning" may lead to a functional deadlock, in which inhibitory (primary fearlike) responses are so reinforced from the neocortex as to disrupt or virtually paralyze other activities of that system.

To the extent that electroshock causes gross disruption of patterned activity generally, it may tend to break up such circular interactions and relieve acute depressions even though (to quote Sperry) at the cost of wearing "blankness and confusion into the brain." Sherwood's work with intra-ventricular cholinesterase, together with Nachmansohn's recent model suggesting the mode of action of acetylcholine-cholinesterase at the membrane surface,[52] strongly implies that in catatonia the circular interaction just described may have long-term metabolic *sequelae* which in effect entrench the disorder.

The projections of the thalamic reticularis to the midbrain (Schlag *et al.*), conceivably constitute one route by which neocortical activities, e.g., preparatory to overt behavior, evoke appropriate degrees of activity in the core pleasure and/or punishment systems, other pathways being those from the frontal and temporal systems which reach the midbrain via the rhinencephalon; or those from the neocortical "strip" regions to the septum and thence to the midbrain.*

The longer latency of the rostrally projecting tonic midbrain system vis-à-vis that of the thalamic reticularis (see Jasper above; also note 45) seems to support the distinction made here between caudally and rostrally directed outputs of the RF. For whereas the former outputs may precede and tonically "set up" pyramidal outflows, and may also supply some of the phasic components of final effector outflows arising in this way, the latter or rostrally directed outputs of the midbrain RF may be automatically fractionated such that the phasic component, of thalamic origin, is shorter in latency and owes its form perhaps in good part not to the RF at all; while the tonic component, of midbrain origin, follows some msec in its wake. Even with due allowance for reticular "gating" of inputs, e.g., in the gracile and cuneate nuclei or in the bulb,[53] this arrangement may serve to give primary sense-reception in neocortex a slight headstart over tonic nonspecific inputs resulting from the same group of stimuli (cf. note 54).

Finally, where inputs to neocortex from the tonic midbrain system are concerned, it appears that there may be important areal differences in the effects which these produce. The chief difference is perhaps between intrinsic and extrinsic sector effects. The latter are exemplified in a recent paper by Fuster,[55] and by evidence cited earlier, showing that reticular stimulation tends to reduce the latency of sense-reception. By both intensifying and shortening the duration of given patterns of extrinsic sector excitation and inhibition, it effectually increases the number of discrete "bits" of sensory data which can be distinguished per unit time from the flux of concurrent inputs.

According to Arduini "the highest responses to reticular stimulation were found almost constantly in the frontal areas"[56] —a fact possibly related to effector or action-organizing functions of those areas (cf. Chapter VIII, part ii, below). Jasper[57] reports that "in another series of experiments, Ricci has found

---

* That the neocortex does in fact exert a control of this kind over the RF is further shown in a recent study by Hugelin and Bonvallet (*EEG clin. Neurophysiol.*, 1961, 13, 270–284).

that direct stimulation of the brainstem reticular formation causes blocking of slow activity in the EEG, and more commonly causes a decrease or arrest of unit discharge in the temporal lobe."

These observations suggest certain parallels with the psychic changes occurring during intense motivational-affective states, in particular fear. In these, processes equivalent to peripheral or reflective thought-activity are brought to an abrupt halt—this perhaps corresponding to the diminishment of unit activity in the temporal lobe as reported by Ricci. At the same time perceptual acuity is increased (Fuster) and attention riveted on those parts of the perceptual field usually, though not invariably, representative of actual danger to the organism. This phenomenon may in varying degrees involve activation of the subcortical (perifornical) "sensory fixation" mechanism,[58] the latter substituting generalized all-purpose responses (e.g., fixation on anything moving in the organism's visual field) for the temporarily disrupted and more selective mechanism of "partitioning" described in Chapter V here.

It is then on the rebound from such primary emergency states—i.e., in consequence of subcortical answering effects mobilizing the pleasure system and accompanied by widespread facilitatory release in the neocortex—that we begin to act, often with an improvisatory brilliance proportioned to our preceding fright and mental paralysis. Conversely, when such rebound does not promptly or fully occur—i.e., when fear is prolonged or chronic —the tendency is for our thought-processes to remain hampered and our behavior ill-adapted, repetitive, and crude. Memory-defects frequently accompany such states (e.g., stage-fright or chronic anxiety). These facts argue that high levels of tonic nonspecific input produce diffuse inhibition selective for the thing memory apparatus of posterior intrinsic cortex and for the labile neocortical activities associated with it (cf. Chapters VIII and IX).

The point of importance here is that rises in tonic nonspecific input to high levels, corresponding to intense activity in the subcortical "punishment" or dynamogenic emergency system, may serve to enhance those neocortical activities most directly arising out of the specific system, in the way illustrated by

Fuster's data,[55] while causing some disorganization or inhibitory suspension of those mediated via the thalamic association and nonspecific nuclei. Hence the fact, noted by Jasper, that high-frequency midbrain stimulation may block recruitment from the thalamic reticularis,* may have certain clear parallels in the electrocortical and psychological events accompanying acute fear or activation of the longer latency tonic midbrain arousal system. What these relations also demonstrate is the point made above—namely, that in the case of rostral output of more cephalad portions of the RF, a clear separation of phasic and tonic components seems to have occurred, the former or phasic component deriving its informational content from systems external to the RF, while the tonic component originates in the midbrain proper and conveys no information to neocortex.[59]

The experimental prediction which follows is clear. If the thalamic reticularis is both as important to "intrinsic" neocortical activities as many have concluded, and if it also largely owes the phasic component of its activity *to* neocortex, then any operation which deprives neocortex of the influx of precise sensory information necessary to its proper activity will likewise disrupt normal functions of the thalamic reticularis. Nonspecific input will then no longer further, and may impair, "intrinsic" activities of neocortex; near obliteration of the phasic output of that system will release primal (normally vehicular) motor mechanisms and cause failure of the reticulospinal and peripheral apparatus which normally subserves attention by the selective "gating" of sensory inputs. In effect, "central integration" will collapse.

Such seems to have occurred in Sprague *et al.*'s bilaterally lemniscal cats, and that notwithstanding the fact that in these animals, olfactory and visual afferents, and collateral sensory

---

* Implying functional competition between these divisions of the RF, the thalamic reticularis perhaps having become, as suggested here, a dependency of the neocortex. If the latter and TR are cholinergic, arousal obtained by "backward action" of TR on the midbrain RF may be of the answering-effect type. That is, the primary effect of TR-RF outflow may be inhibitory for the activating system and may be followed by rebound of that system. This pattern of response may figure in the momentary arrest of activity accompanying the "regarding reaction" and can also be obtained from stimulation of the cortical "strip" regions (French).

inputs to the RF, were evidently intact. It was, in short, not necessary to deprive the neocortex totally of patterned inputs from the periphery, to bring about a seemingly permanent shift in functional dominance from neocortex to systems of the core.* Nor were the latter when dominant but also subnormally "informed" (i.e., released from phasic neocortical control; see the model of intersystemic relations given above) capable of maintaining the minimum of behavioral organization necessary to survival in a natural state.

On these grounds, I believe that central integration in mammals must be regarded as a synergy[60] of the kind proposed in this and earlier chapters. Conversely, the notion that central integration has a "seat" or is in some way finally accomplished in any one subsystem of the CNS seems to me, on the evidence no longer tenable.

---

* A similar but far less complete or intractable shift toward core-dominance appears to have occurred in Thompson and Melzack's Scotties (Chapter II, note 19). Melzack has since produced roughly the same effects in beagles by early restriction of visual experience (*Science*, Sept. 21, 1962, 137: 978–979). The excitability and irrational (inappropriate) behavior of these animals at maturity I have supposed to result from an inadequately developed neocortical type memory-apparatus, it being the latter which assorts or organizes specific inputs and is therefore prior to "intrinsic" activities of neocortex generally, phasic outputs included.

The behavior of Sprague's cats suggests the second stage in insulin-induced hypoglycemia in man, described by Himwich—the stage of rhinencephalic-diencephalic dominance (see *Biol. Ment. Health and Disease*, 552–553). It is interesting that adult psychically normal humans can undergo quite drastic reductions of forebrain input *à la* Sprague (e.g., by bilateral section of the medial lemniscus and spinothalamic tract) without obvious impairment of conscious mental activity (Glees, *op. cit.*, note 57, 357).

CHAPTER VII

The Limbic System

THE three-part olfactory system of Pribram and Kruger here referred to interchangeably as the limbic system or rhinencephalon (Introductory, note 8), is described in their paper as follows: "The first system consists of the olfactory tubercle, area of the diagonal band, prepyriform cortex, and the corticomedial nuclei of the amygdala. This system has direct connections with the olfactory bulb. A second system has only secondary connections with the olfactory bulb. It consists of the basolateral nuclei of the amygdala, the septal nuclei, the frontotemporal (and possibly subcallosal) juxtallocortex, and probably includes basal parts of the striatum.* On histogenetic grounds, the structures grouped as first and second system (semicortex and perisemicortex) were distinguished from Ammon's formation and related cortex (archicortex and periarchicortex). This distinction is supported by axonography. [As will be apparent presently, however, it may have to be qualified in the case of the septum, vis-à-vis the third system.] The third allo- and juxtallocortical system composed of Ammon's formation and cingulate and entorhinal cortex has abundantly demonstrated electrographic as well as histological intraconnections and is only remotely related by any technique, to the olfactory bulb."

Several anatomic points about these systems require mention. MacLean[1] shows the lateral olfactory tract distributing to

---

* Hence occasional later references to this as the strio-amygdaloid complex, a designation also used by Herrick in *Brain of the Tiger Salamander*. It is probably significant, however, that caudate spindling in the cat can be evoked in the septum but not in the amygdala (Buchwald *et al.*, *EEG clin. Neurophysiol*, 1961, 13, 509–538).

the amygdala and the medial tract to the septal area—the intermediate olfactory tract distributing to the diagonal band area and olfactory tubercle.[2] Papez[3] states that "the medial olfactory tract passes deep to the cortex and ends in the region of the subcallosal gyrus. This is the region where the medial bundle of the forebrain takes its origin and passes back into the lateral portion of the hypothalamus for visceral responses." At least some of the latter appear to be feeding responses,[4] "satiety" (or better perhaps mechanisms inhibitory for feeding behavior) having more medial hypothalamic representation.

"The diagonal band of Broca" (Papez continues) "extends from the region of the lateral olfactory nucleus across the anterior perforated substance in front of the optic tract and ends in the medial parolfactory area. It effects some correlation beween the lateral and medial areas"—i.e., between the amygdala and septum. (For interconnections of the latter, in some detail, see Herrick, *op. cit.*, note 11 below, 255–256.)

Three other groups of septal connections are probably of special importance. The first of these are the cortico-septal fibers described by French.[5] The second are the two-way connections of the septum with the hippocampus via the precommissural fornix—septal efferents evidently figuring in the regulation of hippocampal theta activity.[6] The third consists of those septal fibers which according to Nauta (as cited by Petsche *et al.*[7]) "form one of the most massive roots of the medial forebrain bundle. Most of the fibers which arise in the septum are distributed either directly . . . or indirectly . . . to a zone in the tegmental area."

In this same zone, which MacLean has called Nauta's limbic midbrain region,[1] ends "a most primitive motor path" (Papez) which in its full extent comprises the olfacto-habenulo-interpeduncular system. It evidently arises in the *nucleus basalis* of the anterior perforated substance (passing thence to the lateral habenular nucleus via the olfacto-habenular tract); and in projections of the septum to the habenula via the stria medullaris.[3,8] In addition, the medial habenular nuclei receive projections from neocortex. Habenular outflows chiefly reach the interpeduncular nucleus via the *fasciculus retroflexus* of Meynert, from which "a massive fiber system, Ganser's tegmental tract of the interpeduncular nucleus, distributes to paramedian regions of the caudal midbrain tegmentum* including Bechterew's superior central nucleus and the tegmental nuclei of Gudden. In the rat the septal region also projects directly to this tegmental region. Furthermore part of the fornix bundle" (i.e., the post-commissural fornix) "must be assumed to articulate in the mammillary body with the mammillo-tegmental tract, which likewise distributes to medial tegmental regions of the caudal midbrain, possibly including Gudden's deep tegmental nucleus" (Nauta[8]).

Additional projections from the limbic system to the midbrain include those from the basolateral nuclei of the amygdala, damage to which reportedly causes hyperphagia in cats and rats (Adey[9]); those from entorhinal cortex (*ibid.*); and those from the hippocampus, via the fornix, to the periaqueductal grey (Nauta[8]).

The projections arising in Nauta's limbic midbrain region are of equal interest. Nauta[8] points out that "reticular projections to the hypothalamus and limbic system appear to arise only from medial regions of the caudal midbrain which . . . are largely situated outside the mainstream of ascending reticular pathways enclosed in Forel's . . . system" (i.e., the *tractatus fasciculorum tegmenti* which evidently bifurcates rostrally into the dorsal and ventral components described by the Scheibels; cf. Chapter VI, note 47). Reticulo-hypothalamic projections include the system of the mammillary peduncle which originates in the medial tegmentum rostral to the isthmus—"possibly" including Gudden's deep tegmental nucleus—and in the ventromedial tegmental region or Papez' "nucleus of the mammillary peduncle."[8] It should be added that components of the system of the mammillary peduncle continue forward in the medial forebrain bundle to reach the lateral hypothalamus and preoptic region, and the

---

* It is possibly relevant, in this connection, that many reticulospinal fibers arise in medial portions of the RF, notably the medullary part of the *nucleus reticularis gigantocellularis* which according to Glees (*op. cit.,* Chapter VI, note 57) "extends over most of the medial two-thirds of the reticular substance" in the cat and rabbit. In man, this nucleus is reportedly much reduced.

medial nucleus of the septum. The last is probably of special importance in view of the apparent role of that septal nucleus in the regulation of hippocampal theta activity.[6] In addition, fibers of the medial forebrain bundle distribute to the amygdala. A second fiber system, the dorsal longitudinal fasciculus of Schütz, is, according to Nauta, "composed mainly of fibers which ascend from the periaqueductal grey midbrain substance to caudal regions of the periventricular zone of the hypothalamus."[8]

Finally, Petsche et al.[7] point out that in the same midbrain region, comprising Gudden's dorsal and ventral nuclei, the "paramedian reticulum,"[1] periaqueductal grey and ventral tegmental area of Tsai,[8] there arise ascending fibers which reach the thalamic reticularis "via the ascending component of the *fasciculus longitudinalis dorsalis*" (of Schütz).

Before discussing the functional meaning of some of these arrangements, I will briefly consider them from the standpoint of comparative morphology, and also in the light of certain ideas presented in earlier chapters here.

Sherrington[10] long ago pointed out that "the earliest cerebral cortex is formed in connection with the neuron-chains coming into the central nervous organ from the patch of olfactory cells on the surface of the head. The region of the cerebrum thus developed is the so-called olfactory lobe and hippocampal formation" (or, respectively, the *pallium basale* and *pallium marginale*). "The olfactory lobe is well formed in selachian fish. In the reptilian cerebrum . . . the *pallium marginale* coexists in addition. These are both of them olfactory in function. Even so high up on the scale as the lowest mammals, they still form one half of the entire pallium. But in the higher apes and man, the olfactory portion of the pallium is but a small fraction of the pallium as a whole. . . . The olfactory part of the pallium exhibits but little variation in form as traced up through the higher animals."

Three of Herrick's figures are likewise instructive. The first[11] shows, in transverse vertical section, the arrangement of major structures in the brain of *Necturus* as follows. Mediobasally in the hemisphere lies the medial forebrain bundle and above it the fornix. Superior to these, medially, is the hippocampal pallium;

superior to the latter and traversing the dorsal eminence of the hemisphere is the dorsal pallium or innermost grey substance, upon which lie the dorsal neuropil and white substance in that order. On the lateral aspect, dorsally, begins the pyriform neuropil extending basally to the strio-peduncular tract and strio-amygdaloid neuropil, these lying but a short distance from the medial forebrain bundle.

A second schematic view[12] of similar sections made through the brains of *Necturus,* the box tortoise *Cistudo,* the Virginia opossum *Didelphis,* and man, shows that the progressive evagination of the dorsal pallium has gradually displaced both the hippocampus and pyriform-amygdaloid system until these lie in their present mediobasal position in human brain.

His third figure[11] shows the brain of *Amblystoma* in two horizontal sections, as seen from above, the plane of one section being somewhat dorsal to the other. In these the approximate extent of sensory (olfactory) and motor zones is shown in one hemisphere, and the corresponding anatomical formations in the other. In the more basal section the motor zone extends laterally and anteriorly roughly as far as does the pyriform neuropil. In the lateral surface, the sensory zone runs posteriorly almost to meet it, while (on the medial aspect of the hemisphere) it extends into the septal region. The second and more dorsal section shows that at this level the motor zone ends anteriorly in the dorsal thalamus, the sensory zone having a distribution much like that at more inferior levels.

To the foregoing one might add MacLean's statement[1] that "Johnston, who was one of our greatest comparative neuroanatomists, said that the hippocampal cortex is just an outgrowth of the hypothalamus"; Herrick's[11] that "in Ichthyopsida the hypothalamic influence is much stronger than the thalamic, a relation which is strikingly reversed in higher vertebrates," and his observation (*ibid.*) that the medial septal-hippocampal system is olfacto-visceral in function in contrast to the lateral strio-amygdaloid and strio-peduncular system which is olfacto-somatic; Le Gros Clark's suggestion that the system of the mammillary peduncle is to the hypothalamus as the lemniscal system is to the thalamus;[13] and Bureš'[14] that the hippocampus and neocortex may be "end-stations of two systems which are independently aroused by a common subcortical mechanism."

OLDS reports[15] that in rats "extreme escape behavior" results from stimulating in the dorsomedial tegmentum, while extreme self-stimulation—presumably pleasure—can be got from electrodes placed in "ventralmost portions of the tegmentum," arousal reactions arising from "a fairly lateral strip halfway up." "A region yielding extremely high self-stimulation rates runs in a broad path along the medial forebrain bundle region of the ventro-lateral floor of the hypothalamus."

Although there are some midbrain areas yielding low self-stimulation rates, it seems that in general rates are highest at this level and diminish as one moves into the diencephalic and limbic regions.[16] In rats, for example, self-stimulation rates in the posterior hypothalamus (but not in the mammillary body) are very high.[17] Rates diminish as one moves forward in the "tegmental hypothalamic system" along the ventromedial surface; are relatively low in the anterior hypothalamus; "rise slightly" in the preoptic region; and "fall sharply to about 200 an hour . . . [in] cortical parts of the rhinencephalon." "In all cases" Olds adds, "we find extreme stability of self-stimulation rates from day to day when the electrode stays in a given place."

The experimental situation here is one in which the animal receives current only when pressing a lever which turns it on. The fact that self-stimulation rates reach stable ceiling values at all sites tested, and that these values may differ enormously—in the case of tegmental vis-à-vis rhinencephalic cortical stimulation, by a factor of 40—suggests that reversals of effect, from reward to punishment, may begin to occur above the stimulation rate optimal for any given site, such reversals probably not being due to factors such as tissue damage. The latter, if it occurred, would presumably diminish net reward and might therefore lead to a transient rise in self-stimulation rates, followed by a fall when this increase in input had failed over a sufficient interval either to increase or maintain previous net pleasure. This pattern has not been reported. In any case, the range in ceiling input-rates (from 200 per hour in rhinencephalic cortex to approximately 700 per hour in the diencephalon and 8000 per hour in the tegmentum) is so great as to rule out the factor of tissue damage, since it is unlikely that the brain-structures concerned differ that much in their vulnerability to applied currents.

If maximal self-stimulation rates are determined negatively —that is, simply by failure of further increments of pleasure to result from increases in input above ceiling—the question is why periodic overshooting of these maxima does not occur, particularly in areas where ceiling rates are relatively low and so present no problem in motor execution. I suspect that in fact ceiling rates are positively determined, that is, by reversals of reward to punishment when the optimal rate at a given site is exceeded. This conclusion is supported by data cited below, showing that great restriction of reward areas occurs when the animal receives current automatically and can only turn it off.

Earlier I postulated that motivational-affective states in general involve participation of both basal core-systems, one or the other being functionally dominant and its "opposite" in varying degrees playing a supportive role. An example of this mechanism is given in Chapter IX, involving a CR by which animals obtained food. In the preliminary (food-getting) phase, activity in the dynamogenic emergency system may equal or somewhat exceed that of the (alimentary branch of) the pleasure system. In the later consummatory phase, or during eating, activity in former normally subsides, leaving the latter dominant. In the study cited, it was shown that amphetamine did not interfere with the preliminary phase but in sufficient dosages would block the consummatory phase, presumably by preventing the normal subsidence of emergency system activity as just described, or a shift in dominance, e.g., to the far-lateral hypothalamic "feeding" centers.*

These relationships can be pictured by means of a simplified model. Assume the normal survival (pleasure) system A and dynamogenic emergency (punishment) system B each to exert a

---

* Which also give "reward" upon self-stimulation. See Olds and Margules, *Science,* Nov. 2, 1962, 135, pp. 374–375; also Hoebel and Teitelbaum, *ibid.,* pp. 375–377.

mixture of facilitatory and inhibitory effects upon the other. Secondly, assume the latter system, by analogy with the sympathetic, to be the more diffusely organized and massively acting. Thirdly, assume a rate of inhibitory input q to be critical for A, in that that rate of input is capable of damping back activity in A even when A is at or near peak levels of activity. Finally, assume that B is capable of an inhibitory output rate equal to q at levels of activity well below the maximum for B.

When activity in B reaches a level at which its inhibitory output to A equals q, A's activity, and *pari passu* its inhibitory control over B, will begin to diminish. With this, activity in B may show escape or be virtually decontrolled, going on to reach supernormal maxima whose durations are determined by crude physiological factors such as fatigue. Something of this kind appears to occur when we succumb to panic or during prepsychotic crises. It also seems to be demonstrated in the case of Lilly's monkeys (see below) subjected to crescendo stimulation of the anterior midline hypothalamus.

During sexual excitement or rage, pleasure or (in rage) a kind of elation will persist so long as A's inhibitory control of B keeps the latter in a supporting role. (In this situation, pleasure increases as the participation of B, because of the metabolic acceleration involved.) By analogy with the parasympathetic system, A's outputs to B are perhaps more highly differentiated than are B's to A. (See later chapters on the evolutionary origins and comparative morphology of forebrain components of these systems.) Thus like the neocortex vis-à-vis the midbrain RF, A may in part make up in phasic what it lacks in tonic control over B. The inherent danger to the organism during both intense sexual excitement and rage is that circumstances may intervene to upset the balance of power in favor of B. Because in such states, B is very nearly at the level of activity at which its inhibitory output to A approaches q, any external event which selectively heightens activity in B may reverse the order functional dominance between these two basal systems. Hence interruption of lovemaking at or near the point of orgasm, or the sudden appearance of an overwhelming threat when we are intensely and as it were confidently angry, may in an instant precipitate us into violently unpleasant states, often including a considerable element of fear and mental confusion.

Finally, because of the mode of organization of the midbrain reticular formation, one might imagine that here the differences in internal structure and output characteristics of the "reward" and "punishment" systems, just described, are less pronounced than is the case in the diencephalon or rhinencephalon. In other words, at the midbrain level A more nearly equals B in its capacity for massive action or its resistance to inhibitory suppression. (I.e., q at this neuraxial level is larger.) Hence an animal can self-stimulate to far higher rates in the midbrain before reversals of effect begin to occur.

If the intensity of pleasurable states is in fact proportional to emergency system support (such that A and B are at high levels of activity and B's output is just short of q), then maximal self-stimulation rates, for instance in the diencephalon and rhinencephalon, should be found in areas in which anatomic and physiological evidence indicates a high degree of convergence of the reward and punishment systems. In the diencephalon, this is borne out in the case of the posterior hypothalamus, as mentioned below. High self-stimulation rates are also found in the septal region. Lilly believes this result may be due to the fact that "the sexual system here seems to be combining the effect of the powerful energizing avoidance system and the extreme pleasure of the rewarding" (*op. cit.* note 1, p. 51).

Other experimental evidence suggests that what I have called answering effects figure in "reward" obtained from septal stimulation. Glickman and Feldman[18] have shown that, in sleeping rats or in cats under chloralose, stimulation in midbrain or rhinencephalic sites known to be rewarding does not readily produce "habituation." One might predict that with stimulation at a site from which the pleasure system was mobilized first and the emergency system secondarily, in a supporting role, a pattern of primary electrocortical slowing (rise in activity of A; increased inhibition of B) followed by an electrocortical arousal pattern (escape of B, or the answering effect) would be observed. These authors report that, in chloralose-anesthetized cats, "stimulation of the septal area at voltages producing good rates of self-stimulation also induced arousal, although in one cat the onset of arousal had a consistently long latency and was regularly preceded by high voltage cortical activity. In this animal no evidence of habituation was observed in 45 trials. In the two in which slow cortical potentials did not appear, the arousal response did habituate. However complete habituation was not observed, and the arousal response showed much greater resistance to extinction than that observed with the non-reinforcing electrode placements." One wonders if decreasing the stimulating frequency and/or voltage in the latter two animals might not have produced the pattern of response noted in the first.

Apropos of the foregoing and the mechanisms of cortico-reticular control discussed in Chapter VI, one also wonders if the habituation to direct midbrain stimulation observed by these authors to occur in some of their sleeping rats may not have been mediated from the thalamus and neocortex. It appears from the work of Sharpless and Jasper, cited earlier, that the thalamus alone may mediate this type of response. Steriade and Demetrescu (*EEG clin. Neurophysiol.*, 1962, 14, pp. 21–36) remark that "previous investigations have shown that in the case of fast rhythmic acoustic stimuli (above 10–15/sec) the phenomenon of habituation *generally* takes place first at the level of the auditory cortex" (italics theirs).

In other words, when primarily driven by the subcortical emergency system the neocortex may, in particular from extrinsic sectors, exert a focal inhibitory feedback effect upon the midbrain sites chiefly concerned, this interaction leading 1) to a restriction of extrinsic sector activity to smaller and better-defined *loci*; and 2) to a subsequently observable damping down of activity in the more diffusely organized midbrain RF.

By contrast, other areas of neocortex such as the posterior intrinsic may have a less marked inhibitory influence upon the midbrain RF (whence the importance of basal thing memory-systems in the reinforcement, e.g., of activity of the core emergency system). Therefore, when neocortical input of the core emergency system is more nearly equaled by inputs of the core pleasure system, or when reticular inhibition of intrinsic sector activity is less pronounced, neocortico-reticular feedback is likewise less inhibitory—this being the mechanism which causes "reward" responses for instance evoked by stimulating in the midbrain pleasure system, to show the resistance to extinction observed by Glickman and Feldman.

To return to the work of Olds, it is significant that when the stimulating procedure is reversed, so that the animal is subjected to the current and can only turn it off, the resulting map of "pleasure" and "unpleasure" areas is quite different. When (as Olds puts it) "the environment pumps in the electricity . . . the size of the escape system is thereby greatly increased and the size of the system in which the animal will perform no response to turn it off is limited enormously."[15] This is perhaps because stimulation, in this situation, tends to exceed the maxima described above. When avoidance areas—e.g., the anterior midline hypothalamus—are stimulated in monkeys by the "crescendo" technique described by Lilly,[16] dominance of the emergency system becomes so extreme as to threaten the organism with catastrophe. In this phenomenon, Lilly suggests, endocrine feedback may play an important part, in effect reinforcing a primary fearlike response of neural origin (cf. also Marrazzi, Chapter 1, note 4), which is destructive in proportion as it is not compensated or "answered" by *contrecoup* of the pleasure system. It is important to note that whereas the posterior hypothalamus may yield high self-stimulation rates because of the mixed (sympathetic-parasympathetic) representation there reported by Hess,* the anterior midline hypothalamus, like medial and basolateral parts of the amydala, may more specifically mediate massive inhibition of certain pleasure-system activities during fearlike mobilization. (See note 4, regarding medial hypothalamic representation of "satiety" centers; see also Lilly, *op. cit.*, for marked sympathetic signs in monkeys stimulated in approximately this region.)†

---

* Olds, *Trans. 3rd Macy Conf. Neuropharmacol.*, 1957, p. 352.

† Also Krasne, *Science,* Nov. 16, 1962, 138, pp. 822–823, for evidence that ventromedial hypothalamic stimulation at graded intensities produces inhibition of feeding, exploratory behavior, and finally escape reactions. Discontinuing stimulation has been observed to result in "rebound" feeding.

In certain types of severe mental disorder in man, a similarly massive inhibition of pleasure-system functions appears to occur. In these, as suggested earlier, man's unique neocortical potential may play a critical part. That is, his proneness to non-organic mental-emotional disorders may depend upon the unique capacity of his neopallial memory-systems to reinforce and thus unbalance subcortical motivational-affective processes, and of his frontal intrinsic systems both to drive and be driven by, the dynamogenic apparatus of the core. To date clinical evidence indicates that in the genesis of such disorders, parts of the orbit and dorsolateral frontal cortex, and (in the rhinencephalon) of the gyrus cinguli, may play a far larger part than does posterior intrinsic cortex, the anterior temporal region excepted.[19] The meaning of this apparent fact will be discussed presently.

Following evocation of primary motivational-affective states by stimulation in parts of the rhinencephalon, what I have described as answering effects often seem to occur.[20] In other words, when persistent maintenance of such primary states is discontinued, release or unmasking of some of their components in the "opposite" system occurs. In physiological terms, functional dominance now tends to pass from the primarily activated to the supporting system, in the way that under "physiological" conditions, it would probably have done long before. That this is not simply a default phenomenon due to "fatigue" of the structures stimulated, is suggested by the fact that the activity unmasked in previously unstimulated structures appears often to be well above normal waking-state levels (cf. Chapter I, *passim*, and Chapter I, note 18; also the model of intersystemic relations given in Chapter VI).

From the brief *résumé* of the limbic-mesencephalic and intralimbic connections given in the first part of this chapter, it is clear that pathways exist whereby the rhinencephalon can activate the reticular "reward," "punishment," and "arousal" systems described by Olds, and by which answering effects can occur within the rhinencephalon proper. The question is whether from these and other data (e.g., from stimulation and ablation studies) the two motivational-affective systems postulated in Chapter I above, can be inferred to exist in the rhinencephalon. That is, can the structures comprising each and the pattern of their intersystemic relations be stated in a way consistent with a variety of neuroanatomic and physiological facts?

The answer, probably, is yes, provided that one except certain problems still insoluble, and also avoid the fallacy of trying to localize motivational-affective functions in discrete "centers." Present evidence suggests that emotions or drives are not generated by special self-contained neural engines projecting widely to the rest of the CNS. Rather they are integral to receptor and effector processes and may be accounted for in terms of sets of neurophysiological conditions or intersystemic relations which these establish during the genesis of behavior. These conditions —in contrast to the often diffuse free-floating character which emotions have subjectively—favor certain clearly definable behavioral results. The subjective distinctness, e.g., of fear from rage or sexual excitement, is equally misleading, in that it suggests that emotions are isolable psychological *things*, whereas in fact they may be synergic in origin and composed, more often than not, of "opposites" in varying proportions.

In the case of motivational-affective representation in the limbic system, the untenability of the centers concept* is illustrated by the amygdala which has many emergency functions[21] but which also evidently plays a part in sexual[22] and feeding[1] behavior. While pointing out that the amygdala and other structures of Pribram and Kruger's secondary olfactory system show "a surprising similarity" in function, Gloor[23] adds that "bilateral amygdaloid or other rhinencephalic lesions fail to produce deficits of the very autonomic and somatomotor functions which are so clearly influenced by rhinencephalic stimulation. . . . This noninvolvement of the rhinencephalon in the integration of basic autonomic and somatomotor mechanisms makes it easier to accept the absence of a mosaic of topographical representation of function in this system. It also makes more acceptable the potentially dual character of many rhinencephalic stimulation responses, with op-

---

* I.e., of the notion that each feeling-state has exclusive representation at certain sites, or that certain rhinencephalic structures are in this sense highly specialized.

posite effects upon the same function apt to occur from the same locus of stimulation."

It is unnecessary to point out that the concept of the answering effect and the network of limbic interconnections given in outline above make this duality of responses obtainable from a single site more understandable. As in the case of the impingement of neocortical sensory inputs upon vertical columns in various phases of the excitability cycle, a rhinencephalic stimulus of fixed site and parameters may be expected to have graded effects in a given motivational-affective "modality," or may produce "opposite" effects on different occasions, depending upon the sort of answering effect train upon which it intrudes, and where temporally, in the train, intrusion occurs.

The first point made by Gloor—namely, that many limbic structures do not appear to be indispensable to the functions they regulate—is perhaps explainable as a consequence of the peculiar course followed by the evolution of the brain. In reptiles, according to Herrick (*op. cit.*, 11, p. 105) no longer is "the entire forebrain dominated by the olfactory system"; in them "the great increase in the system of the somatic sensory exteroceptive thalamic radiations is correlated with enlargement of the corpus striatum complex, including an extensive area quite free from olfactory and hypothalamic connections, and the extension of some of the fibers of the thalamic radiation to the dorsal pallial field without interruption in the striatum. Thus the pallial field is subdivided into three well-circumscribed areas." Two of these evidently correspond to the rostral and medial sensory (or olfacto-visceral) areas, and to the lateral and more posteriorly situated motor (or olfacto-somatic) area, in the brain of *Amblystoma* (page 124 above). The third pallial area, in reptiles, is one "emancipated from dominance of the olfactory system"; and with its appearance begins the trend toward the development of an extensive non-olfactory receptor-effector apparatus, and the transfer of functional primacy from the hypothalamus and rhinencephalon to the thalamus and neopallium.

Instead of being modified virtually out of existence, the olfaction-bound, hypothalamus-centered brain of the Ichthyopsida has been bypassed by the explosive growth of the mammalian specific thalamocortical system; and during that growth, as Sherrington noted, has itself undergone but little change. As before, rhinencephalic functions remain closely tied to those of the midbrain RF, and many of the innate reactive mechanisms which Galambos[24] and others have suggested are represented in the rhinencephalon may in fact only be activated from that system via its midbrain projections (cf. Gloor, *op. cit.*, note 23, p. 1409). The point of particular interest here is the scheme of functional relations apparently existing between the rhinencephalon and neocortex.

Whereas the neocortex can be shown to project directly to parts of the limbic system, it appears that the latter may chiefly exert its influence upon the neocortex *in*directly,[25] for instance via projections to Nauta's limbic midbrain area and thence via Schütz's fasciculus to Forel's tract, as described above. In this way rhinencephalic influence upon neocortical activity is blended with that originating in the midbrain RF proper; so that to the degree that rhinencephalic activity is itself extensively modulated by neocortical outflows, the rhinencephalon can (to rephrase Bureš's remark) be regarded as a way station, or interposed modulatory apparatus, by which conditioned responses represented in the neopallium evoke appropriate gradations in concurrent responses of the midbrain.

In other words, in mammals the limbic system may be particularly important in the genesis of *learned* motivational-affective responses. This conclusion is supported by a study of Heath et al.,[26] showing that emotionally charged memories evoked distinct changes in rhinencephalic activity, whereas emotions such as anger relating wholly to events in the present did not. Elaboration of learned responses seems almost certainly to have been a primordial function of the olfactory forebrain (as Herrick, in his work on *Amblystoma*, frequently suggests). That is to say, memory-formation very likely occurs in parts of that system in higher as well as lower forms, complementing establishment of neocortical memories of a more highly articulated kind, and likewise "closure" or reticular trace-formation which Gastaut and others believe to occur in the midbrain during conditioning.[27]

In virtue of cytoarchitectural and input differences, rhinencephalic memories might be supposed to exhibit somewhat greater particularity or elaboration, and somewhat lower rates of change or extinction, than do their midbrain reticular homologues. For the same reasons, they are presumably somewhat less stable and particularized than homologous memory-formations, e.g., of posterior intrinsic neocortex (cf. MacLean, *op. cit.*, note 13 above, p. 1737)

Because of its fine-structure (cf. Scheibel and Scheibel, Chapter III, note 5) and the convergence of inputs into the midbrain RF, establishment there of any particular engram or stable firing-order may be of low probability, while "extinction" or radical alteration of such engrams, once formed, may be highly probable. This order of probabilities then tends to be reversed in pallial systems of the rhinencephalon, and still more so, perhaps, in neocortex—this being the essential reason for the observable differences in conditionability and de-conditionability (Voronin, Chapter II, note 1) which have resulted from rostral migration of the "centers" for learned behavior, in the course of evolution.

According to the present account, conditioning may be a process involving trace-formation at a number of central nervous levels concurrently, the "reluctance" of formation decreasing and probable duration of traces increasing the phylogenetically newer the system concerned.[28] The functional relation between the neocortex and rhinencephalon described above is of biological value in that it in some degree places the cruder receptor-effector apparatus of the olfactory brain (parts of the striatum included) under control of the neopallium, with the result that the "functional unanimity" of these systems tends to be established and maintained by the latter. To the extent that the neopallium projects directly to the rhinencephalon more than conversely, the latter system via its tegmental projections favors neocortical modulation of tegmental activity over tegmental modulation of neocortical activity by the same routes. It is perhaps because the rhinencephalon in higher mammals has come to play the subordinate role just described that Sprague *et al.*'s bilaterally lemniscal cats showed nearly complete failure of adaptive behavior. It is important to note that the foregoing analysis applies more to posterior than frontal neocortical sectors, where

136 / THE PHYSICAL FOUNDATIONS OF THE PSYCHE

direct rhinencephalic influence may be greater (Chapter VIII, part ii).

It is also obvious that the midbrain RF must exert a considerable influence upon rhinencephalic activities—one which, in comparison to that of the neocortex, is tonically massive and phasically perhaps less clearcut. From this it would appear that the mammalian rhinencephalon is both a neocortical and a mesencephalic dependency, likely to amplify the activity and extend the *de facto* control of either system, depending upon which happens to be dominant at the time.

Unfortunately, this functional scheme—more especially in the higher mammals and most of all in man—entails possibilities of integrative breakdown and adaptive failure which are proportioned to the adaptive advantages it seems, for the most part, to confer. Both sets of possibilities can best be understood in terms of the influence which core systems exert upon the "intrinsic" activities of neocortex—the latter as described in Chapters IV and V above. In effect, what we call "states" of emotion or motivation are successions of focal subcortical activities, each with its characteristic neocortical consequences. Some of these last are conducive to functional dominance of the neocortex, and some quite evidently are not. The mechanisms and biological rationale involved thus constitute a special case under the general plan of intersystemic relations outlined in the preceding chapter. The question to ask about a particular drive or emotion is not where is it located, but rather to what neurophysiological transactions* does it correspond, and what orders of functional dominance are thereby favored among the n interconnected subsystems principally concerned? This is the question I shall take up next, with particular reference to the rhinencephalon. Of that system, Herrick wrote: "I have suggested that . . . especially in the corticated mammals, the olfactory sense, lacking any localizing function of its own, co-operates with other senses in various ways,

---

* Including tonic, or gross controlling, and phasic, or regulative informational, components. The order of functional dominance of a given group of systems on a given occasion can then be conceived as a vector digaram expressing the directions in which these influences are chiefly exerted.

The Limbic System / 137

including a qualitative analysis of odors (desirable and noxious) and also the activation or sensitizing of the nervous system as a whole and of certain appropriately attuned sensori-motor systems in particular, with resulting lowered threshold of excitation for all stimuli and differential reinforcement or inhibition of specific types of response" (*op. cit.*, note 11, p. 99).

Apropos of the foregoing, it is interesting that in one modality, olfaction, the rhinencephalon can be supposed to retain something of its ancient primacy as the forebrain system for elaboration of learned behavior. It has been pointed out to me[29] that the olfactory receptors, unlike others, lack afferents such as might selectively restrict input at the periphery, although this is clearly not true in the case of the bulb.[30] In any event, establishment of a CR to an olfactory stimulus can be expected to begin in allo- or juxtallocortical systems and to occur later elsewhere;* and because subject to direct reactivation by the CS without, or some msec in advance of, neocortical participation in the response, it follows that olfactory conditioned responses in general must be uniquely resistant to extinction. This conclusion is supported by Pechtel and Masserman's study showing the remarkable persistence of conditioned olfactory (as compared to auditory or visual) avoidance responses in monkeys.[31]

---

* This doubtless being followed by feedback reinforcement or "consolidation"—i.e., establishment of the CS as an olfactory memory in parts of rhinencephalic cortex, in the same way that neocortical thing memories are established as result of nonspecific or core "support."

The *modus operandi* of the bulb, which differs from auditory and visual receptors in having no "direct line" outputs comparable to those of the foveola and inner hair cells, is discussed briefly in Chapter IV, note 5.

CHAPTER VIII — part i

Limbic-mesencephalic and Limbic-neocortical Relations

WITHOUT prejudice to Sperry's contention that all central nervous processes are ultimately effector, it is still necessary to distinguish subsystems which are primarily concerned in the reception and further processing of sense-data as described above in the case of extrinsic and posterior intrinsic areas of the neopallium. Conserved locally as memory, the cumulative effect of that processing is to increase the number and accuracy of forecasts as to the probable course of external events, which the organism, given certain cues in the present, is capable of making.

Data reviewed below suggest that while the subcortical motivational and frontal intrinsic systems are important in the construction of behavioral schemes conforming to such forecasts, these brain-structures are largely informed from elsewhere and fail in their organizational functions when deprived of that information. Notwithstanding the structural similarity between frontal and posterior intrinsic cortex, the type and average rate of input may in the former be such as to preclude the elaboration of stable well-articulated memory systems of the kind which take shape in posterior sectors, secondarily as it were, to the processes of sensory reception. Much frontal intrinsic cortex can in fact be removed without gross intellectual deficit or collapse of adaptive behavior. By contrast, lesions of posterior intrinsic cortex, in particular of the temporal lobe, appear to attack behavior at its source, producing defects of comprehension rather than of execution,* or in the extreme, a Klüver-Bucy animal (see Akert *et al.*, Chapter VIII, part ii, note 51). In short, while it can be shown that receptor structures, e.g., of the neopallium, are not exclusively that, it also seems probable that intelligence is largely a receptor system activity.

It arises, as suggested above, particularly in generalized eulaminate cortex whose input rates are relatively low or intermittent, and in which the selective formation of enduring detailed basal memories is followed by "processing" of these data, giving rise to an overlying abstract memory or "meta-informational" system. Vis-à-vis primary sense-reception, these second and third order activities require relatively large cortical territories; and, because also extended in time, overlapping the specific occasions of experience, they require maintenance of a predominantly facilitatory climate in the cortex concerned.

On the effector side, the case is rather different. Despite the great evolutionary improvements in the motor apparatus which have occurred, for instance in carnivorous mammals, the degrees of freedom achievable by the organism, as a neuromuscular machine, are limited from the outset. The result is that the second- and third-order receptor processes equivalent to intelligence have consistently and increasingly outrun the capabilities of the effector systems, to the point finally that man has come to realize a further fraction of his imaginings as to the possible by means of tools and machinery. A similar disparity appears to exist in forms as low on the evolutionary scale as *Amblystoma*.[1]

One consequence of this disparity is that effector systems must be arranged with respect to receptor so as to restrict outputs from the latter to those which are physically practicable (in the case of somatomotor outflows) and within physiological limits (in the case of both somatomotor and autonomic† outflows). In part this restriction may be accomplished cytoarchitecturally. In the case of the neopallium, it is illustrated by the large-celled agranular structure of precentral effector areas as well as in basal

---

* I.e., as such. This statement might be thought arguable, for instance in the case of Gerstmann's syndrome. The latter is discussed further, below.

† As suggested in Chapter I, this condition is not always met in the case of the vegetative systems, with the result that visceral "defensive" responses may on occasion damage the organism they help to save.

dysgranular (orbital and anterior temporal) cortex. The function of cortex of this type, I have supposed, is to convert inputs deriving, e.g., via the thalamus, from receptor areas, into a comparatively small number of resultants, a still smaller number of the latter surviving as motor "memories" in consequence of multiple feedback processes confirming (selectively reinforcing) these as successful (practicable) effector output patterns. Included in such feedback are doubtless components representative of basal motives, fulfilled or unfulfilled, and of basal feeling-states, e.g., of pain, frustration, sexual or alimentary pleasure, etc., which are "off" (inhibitory) or "on" (facilitatory) for the particular effector patterns concerned, it being in this way that terminally "rewarding" behavior tends to be conserved, or that animals during learning of a response, more or less automatically show a "win-stay" "lose-shift" stratagem.[2] Effector systems may restrict inputs from receptor areas in another way—namely, by feedback which subjects receptor processes to selective inhibitory restraint, thereby reducing the flow of comparatively diverse and largely impracticable outputs from the receptor to the effector apparatus. Because energetic physical action entails general mobilization of the organism, including increased metabolic rates, cerebral blood turnover, etc., inhibitory restraint of receptor system outputs to the effector systems is then particularly necessary, since these might otherwise result in "flooding" of effector pathways, with consequent functional confusion or paralysis. However, it is also clearly necessary that *primary* receptor processes—e.g., of extrinsic and immediately surrounding neocortical areas—not be unduly interfered with since these contribute information vital to the guidance of present actions.

Accordingly, the influence which effector systems exert by playback upon receptor must show an increase in its inhibitory component which is proportioned to the energy or violence of actions then pending or under way, and must be selective for those secondary and tertiary receptor processes I have supposed to be fundamental to intelligence and chiefly to concern the posterior intrinsic sectors in neocortex. And in fact, this seems to be the case (cf. Chapter VI, pp. 116–117, and note 57).* At the same

---

* I.e., reticular "activation" figures in general mobilization preparatory

time, such playback must facilitate primary sense-reception and the activity of those systems concerned in the organization, e.g., of temporal sequences of behavior—notably extrinsic and frontal intrinsic neocortical sectors and motor-sensory areas of the vertex. This selective facilitation seems to occur also (Chapter VI as noted, and reference 56). As mentioned, these processes, reinforced by endocrine changes,[3] serve during intense fear or rage or sexual passion to reduce greatly or extinguish peripheral thought-activities and the rational perspective which these give us upon present events, our own behavior included.

In the same way, partitioning, or the selective reinforcement of certain extrinsic sector data by playback from posterior intrinsic sectors, is impaired. The organism is thus thrown back upon its type (extrinsic and peri-extrinsic) memory systems and tends to show "stimulus generalization" or a diminished capacity for perceptual discrimination.

Conversely, receptor systems when functionally dominant can be supposed to exert an inhibitory action upon the effector apparatus conducive to their own mode of functioning.* This is perhaps illustrated by the physical quieting which often seems to occur in the early stages of "attending"† to some stimulus which does not immediately and powerfully arouse the effector systems. It may also transiently occur at the outset even of the more massive forms of arousal, in part accounting for the physical paralysis and (in some species) for the bradycardia which often accompany primary fear. Davis[4] has reported bradycardia in humans upon sudden arousal of sexual desire. The phenomenon as a whole—that is, the appearance of a predominantly parasympathetic state, with facilitation of the receptor systems and inhibition of the effector—can be regarded as a stage in incipient arousal at which

---

to action and has the selective neocortical effects described in these references. Frontal intrinsic cortex, as an effector area, and one with important two-way connections with the RF (see below) presumably figures in this type of build-up, and thus indirectly influences neocortical activity elsewhere.

* I.e., to a facilitatory climate in receptor systems proper.
† Cf. Herrick, *op. cit.*, note 1 above, re the "regarding reaction" and the possible role of the olfacto-habenulo-interpeduncular system in this response. Also note 54, below.

nonspecific input has not yet risen into the high, or maximally inhibitory range, the result being a transient facilitation of receptor processes generally,* and transient parasympathetic dominance in the body.

The crux of the argument here is that the major components of the emergency or dynamogenic motivational-affective system may lie on the effector side, and the major components of the "normal survival" or pleasure system may lie on the receptor side, of the CNS. In turn this means that the neocortex itself can be fractionated in this respect—a point I shall return to later. An immediate consequence of this conclusion is that structures of the extrapyramidal system must have "arousal" functions vis-à-vis neocortex which resemble those of the midbrain RF. A recent study by Fox and O'Brien[5] of the electrocortical results following upon caudate stimulation in the cat demonstrates what these authors describe as "a striking functional similarity between the caudate nucleus and the reticular formation of the brainstem." It is, one might add, as an effector system itself† that the midbrain RF may exert the inhibitory restraint it appears to do in particular upon those second and third order receptor processes of posterior intrinsic cortex.

These relations presumably have parallels in the rhinencephalon and may provide an important clue as to how the motivational-affective functions of that system are organized. In Chapter I, I postulated that the emergency system mediated behavior arising chiefly in response to external circumstances while the "normal survival" or pleasure system mediated behavior chiefly arising out of inner need. Herrick's horizontal sections of the brain of *Amblystoma* (page 124 above) show the forebrain sensory area extending laterally to, but not into, the strio-

---

* That is, including secondary and tertiary or posterior intrinsic sector activity, it being these that high levels of nonspecific input may selectively discourage—whether by true inhibition, or by occlusion, or critical rises in the noise-to-signal ratio is not clear, and operationally does not greatly matter.

† I.e., at higher than normal waking-state levels of activity, during which its caudally indirected output "setting up" spinal motor outflows is paralleled by an increase in its tonic output to neocortex.

The caudate may specifically figure in inhibition of neocortical activity, in particular at certain input frequencies. See note 54 below.

peduncular and strio-amygdaloid motor zone, and medially into the septal area. In view of the importance of septal-hippocampal projections (Chapter VII, notes 6 and 7) one can perhaps conclude that in this brain, receptor processes more directly concern the hippocampus, the principal structure in Pribram and Kruger's tertiary olfactory system. On the other hand, according to Herrick, effector forebrain processes chiefly concern Pribram and Kruger's secondary olfactory system, with the exception of the septum. To judge by its rhinencephalic and midbrain projections, discussed earlier, and Lilly's observation concerning its functional duality (Chapter VII, note 18), the septum in higher forms may be a structure mediating answering effects or joint action of the rhinencephalic emergency and "normal survival" systems. Finally, the emergency system may be chiefly represented in higher forms in structures homologous to Herrick's "olfacto-somatic" area in the brain of *Amblystoma*, while the "normal survival" or pleasure system may be represented chiefly in the structures homologous to the "olfacto-visceral" area, including those parts of the later nonspecific reptilian pallium which he describes as free of olfactory influence, (that is, the primordium of mammalian neocortex).

These systems correspond essentially to the secondary and tertiary olfactory systems of Pribram and Kruger, except that the septum may be junctional between the two rather than a member of the former as these authors originally classed it. These conclusions are consistent with many of the functional characteristics which have been inferred for the rhinencephalic structures concerned.

The facilitatory pleasure-system functions of the septal-hippocampal complex in higher forms are illustrated by the fact that stimulation of parts of it evoke sexual responses in animals;[6] by the pleasure-reactions apparently obtainable by septal stimulation in animals[7] and also in man;[8] and by the apparent "gating" action of the hippocampus upon neocortical nonspecific inputs,[9] which I have supposed serves to maintain a facilitatory climate in neocortex favorable to the processing of sense- and memory-data.

The emergency and inhibitory functions of areas homologous

to Herrick's pyriform-strio-amygdaloid and strio-peduncular complex are illustrated by the fact that bilateral amygdalectomy in animals decreases apparent fear and impairs behavior mindful of learned precedents[10] as if by release from previous inhibitory restraints; that it causes some but not necessarily lasting release of sexuality[11] and appears to diminish dynamogenic support of rage or ferocity states, with the result that operated animals, when challenged by their cage mates, fail to respond adequately and as result drop to the bottom of the "pecking order";[12] and that stimulation of the amygdala in waking humans produces, at low intensities, sympathetic signs (pupillary dilation, tachycardia, blood pressure rises), and at higher intensities, startle reactions, "fear, fright, visual hallucinations [and] depersonalization" frequently followed by amnesia for these events.[13]

Herrick's classification of the primordia of Pribram and Kruger's secondary (the septum excepted, as noted above) and tertiary olfactory systems as respectively olfacto-somatic and olfacto-visceral in function may be incorrect, or at least may not apply in higher forms. According to Kaada,[14] "Thus far all of the experimental data have confined the . . . [rhinencephalic] areas which influence autonomic activities to a rather limited portion of its rostral part, comprising the anterior cingulate, orbito-insulo-temporal polar region and the amygdala." It is worth noting that somato-motor as well as visceral effector pathways are evidently activated from parts of the secondary system. Motor effects such as rotation of the head and eyes are reported to result most commonly from focal epileptic seizures of the anterior* temporal lobe in man.[15] The cingulate is reported to play some part in vocalization in monkeys;[16] likewise speech difficulties have been found "in humans having frontal parasagittal tumors near the anterior cingulate" (*ibid.*). Stimulation of the amygdala in various animals has been observed to evoke defensive and feeding behavior;[6] also mounting reactions[17] and ovulation[18] (or both skeletal motor and autonomic components of sexual behavior). The last-mentioned evidence casts some doubt on MacLean's hypothesis (*op. cit.*[6]) that structures of Pribram and

---

* Vis-à-vis mid- or posterior temporal *foci*.

Kruger's secondary olfactory system are concerned in feeding and defense, or preservation of the self, whereas structures of their tertiary system—notably the hippocampus and gyrus cinguli—are concerned in sexual behavior or preservation of the species.

The essential fact, perhaps, is not that these two systems are "centers" for particular types of instinctive behavior, but rather that they figure in characteristic ways at different temporal stages of a variety of such actions—the order and degree of participation of each system being determined by the particular functional requirements of the actions concerned, and by the answering-effect or joint-action principle described here.

For example, the hippocampal-cingulate areas from which sexual responses have been obtained in animals may figure in the facilitatory onset phase of primary sexual desire, rage, or fear—this phase being in general longest in the case of sexual desire, shorter in the case of rage, and shortest in the case of fear. When activated in this way, the tertiary system may more or less transiently* inhibit parts of the dynamogenic secondary system and its midbrain homologues. (Hence flushing at onset of rage, or transient vagal depression of the heart rate at onset of fear, rage, or sexual excitement in man.)

At the limbic and midbrain level, the effect of this transient dominance of the tertiary system is to entrain answering effects or proportionate post-inhibitory rebound at functionally corresponding sites in the dynamogenic system—e.g., during sexual arousal in animals, rebound will occur in those parts of the amygdala concerned in mounting reactions. Conceivably, the controlling inhibitory functions of the tertiary system figure in the search for food. For instance, they may inhibit orbital area 13 of the secondary system and adrenergic midbrain arousal systems, thus releasing the (possibly cholinergic) midbrain areas concerned in rhythmic movement.† Likewise they may inhibit those midbrain areas which, during arousal, may restrict receptor activities, for instance by "gating" olfactory inputs at the bulb.

---

* I.e., for intervals often, though not invariably, maximal in the case of sexual arousal, shorter in the case of rage, and minimal in the case of fear.

† Cf. Chapter VI, note 40.

The consequence is that when hungry an animal shows graded locomotor release and olfactory facilitation (roams and is sensitive to a variety of odors). An intense odor meaning that food is probably close by will then transiently increase activity in the secondary system mediated by parallel rises in the tertiary, the latter, if all goes well, outlasting the former or alerting phase of the response. The result is activation, e.g., of feeding mechanisms represented in the hypothalamus and amygdala, of reticular outflows inhibiting miscellaneous sensory inputs at the peripheral and spinal levels (an attentional mechanism), and of locomotor inhibition mediated from orbital 13 (a mechanism permitting the animal to pause and orient to the stimulus). Having oriented, the animal may then proceed more energetically than before in the appropriate direction, a dynamogenic phase ending when, or if, it finds food (and one which, as noted earlier, can be prolonged by amphetamine and preclude eating).

In general, dynamogenic or highly energetic effector states may entail an inhibition of the tertiary olfactory system and its equivalents at other neuraxial levels, which is proportionate to the violence of actions pending or under way. Thus sexual excitement, in its final stages, drastically restricts conscious thought (or as one writer puts it, "Orgasm narrows attention"). A similar progressive restriction of our thought-processes occurs during the build-up of rage. At the outset, or when merely piqued, we are frequently capable of wit. As we grow angrier, our wit is apt to become clumsier and more assaultive. At the peak of rage, flushing may give way to pallor, and verbal to literal assault. In effect, a transfer of dominance from receptor to effector systems has occurred, and with it, a maximal inhibitory restraint on those second and third order processes of posterior neocortex equivalent to mentation or "consciousness." Neurophysiologically, the basic mechanism may be the same, whether the dynamogenic state concerned be sexual or arise out of fear or rage.

Functions of the cingulate have so far remained more of a puzzle than those of other parts of the rhinencephalon.* Morphological and some neurophysiological data seem to relate it

---

* However, see notes 52 and 54, below.

primarily to the hippocampus.[6] Other studies, particularly those of Kaada,[14] appear to relate it to the amygdaloid complex. Stimulation of the anterior cingulate in cats[6] sufficient to produce after-discharge evoked "freezing" and pupillary dilatation (see below, concerning functions of the "strip" regions), followed by penile erection and grooming reactions. In dogs, rostral cingulate lesions involving cortex immediately above and in front of the genu of the corpus callosum[19] did not produce the rage release noted in similarly operated animals by other authors, but did produce disinhibition of an inhibitory conditioned reflex, and something like indiscriminate optimism, such that these animals appeared to expect food upon presentation either of the appropriate "rewarding" CS or of a negative CS, and also "took the food more vigorously than before." Posterior cingulate lesions produced no observable impairment.

Pechtel *et al.* found that following ablation of cingulate areas 23 and 24 in cats and monkeys (Adey[13]), these animals showed a tendency to "diffuse and precipitate activity, and moderately increased aggressiveness . . . with a lowered threshold of startle and fear exacerbated by isolation." Adey adds that "maternal preemption of food at the expense of a nursing baby was noted. There was minimal relief of phobic, regressive or socially maladaptive behavior but greater amenability to restraining."

The increased amenability to restraint, and lowered fear and startle thresholds, argue some decrease in primary ferocity and some increase in primary (fearlike) emergency reactions. The moderate increase in aggressiveness is possibly a rage-rebound phenomenon*—this in contrast to Pribram's amygdalectomized macaques which showed a release of ferocity behavior which readily collapsed when challenged (i.e., because the emergency apparatus which would normally have caused heightening of primary ferocity via induced fear and subsequent rage-rebound was crucially damaged). Though important, granular area 23 is perhaps not vital to cingulate 24 effector functions, because other pathways still exist by which, e.g., hippocampal outflows may

---

* I.e., a further consequence of emergency system release, which in turn causes ready mobilization of surviving parts of the normal survival (ferocity) system.

reach the latter. Cingulate 24, on the other hand, is perhaps a part of the normal survival system which mobilizes the tegmental dynamogenic system, for instance in "support" of primary rage or ferocity states. Finally rostralmost parts of the cingulate may be those in which secondary system structures, e.g., of the orbit, in particular exert their inhibitory influence; hence the "indiscriminate optimism" of the dogs operated in this area, and the rage release noted in similarly operated animals by others. Conceivably this is one of several target-structures reached by inhibitory projections of orbital 14, the function of these being to impose graded, more or less stimulus-specific restrictions upon ferocity, favoring "behavior mindful of learned precedents" (avoidance).

Apropos of the possible dynamogenic functions of the anterior cingulate, it is significant that Fulton,[20] from a review of the clinical literature, concluded that anterior cingulectomy was the "operation of choice" for paranoid psychotics, whereas electrocoagulation of the midventral orbital quadrant was the preferred operation for depressive psychotics. My fundamental assumption here has been that because of the peculiar physiological advantages enjoyed by the emergency system, many functional psychic disorders in man may arise from a predominance of avoidance conditioning, the latter resulting either from comparatively massive traumatic experience, in particular in early life, or from gross under-development of neocortical "reality principle" functions,* or both. The type of arrest or gross exaggeration of subcortical (rhinencephalic and midbrain reticular) answering effects which then results will in part be determined by inherited constitutional factors, but will in each case produce characteristic clusters of physiological and psychic signs. In depressives, for example, inhibitory functions of the emergency system and consequent gross reduction or enfeeblement of normal survival system activities,

---

* As I hope to show in a later study, many of the psychic disorders of modern Western man may be of the latter or default type, the essential reason being that our current skeptical pragmatism and the complex technological society which has grown up with it have robbed rising generations of the early example and in-formation (sic) they might have had, had our earlier tradition been properly continued, while confronting them with a world even the most fortunate of our forebears might have found confusing.

appear to prevail; hence the apparent role of the mediobasal orbit, or the neocortical extension of the secondary olfactory system, in this type of disorder. In paranoid psychotics, by contrast, persistent rage-rebound reactions, or as it were forced anger and forced, pseudo-rational mental activity, prevail. (In consequence of this driving of neocortical "reality principle" processes by the emergency system, paranoid psychotics perhaps more than those of other types elaborate mental "systems" having a bizarre kind of internal consistency.) Hence, in cases of this type, surgical intervention selectively affecting dynamogenic portions of the tertiary olfactory system may act to block secondary mobilization of ferocity or chronic ragelike states, and so check the elaboration of fantasies of persecution and revenge.

It is interesting in this connection that, in the thalamus, the anterior nuclei are less clearly demarcated in primates than in the carnivora, *anteromedialis* and *anterodorsalis,* which project respectively to cingulate 24 and the retrosplenial region, having regressed in the former.[21] Projections of the mammillary body to these nuclei (which latter reportedly also reach the paracentral lobule, a region evidently having sexual functions in man) may figure in the mobilization of dynamogenic normal survival states (rage or sexual excitement). In line with the view that such states are effector and so involve inhibition-by-feedback of higher level central nervous activities; and also in keeping with the principle discussed below, that a degree of such inhibitory control is necessary to keep neocortical activities relevant or restricted to prime concerns of the moment, it is perhaps logical that damage to the mammillary body, as in Korsakoff's syndrome, interferes with the ordering of neocortical sense and memory-data (hence confabulation, in this disorder). As representative of the dynamogenic branch of the facilitatory pleasure system, the mammillary body may play a vital role in setting limits to facilitation, e.g., in predominantly pleasurable states in which activity of the emergency system is minimal. The fact that self-stimulating animals find the mammillary body a "punishing" area* and that

---

* Similarly, the medial hypothalamic "satiety" area which sets limits to feeding has, as noted earlier, been found to give "punishment" responses when electrically stimulated.

"steep rises" in blood pressure can be obtained from it[22] argues in favor of the foregoing account of its functions. Fulton[21] has suggested that the mammillary body also plays a role in sleep. In fact this may be a default phenomenon, due to inhibition of mammillary activity from functionally antagonistic anterior hypothalamic sites (see note 22).

In addition to the system of the mammillary peduncle, by which the tertiary olfactory or rhinencephalic pleasure system may directly mobilize the tegmental dynamogenic system, there appear to be regions junctional between the secondary and tertiary olfactory systems by which the emergency apparatus can evoke "support" of the normal survival system, or conversely. One such region is the anterior dorsal hippocampus, stimulation of which reportedly produces "very disturbed" behavior in cats.[23] Interestingly, dorsal and rostral portions of the hippocampus are said to undergo regressive changes early in the fetal life of man.[24] Together with the regression of *anteromedialis* and *anterodorsalis* in the primate thalamus, this may be a change tending to diminish the duration and intensity of answering effects at the limbic system level. In turn, the effect of this change may be to reduce the proclivity to violent all-out behavior, and the disruptions of neocortical "reality principle" processes which accompany it. That is, it is a change favoring functional dominance of intelligence, as against basal drives and emotion—a change which in man needless to add has hardly gone far enough.

That these conclusions as to functions of the secondary and tertiary olfactory systems are in a general way correct is suggested by the fact that amygdaloid stimulation in animals causes rises in 17-hydroxy-corticosteroid levels,[25] whereas hippocampal stimulation has been found to cause transient rises followed by prolonged lowering of 17-OH-CS levels.[26] Bilateral resection of the hippocampus is reported to abolish the diurnal drop in 17-OH-CS levels in monkeys.[27]

The results of stimulation of the amygdala and hippocampus in waking humans[13,24] suggest that in man "encephalization" or displacement of their specific primordial functions (e.g., feeding and sexual behavior) to neocortical levels has occurred, what remains being chiefly their nonspecific functions (Herrick, *op. cit.*, note 1, p. 98). Broadly, these may be inhibitory vis-à-vis intrinsic sector activity in neocortex, in the case of the amygdala; and facilitatory vis-à-vis the same, in the case of the hippocampus.

These nonspecific effects may be chiefly mediated via descending projections to Nauta's limbic midbrain area, and thence, as described earlier, to Forel's tract and neocortex. It is possible that intra-diencephalic connections also play a part in this process—e.g., the tract of Clark and Boggon connecting the posterior hypothalamus to the thalamic *n. dorsomedialis*,[28] or the well-known pathways from the mammillary body to the anterior thalamic nuclei, thence to the cingulate, thence to frontal areas.[29]

In neocortex it is significant that frontal or effector areas are reached by the last-mentioned projections, the difference between frontal and posterior sector functions having clear parallels in the dorsal thalamus. Here Pribram distinguishes a core comprised of the intralaminar and midline groups, the anterior nuclei, and *dorsomedialis*, and an overlying shell comprised of the specific relay and association nuclei.[30] The shell-nuclei, it would appear, subserve receptor activities without regard to (not directly arising out of) motivational-affective states; while nuclei of the dorsal thalamic core may mediate neocortical activities in a way which far more directly reflects concurrent subcortical activities equivalent to such states. The situation of frontal intrinsic cortex, between effector areas 4, 6, and 8 superiorly, and orbital viscero-motor areas inferiorly (Kaada,[14]); the apparent importance of this cortex to delayed action performance in animals;[31] the deficits observed following various types of frontal lesion in man;[32] and finally the thalamic afferents which it receives, all suggest that this system is more directly a "motivational" one, and has more direct effector functions than does posterior intrinsic cortex. That is, it corresponds to the dynamogenic systems of the core, and like those, may figure in the effectuation of behavior of both motivational-affective types.

CHAPTER VIII—part ii

The Interpeduncular System; Neocortex, Rhinencephalon, and Midbrain as a Functional Unit

THE olfacto-habenulo-interpeduncular system comprises a group of pathways probably of major importance in bringing reticulomotor activity under control of the rhinencephalon and neocortex. In *Amblystoma* it receives fibers from virtually every forebrain area (Herrick, *op. cit.*, Chapter VII, note 11, pp. 257–261). Its origins in mammals (in the septum and *nucleus basalis* of the anterior perforated substance) and its distribution via Ganser's tract to nuclei of the caudal midbrain tegmentum, are described in Chapter VII above. It should be mentioned that the neocortex projects to two important structures in this system—the septum and medial habenula; and that in mammals including man, two-way connections exist between the ventral habenula and parts of the dorsal thalamus (Herrick, *op. cit.*, p. 260). There are, in addition, a number of indirect routes by which the neocortex might be expected to influence rhinencephalic outputs via the interpeduncular system to the midbrain; for instance, temporal cortex→(perforant pathway)→hippocampus→(precomissural fornix)→septum; or, orbito-temporal cortex→amygdala→septum; or, orbito-temporal cortex→amygdala→anterior dorsal hippocampus→*n septalis dorsalis* (see note 23).

These anatomical features argue the importance of the neocortex as a modulator of rhinencephalic activity. Outputs to the midbrain RF via the septum, habenula, and interpeduncular nucleus can then be conceived as resultants of ongoing activities

The Interpeduncular System / 153

in the two major motivational-affective systems of the rhinencephalon, and of neocortical events in part paralleling and giving rise to these. Papez described the olfacto-habenulo-interpeduncular system as "a primitive motor path" (Chapter VII, note 3) but it appears not to be strictly that.

Herrick (*op. cit.*, p. 205) defines three principal fields in the brain of *Amblystoma*: the somatic sensory, of the tectum and dorsal thalamus; the visceral, of the hypothalamus; and the olfactory, of the cerebral hemispheres. He goes on to say:

"The interpeduncular complex is separated from this great system of activators except at its upper and lower ends. It is activated from the same three physiologically distinctive regions and its efferent impulses are discharged into the same lower motor fields. These relationships are in some respects similar to those of the cerebellum with the activators of the skeletal musculature. The cerebellum does not pattern behavior but it acts upon the motor systems as going concerns. . . . The structure and connections of the interpeduncular nucleus suggest that it is similarly related with the great descending extrapyramidal systems of the cerebrum, and specifically with those concerned in feeding reactions. . . . The efferent activating systems of patterned behavior discharge through the basal forebrain bundles and the tegmental fascicles. Above and below this central core of activating fibers, and parallel with them, there are inhibitory systems of fibers which have the same origins and terminations . . . but which pursue different courses with different connections. Dorsally there is an olfacto-visceral inhibitory system centered in the mammillary region. . . . Both these inhibitory systems converge in the interpeduncular nucleus." (Concerning the similarity in terminal distribution of fibers of the mammillo-tegmental and interpeduncular system in mammals, see Chapter VII above).

In fact, neither the mammillo-tegmental nor the interpeduncular system may have the predominantly inhibitory functions Herrick attributes to them. Morphologically they are of interest in that the former is hypothalamus-centered and the latter, thalamus-centered, as are the tertiary olfactory system and neocortex, whose similarities in plan of organization are discussed later in this chapter.

A recent study by R. Thompson[33] shows that in rats, following electrolytic lesions which destroyed 35 to 85 per cent of the interpeduncular nucleus, a conditioned motor response (jumping to avoid shock upon presentation of a 5–sec. warning light-signal) was impaired or abolished. On receipt of the CS, the animals gave evidence of fear (squeaking, respiratory changes) but tended not to jump *until* shocked, when they evidently did so quite normally. The author points out that this result "is not readily explainable on the basis of a motor disturbance." A second group of six rats which had sustained mean 48 per cent interpeduncular damage but had no prior experience of the test situation failed to show signs of fear when exposed, for ten trials each, to the light-shock sequence.

Of a group of six pretrained rats without interpeduncular damage but with "virtually total bilateral ablation of the visual cortical areas," three showed fearlike responses to the CS on trial one, and another showed such a response on trial two. In all six animals, this operation "only partially impaired the conditioned jumping response."

In still another group of animals, Thompson made bilateral electrolytic lesions in "a region of the posterior thalamus, medial to the lateral geniculates" (not further specified). By analogy with the human thalamus, the structures affected may have included *lateralis dorsalis, medialis dorsalis,* the pulvinar,* and the habenula. In these animals both the conditioned jumping response and the anticipatory fearlike response to the CS seem to have been significantly impaired.

Several other facts require mention in connection with the foregoing. It appears that there may be important species differences in interpeduncular functions since destruction of that nucleus in cats (Bailey and Davis; cf. Herrick, *op. cit.*, p. 208) releases "obstinate progression." In respect of the distribution of the "reward," "punishment," and "arousal" areas in the midbrain tegmentum as reported by Olds in the rat, species differences among mammals may be less, or the basic plan of organization much the same. Apropos of the dorsal longitudinal fasciculus of Schütz (page 123 above), Herrick cites a second study by

---

* This nucleus, however, is not well developed in the rat.

Bailey and Davis in which cats were subjected to extensive electrocoagulative lesions of the periaqueductal grey, lesions which "must have involved the dorsal longitudinal fasciculus and the dorsal tegmental nucleus." Postoperatively, the animals were silent, flaccid, and never showed spontaneous activity again. According to an old report in the literature,[34] encephalitis lethargica in man is accompanied by swelling and other evidences of pathological change in the periventricular and periaqueductal grey. Mirsky and Cardon[35] cite earlier evidence implicating medial parts of the midbrain tegmentum in the maintenance of waking in animals and suggest that lateral areas (possibly corresponding to those from which Olds obtained arousal responses) also participate in the support of "consciousness." Finally, Hess and Hunsperger have reported that in intact preparations, rage can be evoked from stimulating in the perifornical region of the hypothalamus (i.e., parts of the tertiary olfactory system) or in the mesencephalic central grey.[36]

It may be that central dynamogenic states of both fearlike and ragelike or "punishment" and "reward" types arise in similar regions of the midbrain.* Thompson's results on the other hand suggest that the olfacto-habenulo-interpeduncular system specifically projects to the reticulomotor apparatus but not to these basal motivational-affective areas subserving general central nervous mobilization. Interpretation of his results requires an analysis distinguishing the mechanisms of learned from those of unlearned behavior, and also learned motor from learned affective responses.

I have supposed that during conditioning, trace-formation occurs at several levels—notably the midbrain reticular, rhinencephalic[37] and neocortical—and involves circular interaction between the systems concerned. One effect of this interaction is to establish ("consolidate") neocortical thing memories which when later activated (by presentation of the corresponding CS's) give rise to clearly defined phasic outputs from neocortex to the

---

* See Chapter VI, note 40, concerning the tonic activating system involving the posterior hypothalamus, the periventricular and periaqueductal grey, and the midbrain tegmentum, as postulated by Demetrescu and Demetrescu.

rhinencephalon and midbrain. In this way neocortical participation in the genesis of motivational-affective states becomes conditional upon sensory inputs of highly specific configuration; while the resulting highly organized outputs from neocortex tend to establish activity at subcortical levels precisely appropriate in kind and intensity to the situation in hand. In proportion as its output is "informed" in this way more particularly in the extended sense described in Chapter V,* the neocortex acts as a controlling element or check-valve in the circuit:

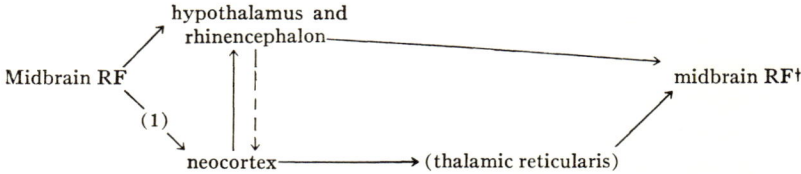

Conversely, when minimally informed, the neocortex may readily permit reactions of the arousal or orienting reflex type (Chapter II, p. 34).

Receipt of a CS also entrains a second set of central nervous events—namely, activation of effector from receptor system sites, a phenomenon not precluding more direct prior activation of the former.[38] In other words, there shortly occurs a shift from an attentional state, characterized by a predominance of receptor system activity and a build-up of "drives" or emotions, to an overt behavioral state, characterized by functional dominance of the effector systems and some inhibition of receptor system activity,[39] with consequent lessening in the circular build-up of motivational-affective states (pp. 139–140 above). This last is perhaps essentially the mechanism responsible for the fact that actions—even relatively futile ones—tend temporarily to lessen the pressure of drives or the intensity of emotion.

---

* I.e., by abstract memory-formations. The greater the neocortical potential of the organism, the more important such further patterning of neocortical output becomes, since when *un*patterned, such output may equally disrupt functioning of the CNS, as described earlier.

† (1) includes the thalamic and extrathalamic paths described by the Scheibels. The dotted arrow indicates pathways such as the "diffusely projecting" hippocampal-cortical fibers (Purpura *et al., Science,* Sept. 15, 1962, 134, pp. 729–730).

The Interpeduncular System / 157

One consequence of progressive encephalization, as Herrick has pointed out, has been to lengthen the period of delay or attending before action results in a given situation, it being in this way that the informational resources of the organism are most fully brought to bear (cf. Chapter II above, on the relatively long latency of "specific recognition"). So with the exception of certain protective reflexes,* possibly including fast visual reflexes mediated by the basal optic tract (Chapter VI, note 54), the tendency of collateral sensory inputs into the midbrain RF of higher forms is perhaps not to activate the reticulomotor apparatus directly, but rather via the RF to cause general forebrain excitation and possibly preparatory facilitation of the spinal motor apparatus, accompanied by some peripheral gating of sensory inputs.[40] In fact the midbrain RF appears to be so organized that its main lines of conduction run longitudinally, the dendritic shafts of these fibers being "arranged primarily perpendicular to the long axis of the brainstem, with a secondary and much less extensive system projecting rostrocaudally. . . . The rostrocaudal axis is followed by all efferent axons. . . . Thus the two main orientations of reticular dendrites mirror the orientation of adjacent axonal components, and make for parallel axon-dendrite appositions, allowing for repetitive axodendritic synapses" (quoted from Scheibel and Scheibel, Chapter III, note 5, second reference).

The functional result of this anatomical arrangement may be that except for inputs corresponding to extremely intense or painful stimuli, which may be capable of activating the reticulomotor apparatus as it were transversely, via the dendritic network just described, activity produced in the midbrain RF by collateral sensory inputs may chiefly be relayed elsewhere. Similarly, reticulomotor outflows may originate at forebrain levels via outputs so arranged that they activate the appropriate descending axon systems of the midbrain, it being in this way that

---

* Apropos of this point, Hagbarth and Finer (*EEG clin. Neurophysiol.*, 1962, 14, 590) report a short latency (60–80 msec) presumably spinal reflex in man which occurs rather rigidly (e.g., often inappropriately) and a longer latency (120 msec) response which was more variable and perhaps centrally mediated. Both involve limb-movement.

in the course of evolution, the "centers" for determining motor behavior have been shifted rostralward and reticulomotor outflows have come to act as "carriers" for effector outputs originating at higher neuraxial levels (see Chapter VI).

Finally, this scheme of relationships includes two safety factors—one such that midbrain sensory inputs may if sufficiently intense, directly touch off reticulomotor responses comparable to those medullary autonomic reflexes which Ingram has described as functioning "only for the needs of the moment" (Chapter I, p. 16). Secondly, intense activation of the midbrain RF by sensory collaterals, while not sufficient to trigger such reflexes, may nonetheless foreshorten the processing of immediate sense-data, e.g., in neocortex, by inhibitory action selective for posterior intrinsic cortex, thereby reducing prebehavioral delay* and achieving promptness of action at some cost to its informed character or precise appropriateness.

In Thompson's conditioned interpeduncular rats, jumping occurred on receipt of shock—illustrating the reflex mechanism just described. Blocking of forebrain output to the reticulomotor apparatus via the interpeduncular nucleus made it impossible, however, for the forebrain to activate that apparatus on receipt of the conditioned stimulus, the pyramidal system in these animals evidently being unable to mediate the response without reticular participation. In effect, this motor blockade arrested the CR as a whole in the receptor or primary excitatory build-up stage;† whereas normally, prompt entrainment of motor outflows or a shift from receptor- to effector-system dominance would also have entailed an increase in inhibition of receptor by effector systems serving to check the circular build-up of primary central excitation.

In the operated conditioned animals, this "answering effect" cannot occur except on delivery of the shock itself. Thus between presentation of the CS and delivery of the shock, they

---

* I.e., by virtually eliminating the final stages in the processing of sense-data while accelerating the primary (extrinsic sector) stage.

† This account predicts that upon sufficient exposure to shock, Thompson's unconditioned interpeduncular group (which showed no evidence of fear over ten trials) would have developed a response similar to that of the preconditioned group.

The Interpeduncular System / 159

exhibited a marked build-up of the central excitatory state of fear, exemplifying the principle stated in the Introductory that, with sufficient intensification, what we call a "drive" turns into what we call an emotion. Also, any drive whether pleasurable or not, when sufficiently intensified, turns into more or less the same emotion—namely, the fearlike agitation or inhibition appearing in animals or human beings when grossly frustrated.[41] Apropos of the tendency of actions to check the build-up of motivational-affective states, it is reported that drugs such as phenacetylurea, which block motor effects in psychomotor seizures, are also apt to worsen the psychiatric disorders accompanying seizure.[42]

In Thompson's rats which had sustained visual cortical ablation (but in which the interpeduncular system was intact), some visual information was presumably available via the tectum. In neocortex, however, the response could not proceed as efficiently as before, since a one-to-one match between the input and the corresponding pre-established visual memory could no longer be made. The result was then a deficiency in precise phasic outputs from neocortex to lower levels and a corresponding deficiency in neocortical control of central excitatory build-up. Hence some of these animals showed fear, paralleled by partial impairment of the jumping response.

Finally, it appears that damage to a posterior thalamic area quite possibly essential to the distribution and neocortical processing of sensory information resulted in animals which showed impairment both of motor and motivational-affective conditioned responses. This finding argues that in mammals, the neocortex is as essential to the genesis of motivational-affective states as it is to the guidance of actions arising out of and tending to terminate them (see also note 51, below; and the data of Sprague *et al.* reviewed in Chapter VI). To the degree that when informed (e.g., as to a present external situation) the neocortex may act to limit such "states" at the rhinencephalic and midbrain levels, it may also when un- (or mis-) informed contribute to their diffuse augmentation and so, on occasion, to disorganization of neocortical activity proper, with consequent adaptive failure. It is for this reason that the radical increase in neocortical potential which has occurred in man has proved a two-edged blessing, producing a creature uniquely rational and self-controlled but also one uniquely subject to functional central nervous disorders—many of the latter neither occurring in animals in a state of nature nor apparently reproducible in them experimentally.

Because the rhinencephalon appears to have been bypassed in the course of mammalian evolution and become, as it were, a second-string brain, a number of whose specific functions in man have "migrated" to the neopallium,[24] it is no longer essential to many of the activities it nonetheless continues to regulate (cf. Gloor, Chapter VII, note 23). It is perhaps for this reason that with the exception of limited intervention in selected cases—for instance the operation performed by Turner,[23] electro-coagulation of the ventromedial nuclei of the hypothalamus (for relief of catatonia[43]); or the midventral orbital quadrant coagulation and anterior cingulectomy, discussed by Fulton[20]—rhinencephalic resections have so far failed to be of great value in the relief of human mental disorder or to produce alterations as profound as those resulting from frontal lobotomies or topectomies.

The foregoing interpretation of Thompson's data suggests the sequence of events which during conditioning leads to "habituation." Briefly, as thing memories corresponding to the CS and its related "model" of behavior (the CR) take clear form, and as the paths of subcortical outflow from their neocortical areas of representation become with use more clearly defined and efficiently acting, the tendency is for the preliminary general-excitatory phase of the response to shorten to the point of disappearance.

In other words, on receipt of the CS, neocortical control of reticular activation is established with maximal promptness, as are forebrain effector outflows, which act as described above to restrict preparatory general excitation still further. The net result is that as a learned response becomes habituated, generalized neocortical desynchronization, on presentation of the CS, ceases to occur and more focal patterns of electrocortical activity appear at the outset.

When, however, a CR cease to be effective (produce terminal reward or relief), this pattern of change in the form of the response is reversed. Essentially what occurs may be this: On termination of the now unrewarding response, its motivational-affective state of origin is not superseded but continues and perhaps intensifies.* With sufficient intensification it becomes, whatever its original motivational-affective type, an emergency state (frustration). The result is that during extinction of a learned response, there is a return of generalized neocortical desynchronization, accompanied by increased variability in behavior (as reported by Antonitis *et al.*; cf. Chapter III, note 12) in response to the CS. If frustration is prolonged and severe, disorganization of neocortical activity, as in acute fear, may result, paralleled by a tendency not to variable but to automatized, ineffective "superstitious" forms of behavior (41; cf. also Maier, *op. cit.*, Chapter 1, note 10).

However, except for problems which the organism finds excessively difficult—for instance, Maier's "no-solution" problem, in which the animals were physically confined and had no alternative but to continue responding in some fashion to a punishing situation—the mechanism of frustration, like that of primary avoidance, ordinarily results in some form of action, if only withdrawal, before circular build-up of an emergency state becomes sufficiently intense to disrupt neocortical control and automatize behavior as just described.

Acute frustration thus involves functional alteration, e.g., of memories representing CS's triggering some form of normal survival (gratificatory) behavior. In the case of neocortical memories, this process can be conceived as a circuit change or switch in preferred pathways of subcortical distribution, possibly occurring in the rhinencephalon and at or below the level of the thalamic reticularis (cf. the data of Schlag *et al.*, reviewed in Chapter VI). Simply because emergency or avoidance reactions tend to be the more massive, reassociation of neocortical thing memories representative of normal survival responses may occur with relative ease. That is, it is probably easier to convert a "good" CS into a "bad" one than conversely.† It is also probable

---

* Equivalent to receptor-system rebound following upon cessation of overt activity or effector-system dominance.

† A famous study of Lewin's with groups of school children organized on "democratic" and "totalitarian" lines appears to bear this out be-

that such reassociations are never absolute, but give rise to motivational-affective responses which are more or less ambivalent, i.e., accompanied by mixed autonomic and subjective-psychological signs and behavioral "conflict" or a degree of vacillation. Particularly in civilized urban man, whose daily experience is relatively diverse and who is relatively informed and sophisticated, such ambivalent responses may tend to predominate—and with them, a qualified, skeptical outlook on life. By contrast, men growing up in simpler, more rigidly orthodox societies perhaps exhibit patterns of conditioned response more of the black or white type, their moral judgments, affections, and hatreds being correspondingly absolute and unclouded by second thoughts. Something of this difference can be seen in the politics and social customs of the Protestant vis-à-vis the Catholic countries of our civilization. It might be added that the tendency of the mind to think in "opposites" (cf. McCulloch, Chapter III, note 4) may be more a consequence of the duality of the motivational-affective systems of the core than of the fact that brains act primarily as digital computers (which it now appears they may not do).*

For purposes of discussion, it is convenient to divide nonspecific neocortical input from the midbrain into a three-part spectrum. The lowermost range corresponds to that characteristic of sub-waking states—there evidently occurring in sleep periodic shifts in functional dominance, as e.g., during Jouvet's "rhombencephalic" stage. The middle range of nonspecific input corresponds roughly to that of normal waking state activity and is perhaps predominantly, although not exclusively, facilitatory in its effects. Transition from the lower to the lower-middle range has been observed by Evarts *et al.*[44] to be accompanied by some decrease in over-all unit activity and some increase in the vari-

---

haviorally. He found the democratic group could be more readily totalitarianized than the other way round. He also found the totalitarians to be poorer producers, confirming some animal studies which show punishment to be a less effective incentive to organized behavior than is reward.

* E.g., dendritic networks may constitute an analogue apparatus, and each neuron an analogue-to-digital converter, reconversion occurring beyond the axon terminals.

ability of the activity of individual units. In the uppermost range, corresponding to intense prebehavioral excitatory states (e.g., fear, sexual arousal, and primary or rebound rage) gains in nonspecific input may be accompanied by a further relative increase in reticulocortical inhibition,[45] in particular, perhaps affecting activities in those neocortical territories (e.g., the posterior intrinsic) in which fibers of the thalamic reticularis are the principal, or only, thalamocortical afferents, and the influence of the specific system therefore minimal.

It is, I have supposed, in the accelerative and decelerative phases, or just before and just after such peaks of nonspecific "activation" that learning is most apt to occur, in part because of the de-differentiative effect which very high levels of nonspecific input may have, principally perhaps upon the more labile "abstract" memory formations of the external lamina, though possibly also upon basal memory formations of layers V–VI. Reticular driving may, in short, be conducive to the subsequent formation of new from old action-patterns, although in the case of thing memories, use of existing components in new configurations does not necessarily replace old: it merely diminishes the probability of the latter as future routes for the "irradiation" of cortical activity, by helping to increase the total of such routes available. Thus in the preliminary "attending" phase of an arousal response, neocortical activity is perhaps predominantly facilitated. At the peak of that response, the combination of intense driving and intense inhibition is perhaps largely de-differentiative both of ongoing neocortical activity and of pre-established action-patterns. With overt action, or a shift to effector-system dominance, nonspecific input again falls, and neocortical activity of the new-learning or reorganizational phase begins.* This, in brief, is Whitehorn's acute emotional episode (Introductory, note 1).

In frontal as opposed to posterior intrinsic cortex, the situa-

---

* In this connection, Steriade and Demetrescu (*EEG clin. Neurophysiol.*, 1962, 14, p. 30) point out that "the facilitatory after-effect of reticular arousal is often observed," although in the same phase of the response, extrinsic sector activity (normally dominant *during* arousal) may be depressed.

tion may at all times be somewhat different, in that this cortex evidently receives a larger share of nonspecific input (Arduini, Chapter VI, note 56) as well as projections representative of motivational-affective systems of the rhinencephalon. This combination of inputs may make for consistently higher transaction rates in frontal (vis-à-vis posterior) generalized eulaminate cortex, with correspondingly high rates of de-differentiation and re-formation of frontal intrinsic action-patterns. This combination of high turnover in input and high levels of nonspecific inhibition may make for skeletonization of information represented there (i.e., for an erosion of detail similar to that occurring in extrinsic cortex), as well as for comparatively fugitive representation of any particular "bit."

As proposed below, these "bits" may originate posteriorly, and their relay to frontal sectors so as to form blueprints of imminent behavior may involve a special type of convergence mechanism serving a special biological purpose. Briefly, whether activated from the core or in the course of "reality principle" processes equivalent to thought, basal posterior sector memories tend to entrain emotions or "motives." Frontally, both motivational-affective systems of the rhinencephalon are represented (amygdala→posterior hypothalamus→tract of Clark and Boggon →dorsomedialis; hippocampus→mammillary body→anterior thalamic nuclei→cingulate→). Thus if we assume that designs of action are constructed in detail posteriorly; that this construction involves basal memory formations; and that the resulting designs are duplicated in outline frontally—then it is clear that the second stage of this process involves or is paralleled by neocortical-rhinencephalic outflows, which in turn, via the diencephalic routes just mentioned, will converge in frontal sectors with information relayed thence in part by the same routes (e.g., posterior intrinsic cortex→thalamic reticularis→dorsomedialis). By this convergence mechanism, those features of a given design of action which to the organism are *key* features, or most motivated, are perhaps those which selectively come to have frontal representation—the short-term play of basal inclination or impulse giving rise to somewhat longer-term or delayed-action schemes of behavior via frontal intrinsic holding action.

The Interpeduncular System / 165

Posterior sector memories of a given event do not in man appear merely to represent CS's, but rather are complexes of recalled particulars including sensorimotor components corresponding to certain of the organism's actions on that past occasion. Presentation of a CS therefore evokes parallel response trains of several somewhat different types—e.g., facilitation of related posterior sector audiovisual memories may prepare the organism to perceive the same sight and sound sequels to the stimulus as have resulted previously in its experience. (Given certain cues, we anticipate or are "reminded" of the corresponding earlier event.) Simultaneously, via the thalamus, in both pre- and post-central cortical areas, "motor memories" corresponding to actions on that previous occasion, may also be facilitated. These are preparations for the simple (unmodified) repetition of a CR.

Two sets of modificatory influences, however, are also brought to bear upon this nascent response, the "model" of which is perhaps principally laid down in various posterior receptor areas and in granular and dysgranular motor regions at and anterior to, the vertex. The first set involves neocortical "reality principle" processes which serve to analyze the present situation by the multiple comparison process described in Chapter V—a process essentially involving those generalizations from previous experience embodied in abstract memories. To the degree that this analytic process reflects the organism's intervening experiences, and also objective differences between this present occasion and its precursor, the evoked patterns of neocortical activity are on this occasion also different, which in turn alters cortico-subcortical outflows to the rhinencephalon and midbrain—the result being that the organism's motivational-affective response to the CS is now different than it was formerly. In addition, these cortico-subcortical outflows may impinge upon some precurrent, or as it were baseline, state possibly quite unlike that in which the CS was originally formed. If sufficiently intense, this motivational-affective state may resist modification by cortico-subcortical outflow, and itself may become the prime modifying agent of the response which follows upon presentation of the CS. Conversely, if that state is not intense, or if the neocortex be highly and extensively organized and so capable by its phasic subcortical outputs of controlling even quite intense core-activities, then alteration of the CR (present response to the CS) will chiefly reflect "reality principle" processes, and consist both of actions and feeling-states more rationally appropriate to the occasion (i.e., these will be to a degree, logically improvised).

In other words, presentation of the CS—the more so the greater the neocortical potential of the organism—does not lead merely to a "mental" rerunning of the CR but to extrapolative processes of one of two basic types. The first form of extrapolation results in a new neocortical "model" of action more or less accurately representative of actually feasible behavior and a rationally desirable outcome, with a subcortical motivational-affective "set" to match.* The second form results from an evoked or pre-existing motivational-affective "set" so powerful that this order of functional dominance is reversed. Instead of activities from the top of the neocortex down determining the flux of subcortical events, the latter establish circular (subcortico-cortico-subcortical) interactions which, e.g., via axosomatic nonspecific fiber connections with cells of layers V–VI (Lorente de Nó, *op. cit.*, Chapter IV, note 1), favor activation of basal memory-formations in certain areas, hence neocortical activity from the bottom up, hence conditioned *reflexes.*

When such rises in nonspecific input occur, they presumably impinge upon cortico-thalamo-cortical transactions in progress, it being the latter which tend to determine the more focal effects of the former. To the degree that for instance nuclei of the thalamic reticularis figure in intracortical communication, rises in nonspecific input via the same nuclei will enhance the neocortical activities being mediated by these, but in a differential manner, such that the memory apparatus of layers V–VI may now tend preferentially to be driven. As this occurs, activity in the overlying layers of the n vertical columns concerned will tend to become secondary to that of the internal lamina and will no longer determine the sequences in which such basal memories and their corresponding core-processes are brought into action. In psycho-

---

* I.e., with motives or emotions permitted by reason.

The Interpeduncular System / 167

logical terms, our thinking ceases to be free in that it is no longer determinative of, but is now largely determined by, the flux of our basal states. Moreover, activation *en bloc* of a large group of basal memories of one motivational-affective type may reinforce the core-activities leading to this dominance of "pleasure principle" processes, to the point of producing an arrest of the normal progression of subcortical answering effects in a particular phase, with corresponding entrapment of neocortical processes equivalent to conscious thought.* A mechanism of this kind may figure in obsessions and lead to the incessant return of certain ideas, recollections, etc., accompanied by a stubbornly dominant "mood." Similarly, thought-activity determined from the core, or the bottom (of neocortex) up, reflects sequences of desire, aversion, etc., translated *en passant* into more or less logical forms (fantasy, rationalization). In contrast to "reality principle" processes proper, these are generally recognizable as substandard mental productions, as are the things we often say when frightened or enraged.

The representation of key or "most motivated" features of action-sequences in frontal intrinsic cortex may likewise involve projections from these sectors to the rhinencephalon and midbrain which reinforce the corresponding basal states, in this way offsetting the inhibitory action which the effector systems, when dominant, have upon the receptor.

In other words, while frontal intrinsic cortex may participate in the genesis (or pre-effector stage) of behavior, its prime function may be to maintain *during* effector states (as posterior intrinsic sectors do during receptor) a continuity of motivation such that adequate and appropriate drive-levels are sustained through successive stages in the execution of a given behavioral plan. When lobotomized, we do not lose the capacity to plan, as such; rather we become too fluid and shallow in our basal feeling-states for our plans to cohere in action. The essence of this type of distractibility is that the machinery is lacking by which subcortical answering-effect trains are systematically made to parallel and physiologically support the train of informed actions comprising a projected behavioral sequence.

---

* That is, confinement of these to certain subcortically determined *loci*.

Frontal intrinsic cortex is thus peculiar in that it has functions in a sense receptorlike, acting during effector states to conserve as a functional unit the essentials of behavioral models elaborated elsewhere, and likewise guaranteeing maintenance of motivational-affective states appropriate to these. Transient frontal memory-formations may thus exert a holding action on two sets of central nervous events simultaneously. Via the thalamus they may act during effector states to reinforce those posterior sector activities in which they originated, thus guaranteeing the relevance of concurrent "thought" processes to actions under way. Secondly, and perhaps in particular via frontal projections reaching the secondary olfactory system and midbrain, they may act to redirect the normal flux of subcortical states arising either spontaneously or in response to passing sensory inputs. In the process they may help to guarantee certain key features of attentional states—for example, reticular gating of peripheral sensory inputs favoring enhancement in some modes and suppression in others.[40] Except that its consequences are more complex, this action of frontal intrinsic sector memories is perhaps essentially similar to the holding action which I have supposed type memories of the extrinsic sectors* to exert upon the flux of our moment-to-moment sensory experience. There is evidence that frontal cortex projects subcortically as just described.[46]

Some of these conclusions as to frontal intrinsic functions have been drawn by others ([31, 32]) and have been criticized, notably by Teuber.[47] A close examination of the data presented by Pribram[31] suggests that the frontal system is indeed important in maintaining the core "driving" of behavior in the way proposed above. That posterior sector memories may also include timelike features (i.e., may represent episodes in their original temporal sequence) suggests that posterior sectors can also mediate behavioral sequences, but may do so somewhat less energetically or efficiently. This conclusion is supported by a study (Akert *et al.*,[48]) which showed that bilateral ablation of dorsolateral frontal cortex in newborn rhesus monkeys does not impair later delayed-action performance (in contrast to Pribram's animals,

---

* Which in fluidity and generalized character they resemble.

The Interpeduncular System / 169

operated at maturity). However, in these animals the early stage of learning is slower—implying less prompt emergency system support—and discrimination is somewhat improved—implying proportionately less inhibitory interference with posterior sector activities.

The hypothesis that the hippocampus may act as a brake upon rises of nonspecific input, and consequently may favor posterior sector over frontal-dynamogenic activity, has these data in its favor. The hippocampus receives important posterior sector projections (e.g., via the perforant pathway); except for anterior parts, it has been shown upon stimulation to produce hormonal changes interpretable as anti-dynamogenic; and desynchronized hippocampal activity has been reported not to parallel, but to show an inverse relation to rises in activity of the midbrain RF. In this respect it has an interesting resemblance to the cerebellum which has been found, e.g., in cats to show a "slow" (20–40 sec.) rhythm in response to reticular arousal.[46,49]

If in fact the hippocampus exerts a damping action upon nonspecific input (e.g., via pathways discussed in Chapter VII), stimulation of parts of it in an animal should block massive arousal and the subsequent new-learning or reorganizational phase, while not significantly affecting neocortical activities arising out of memory-formations already in being. I.e., when so stimulated an animal should be able to perform a previously learned response but should resist learning a new one. Stimulation of the amygdala on the other hand should, if sufficiently intense, bring on an emergency state accompanied by nonspecific input capable of disorganizing neocortical activities mediating learned behavior and (while maintained) of blocking further learning as well. This prediction is apparently confirmed by a study of Olds,[50] who obtained these differential effects from stimulating in the hippocampus and perimygdaloid cortex.*

It is less clear why Scoville and Milner's patients (Chapter II, note 31) following bilateral removal of the anterior two-thirds of the hippocampus did not show other changes paralleling the loss of "recent memory" (i.e., of the capacity to form new lasting

---

* Animal unspecified. Cingulate stimulation at the same intensities produced no effect.

memories). Removal of the uncus and amygdala alone reportedly does not produce this effect, which therefore cannot be attributed to interruption of the rhinencephalic emergency system. It may be that with bilateral loss of both the amygdala and hippocampus a vital closed circuit (temporal cortex→rhinencephalon→midbrain→neocortex) is broken. As result, circular processes equivalent to the internal reinforcement of nascent thing memories become impossible. Such processes, incidentally, may in the aftermath period of very intense motivational-affective arousal give rise to the "one-take" memory formation mentioned by McCulloch (Chapter III, note 4). The question is why noticeable emotional changes did not accompany this memory defect in Scoville and Milner's patients; or why, if conditioned emotional responses were still normal (mediated, e.g., by the septum and MFB, or by cortico-thalamo-mesencephalic paths) these or similar unconditioned responses did not lead to new thing-memory formation under certain circumstances. Possibly the tendency of the hippocampus toward prolonged post-stimulatory activity[23] is crucial to the maintenance of neocortical conditions suitable to the "consolidation" of new learning.*

IN this and the preceding chapter I have attempted to define the mesencephalic reticular, rhinencephalic, and neocortical equivalents of the dual motivational-affective system described earlier. The arrangement of these is such that in any given basal "state," functionally corresponding systems at each of the neuraxial levels concerned tend to be called into action. Vertically, or between levels, the relation between the systems activated is hierarchical, with the qualification that given a sufficient degree of general activation, output from lower to higher levels may set aside the more usual hierarchical order of control,

---

* That the hippocampus does exert a damping action upon evoked cortical (striate) potentials in unanesthetized animals has been shown by Redding and Siegfried (*EEG clin. Neurophysiol.*, 1962, 14, 588), who interpret this effect as possibly involving inhibition of the ascending reticular activating system, or of neocortex, or both. Why, then, did Scoville and Milner's patients show no signs of central disinhibition?

The Interpeduncular System / 171

thereby causing behavior to be determined in phylogenetically older structures of the CNS.

Horizontally, or at each of the neuraxial levels concerned, component structures of the reward-and-punishment or normal-survival-and-emergency systems interact according to the answering-effect principle, with the result that all orders of functional dominance as between such components tend to show reversal, both at that and other levels. In the rhinencephalon, the reward (septal-hippocampal-cingulate) and punishment (orbito-insulo-temporo-amygdaloid) systems may be supposed to interact both locally—e.g., over pathways described above and in note 23—and indirectly via their midbrain projections, the outputs of the olfacto-habenulo-interpeduncular system presumably being resultants of this interaction. The foregoing is, in its essentials, the mechanism giving rise to the continuous cyclical recurrence of basal "drive" states or (in Sherrington's phrase) to a "serial variety" of motivation or emotion comparable to that guaranteed at the spinal level by the arrangement of motor reflexes. This process, needless to add, is integral to that by which the components of a given "state" are assembled, since the temporal order of assembly of these likewise establishes, with a high degree of probability, what the components of the succeeding "state" or action are likely to be. Thus—to repeat—the answering-effect principle is a generalization from Sherrington's principle of successive spinal induction and states that the neuronal connections and/or neurohumoral agents which determine the components of a given central nervous event also determine its most probable successors, the potential variety of the latter increasing with the evolutionary elaboration of the brain. In turn, this means that the higher the organism, the more complex become these inner dynamics, and the more potentially diverse or unpredictable its behavior under a given set of circumstances. In the sense that, as described earlier, the basal memory-formations of the neocortex act to establish a degree of functional unanimity, or parallel answering effect trains, at cortical and subcortical levels, enlargement of memory-capacity has served both to inform and stabilize behavior by guaranteeing the necessary minimum of complementarity among the various central nervous activities in which it originates. Finally, as if as a safeguard against the "escaping tendency" of the neopallium described in Chapter III, core-control of neocortical activity is such as selectively to restrict the least determinate forms of that activity (i.e., activity of the external lamina in posterior intrinsic sectors) and does so more particularly at high levels of central nervous excitation, when acceleration of that activity might lead either to motor incoherence or to fatally impulsive forms of behavioral improvisation.

Analysis of the rhinencephalon according to the sorts of function apparently mediated by its various structures, shows that my previous suggestion that pleasure functions lie chiefly on the receptor side, and emergency functions chiefly on the effector side of the CNS requires qualification. Ablation studies in which the rhinencephalic emergency system is principally encroached upon disclose a paradoxical effect—namely, some release and some enfeeblement of ferocity. See, for instance, Pribram's macaques, note 12. See also a more recent study by Akert *et al.*, note 51. In the latter, immature macaques were subjected to bilateral ablation of temporopolar cortex and of the superior middle and inferior temporal gyri posteriorly "to a line perpendicular to a point halfway up the Sylvian fissure." These animals showed transient hyperorality, post-operatively, and more lasting affective changes, especially loss of fear. However, when restrained they struggled more than did the controls and tended to bite, though "with substantially less vigor than the normal animals."

The implication is that normal survival "ferocity" functions derive some, but not all, of their dynamogenic support from the emergency system; and further that low-energy or inhibitory functions of the latter system play an important part in setting limits to ragelike behavior—e.g., limits determined by prior avoidance conditioning, the latter being in part represented in anterior temporal cortex. In fact, in the hippocampal "pleasure" system, the mammillary body appears to have dynamogenic functions (see note 23). It might then be more correct to say that with the evolutionary expansion of the brain, new systems were added in which the *proportion* of receptor to effector activities was in each instance increased, it being in this qualified sense that "pleasure" functions lie more on the receptor side of the CNS.

In the rhinencephalon, the primary and secondary olfactory systems* appear to correspond to the *pallium basale* of selachian fish—an ancient forebrain system in which are represented the bare behavioral essentials—that is to say, sexual, defensive, and food-getting activities, or both emergency and "normal survival" functions. The representation of all of these in the secondary olfactory system persists up to quite high levels of mammalian evolution, as Gloor's review of the evidence from stimulation studies of the amygdala clearly shows (Chapter VII, note 23).

The mammalian hippocampal system appears to be a descendant of the later appearing *pallium marginale* (Sherrington, Chapter VII, note 10). Herrick (Chapter VII, note 11) points out that the hippocampus is the first structure in primal brains to exhibit true cortex. With it begins the elaboration of a second hypothalamus-centered forebrain system in which receptor functions play a relatively larger part. While the hippocampal system participates synergically with the structures of the *pallium basale* in the genesis of behavior generally, its appearance also perhaps marks the beginning of a separation of behavior and its corresponding central nervous states of origin into two fundamental classes. These are, respectively, forms of behavior whose time-course must as nearly as possible be geared to external circumstance, and those whose time-course can more successfully be determined by events occurring within the organism proper. Behavior and corresponding central nervous states of the former type perhaps continue to be handled by evolutionary descendants of the *pallium basale* and its corresponding projection areas in frontal neocortex and in the brainstem. The representation of alimentary and defensive reactions in closely adjoining sites of the amygdaloid area in cats (MacLean) suggests an arrangement which tends to offset the placidity likely to accompany feeding by permitting a rapid switchover (reversal of facilitation-inhibition patterns) from normal survival to emergency behavior upon presentation of appropriate

---

* Of Pribram and Kruger.

olfactory or other sensory cues. The essential point about such emergency reactions is that they are maximally stimulus-bound, or involve a minimum of facilitatory delay and processing of inputs before resulting in motor outflows and action. As if in acquiescence to external *force majeure,* fear behavior even in the highest forms continues to be forced behavior, and for that reason has remained a prime function of phylogenetically older systems of the CNS—i.e., those in which the processing and storage of information is minimal and whose connections with other systems are such that when dominant, they maximally restrict that processing elsewhere.

In contrast, those forms of behavior whose success more largely depends upon extended, or extensive, processing of primary sense-data, perhaps came to have representation in protocortex of the *pallium marginale;* and in higher forms have their chief representation in descendants or homologues of that system. By their nature they require a longer delay period to materialize in actions, and moreover one in which a suitably facilitatory climate is maintained in the receptor systems concerned. Thus the normal survival system is so arranged, vis-à-vis the emergency, that when activated it tends to inhibit the latter (including those structures of the emergency system inhibitory for the normal survival). The functionally antagonistic relation between these systems is therefore reciprocal, arousal responses generally presenting an appearance of suddenly accentuated competition between the two—witness the bradycardia in some species at onset of fear, the frequently mixed autonomic signs in intense fear or rage, and (subjectively) the sense of being internally threatened* which often accompanies even intensely pleasurable feeling-states. In fearlike alerting, the basic competition is between the "attending" reaction (cf. Herrick, *op. cit.,* p. 38) which tends to defer behavior until a rational course is clear,† and the basal fear, or emergency-system response, which tends to cancel these receptor-system activities in favor of im-

---

* I.e., by lapses into mental disorganization and intense, unpleasant fearlike states.

† Concerning the possible role of the caudate and ventralis anterior in the "attending" reaction, see note 54.

mediate violent general-purpose actions. That this competition is frequently one-sided reflects the biological rationale mentioned earlier—namely, that survival is the necessary prerequisite of all other creature activities, and is on the whole more apt to be favored by swift minimally informed behavior than by actions which, though better suited to the situation, might come too late to serve at all.

This brings me to my final point, which is that the neopallium and hippocampal-cingulate system exhibit striking similarities in their plan of organization, reflecting the fact that they are perhaps successive evolutionary manifestations of the same basic trend.

In neocortex, receptor functions are represented posteriorly, overlapping with and giving way to effector functions in the region of the central sulcus. Moving forward, we then pass into cortex under the influence of projections of the dorsal thalamic core nuclei and rhinencephalon.

MacLean and Pribram[6] have commented on the fact that the cingulate appears morphologically to be an outgrowth of the hippocampus. Data cited earlier here indicate that (perhaps by homology with precentral neocortex) parts of anterior cingulate cortex are agranular and have some effector functions as yet not well defined. In the same way that precentral areas may be "informed" via the thalamus from posterior sectors of neocortex, the cingulate may receive the bulk of its instructions* via the hypothalamus and anterior thalamic nuclei from the hippocampus, which in location and functions is roughly comparable to the receptor systems of neocortex.

Rostrally, in the pregenual cingulate region, the hippocampal system appears to come under the influence of the secondary olfactory system (p. 147, above), which is also represented in fronto-basal neocortex and may, via dorsomedialis, exert a similar influence upon activity in other frontal sectors. Just as posterior neocortical sectors may tend to prolong attending reactions

---

* Or phasic as distinct from tonic inputs, the latter perhaps being largely of midbrain origin. In the same way, the neocortex may determine the phasic outputs of the thalamic reticularis, and the midbrain its tonic outputs.

by inhibition of the effector and basal dynamogenic systems, the hippocampus and cingulate area 23 (Pechtel et al.,[23]) may be inhibitory for the midbrain activating system and parts of the secondary olfactory system.

The trend of evolution of the mammalian brain has seemingly been toward increased segregation of receptor and effector functions, fractional effector functions being retained in receptor systems, and fractional receptor functions in effector systems. This pattern of dual motor representation both in mesial supracallosal and cingulate cortex in the monkey is illustrated in a paper by Hughes and Mazurowski.[52] Similarly, "strip" regions mediating arousal reactions are found both in frontal effector and posterior receptor neocortex,* and likewise in the anterior cingulate and *entorhinalis* (or effector and receptor portions of the tertiary olfactory system). Finally, dynamogenic functions of the temporal pole are perhaps paralleled by those of the anterior dorsal hippocampus, as described here earlier. In short, it is as though the phylogenetically older hippocampal complex had been overlaid by its near-duplicate in respect to the arrangement of receptor-effector and motivational-affective "fields" in each.

From this scheme of basic structural and functional relationships, certain others appear to have followed. As primarily an effector system, frontal neocortex—in particular perhaps those sectors (the intrinsic) most directly descended from nonspecific reptilian cortex—may be related primarily to the secondary olfactory system and corresponding midbrain areas. Posterior neocortex—the intrinsic sectors again, in particular—may be primarily related to the tertiary olfactory and mammillo-tegmental systems.

In the sense that it favors maintenance of a facilitatory climate in neocortex, the hippocampus may be construed to be synergic with its posterior neocortical homologue, or constitutive of those second- and third-order "receptor" activities which largely underlie intelligence. Freud's notion that intellectual or "creative" activities and sexuality are related may thus have been in a rough way correct. However, since in man these appear

---

* Concerning these and their possible relation to inhibitory functions of the caudate and VA, see note 54.

to be handled by subdepartments of a highly differentiated neopallial apparatus, and since human sexual functions do not seem to be mediated from the rhinencephalon proper,[24] the concept of "sublimation" (implying that sexual drives are in some way anterior to "higher" mental activity) may have few equivalents in neurophysiological fact.[53]

Finally, the secondary olfactory and frontal intrinsic systems may not be constitutive of processes equivalent to thought, as the hippocampal system is, but may act to maintain nonspecific inputs at levels such that posterior intrinsic sector activities are subject to persistent inhibitory restraint, favoring their restriction to certain "most motivated" forms. In the sense that they mediate this type of inhibitory editing, the frontal and subcortical emergency systems are regulatory of thought. The association of anxiety with intense, rigorous, mental effort is shown by the etymology of the word "meticulous," which literally means "full of little fears."

CHAPTER IX

Conclusion

THE axonal spike-discharge appears to be the quantum of action of neural networks and likewise the most strictly conditional form of neural activity. It is for this reason that I have supposed memories, whose reactivation is often conditional upon inputs of highly specific configuration, may be represented in the form of spatio-temporal axonal firing-orders. Bishop has suggested that axonal activity represents a special adaptation of the properties of nerve favoring rapid conduction with minimal loss over anatomically long distances. Purpura (Chapter VIII, note 45) and Grundfest[1] have advanced views suggesting that apical and basilar dendritic networks, and possibly axonal terminals, are primarily chemoreceptor, the essential function of the all-or-none discharge arising from summated p.s.p.'s being to establish similar changes in standing potentials at the next link in the synaptic chain.

In line with these ideas, De Robertis[2] reports on the basis of electron microscope studies that "synaptic vesicles" or small quantities of neurohumoral substances contained in a membrane 40–50 Å thick may be formed in the perikaryon, synthesis continuing and the size of the vesicles increasing as these move down the axoplasm toward the nerve-endings. At the synapse, De Robertis believes they may then be released at what he calls active points, passing into a "synaptic cleft" some 120–200 Å across, where they presumably act upon similar points in postsynaptic membrane. In addition to this focal action, he suggests that the release of neurotransmitters may also act "at a distance, by way of the circulation." The tonic neurohumoral component of midbrain activation of neocortex apparently demonstrated in

Purpura's cross-perfusion experiment (see Chapter VI, note 46) may involve a mechanism of this kind. More generally, the tonic influence which any neural subsystem exerts upon others may in part be mediated neurohumorally.

Rostral to the midbrain, at least three major interconnected systems are distinguishable: the strio-amygdaloid or secondary olfactory, in which the proportion of effector to receptor functions is high; the hippocampal-cingulate or tertiary olfactory system, in which the proportion of receptor to effector functions shows relative increase; and the neopallium, in which both receptor and effector (but perhaps especially the former) undergo radical expansion. The outstanding characteristic of the latter two systems is that, while including their own effector apparatus, they may in varying degrees also enlist that of the strio-amygdaloid complex and midbrain.

Thompson's work with interpeduncular rats underscores the importance of the reticulomotor system as a carrier of higher-level effector outflows, though species differences in the type of control mediated by the olfacto-habenulo-interpeduncular system may be great (cf. the work of Bailey and Davis on interpeduncular cats, cited in Chapter VIII). Akert's and Pribram's studies of macaques following bilateral temporal cortical ablations and bilateral amygdalectomy respectively, imply that "pleasure-system" functions such as ferocity, while mediated by an effector apparatus in part distinct from that of the strio-amygdaloid complex, also require support of that complex if the resulting behavior is to be sufficiently energetic and under adequate inhibitory control. This combination of massive mobilization and widespread inhibitory restraint is *par excellence* an emergency-system function, simply because the emergency systems are those in which effector functions predominate. Thus the massive central nervous mobilization mediated by these systems is accompanied by graded, relatively high, levels of inhibition serving to simplify the outputs of more rostrally lying phylogenetically newer systems—an arrangement acting, as described earlier, to guarantee that these outputs are practicable as well as prompt.

It seems probable that these systemic subdivisions in the brain and the scheme of functional relationships to which they give rise have neurohumoral parallels and might lead to an account of the complex, rather puzzling, physiological relations between substances such as the catecholamines, acetylcholine, histamine, serotonin, and gamma amino butyric acid. The problem is complicated by the very great species differences in responses to these substances, reported in the literature. See for instance Nozdrachev[3] on the effects of intracisternal and intravenous serotonin on dogs, mice, cats, and pigeons; or Knapp and Domino[4] on EEG changes following i.v. epinephrine and serotonin in dogs, cats, and rabbits transected at the midpontine pretrigeminal level.

In general, the tonic influence exerted by one system upon another may depend upon the balance of neurohumors released, and may be such that the higher the level of excitation mediated in this way, the greater the proportion of inhibitory to excitatory transmitter substances tends to become. Costa *et al.*[5] conclude that cholinergic ganglionic transmission may involve release of norepinephrine, which acts in turn to raise the threshold of postsynaptic membrane. Stein and Seifter[6] suggest that norepinephrine may be a "reward" system neurotransmitter; that is, it may specifically be concerned in effector functions of that system, the concentration of dopamine in the basal ganglia[7] implying that these figure in such functions. Both epinephrine and norepinephrine are reportedly facilitatory for nerve in low concentrations and inhibitory in higher, greater inhibition reportedly being obtainable from equivalent concentrations of epinephrine,[8] presumably an emergency system neurotransmitter.

A recent paper by Monnier and Romanowski[9] reports that in the rabbit acetylcholine, eserine, and pilocarpine elicit neocortical desynchronization, though with somewhat different subcortical concomitants in each case. The response could in all cases be blocked by atropine. Sadowski and Longo[10] report that a conditioned food-reward response in the rabbit was abolished by scopolamine (.1 mg/kg). Amphetamine in low concentration facilitated the CR as a whole, while in higher concentration it effected a separation of two phases of the response, increasing the energy with which the animals pulled a ring to obtain food while blocking eating proper. This suggests that amphetamine acts selectively on the emergency system, e.g., of the midbrain, favoring the comparatively energetic action of obtaining food but likewise blocking an answering effect, so that an appropriate switch to the lower-energy "normal survival" activity of eating could not then occur. (More precisely, midbrain-rhinencephalic output may have maintained activation of the midline hypothalamic "satiety" center for longer than it would normally have done.)

The roles of GABA and serotonin as central neurohumors remain obscure. As in the case of others, the central effects of these substances vary greatly with the mode of administration (i.v., topically, intraventricularly, etc.) and with the species tested.[3,4] Wada[11] observes: "Behavioral and electrographic studies of modified levels of brain neurohumoral agents in cats and monkeys have led to the belief that a change in the level of any single . . . agent may be less important than production of a disequilibrium among the various endogenous agents. In this connection my co-workers and I have found that the paroxysmal abnormalities induced by administration of 5–HTP and Marsilid in conjunction with reserpine are at least partially eliminated by the administration of atropine. This finding is difficult to explain but the possibility that the cholinergic mechanism is involved in such activation is being investigated. A recent report that high levels of serotonin markedly reduced cholinesterase activity . . . seems to support such a possibility." In this connection, the report of Von Euler and Lishajko[12] that reserpine causes release of norepinephrine from "transmitter granules" in tissue *in vitro* is of interest, as is the report of Costa *et al.*[5] that administration of a monoamine oxidase inhibitor favors systemic accumulation of norepinephrine.

At the conclusion of a review of the recent literature pertaining to neurohumoral substances, McGeer[13] writes: "Brodie and Shore . . . suggested that serotonin may be the neurotransmitter for the trophotropic system of Hess, while norepinephrine may be the neurotransmitter substance for the ergotropic system. We have proposed that at least as far the extrapyramidal motor system is concerned, histamine and acetylcholine may be components of one modulating system while the catecholamines and possibly serotonin are components of another. . . . More recent experiments suggest to us that histamine may be of importance to pain or punishment centers in the brain." (Apropos of this point, see Heath[14] who has postulated a septal dysfunction mechanism as figuring in schizophrenia and involving a hypothetical mono- or diamine oxidase inhibitor.)

I have nothing to add to the facts and opinions just cited except to suggest that the fractionation of the central nervous system made here may have traceable neurohumoral parallels, it being for this reason that groups of neurohumors have been found having similar but not identical effects when administered at the same sites, and apparently distinct although overlapping functions in the normal organism. In other words, one test of the ideas outlined in this book is provided by the rapidly accumulating literature on the neurohumoral transmitter substances. If close to the truth, the former should, with modification, be capable of yielding a consistent account of the latter.

THROUGHOUT this discussion, I have gone on the assumption that Purpura's statement (Chapter VIII, note 45) that high levels of nonspecific input are accompanied by gains in reticulocortical inhibition is correct—if not literally, at least operationally. Of the four main routes of intracortical communication mentioned at the beginning of Chapter V, two—the thalamus and plexiform layer—are held in common with the midbrain reticular formation. Moreover, this applies in particular to association cortex, since the same nuclei possibly mediating communication of this cortex with other areas are probably also in direct receipt of midbrain inputs, and may moreover activate the midbrain in the course of subserving neocortical activities as just described (cf. Schlag *et al.*, Chapter VI, note 49). By contrast, in extrinsic cortex, nonspecific influence must compete with that of the specific system, doing so by two routes. The first, suggested by Jasper (Chapter VI above), consists of sensory collaterals to the thalamic reticularis and intrathalamic projections from these nuclei to the specific relay and association nuclei. The second consists of nonspecific projections proper to the extrinsic areas, whose existence is suggested by the fact that recruiting as well as augmenting reactions can be obtained in those areas.[15] If the mode of laminar distribution of nonspecific afferents proposed by Lorente de Nó is the actual one, this means that nonspecific fibers may activate the basal type memory apparatus of extrinsic cortex, and may thus subserve "partitioning," the mechanism of which is discussed in Chapter V above. The net effect of nonspecific input into extrinsic sectors is then perhaps to intensify ongoing activities there in the way exemplified by Fuster's data[16]—(a general or tonic effect mediated midbrain→thalamic reticularis→specific nuclei) and on occasion to intensify certain of those activities selectively (a phasic or "partitioning" effect, mediated, e.g., posterior intrinsic cortex→thalamic reticularis→extrinsic cortex).

The disorganization and diminution or restriction of thought-activity which occur during intense fear may, for the reasons just given, especially involve posterior intrinsic sectors, or those concluded earlier here to be most concerned in the storage and processing of highly detailed information. Psychological evidence indicates, however, that the relation between the motivational-affective type of a memory and its accessibility to conscious thought is not a simple one. It is not true, for example, that all memories of "bad" experiences are "repressed"; many, including unpleasant memories formed quite early, come back to mind with ease and all too vividly. Secondly, there is an evident difference between the spotty forgetting which we experience under stress (e.g., stage fright) and repression proper, which appears to render certain recollections consistently unavailable.

Essentially, the neurophysiological mechanism underlying these phenomena may be somewhat as follows: During intense arousal, or when nonspecific input rises into the upper third of the spectrum mentioned in the last chapter, the neocortex begins in effect to lose control of the thalamus, while tonic midbrain inputs equivalent to "noise" begin to predominate. As this occurs, only the most thoroughly reinforced or clearly patterned "messages" relayed from one cortical area to another tend to survive thalamic transit. Because of the relative influence of the nonspecific system upon extrinsic and intrinsic sectors, this shift is one in favor of extrinsic over posterior intrinsic sector activity or (behaviorally) in favor of strict attention to present events (though "specific recognition" and partitioning may be impaired).

In Chapter VIII I proposed the mechanism by which high levels of nonspecific input may act to favor intrinsic sector activity from the bottom up. The fact that nonspecific fibers also distribute to the plexiform layer may mean in addition that a considerable element of "noise" is introduced into those activities of the external lamina postulated in Chapter IV to be most labile (and therefore involving the maximal metabolic rates implied by the data of Vladimirov *et al.*, Chapter IV, note 13). I have supposed that these activities and the related axonal firing-orders or "abstract memories," e.g., of lower III, may be the neurophysiological substrates of the waking conscious self. The implication is that during intense arousal much of this functional system of the external lamina may effectually be put out of action via the plexiform layer. Its activities, being less strictly predetermined than those of the internal lamina, may be the more readily disorganized. For example, the "flooding" of apical dendritic networks[17] may have occlusive or inhibitory effects reducing or blocking activity in immediately underlying layers; or alternatively, may act to replace discrete patterned processes in those layers by a type of random, virtually patternless activity.[18] It does not, in fact, matter which of these assumptions we make, since reticular "driving" of neocortical activity or diffuse reticulocortical inhibition might have much the same effect, granted the plan of organization of neocortical functions proposed here.

The important point is that intense fearlike arousal states may produce spotty forgetting, not by the inhibition of basal memory-formations or the withdrawal of recalled facts from "consciousness" but by the widespread creation of "holes" or discontinuities in activities equivalent to "consciousness" itself.* This conclusion is consistent with the fact that the paralysis of thought during fear does not preclude the automatic execution of learned actions (implying that basal neocortical memory-formations continue to mediate behavior even when related activi-

---

* I.e., the noise-to-signal ratio may reach a level at which intracortical communication fails. See note 18.

ties equivalent to thought have ceased to play much part in the process). It is also consistent with the observation made, I believe, by Purpura that signs indicating inhibition near the cortical surface may be accompanied by signs indicative of activity in the cortical depths.

Repression may be a phenomenon distinct from the foregoing and basically related to the sequence of events in extinction of a CR. It has been pointed out by Gastaut (Chapter VII, note 27) that extinction is accompanied by suspension of neocortical activity in those areas which previously showed focal activation, suggesting functional thalamic deafferentation. This description is in accord with the definition of avoidance given here (Introductory, p. 9).

I have supposed that during conditioning of a given response, the organism, depending upon its neocortical capacity, forms a more or less complete "model" in memory of the response including its immediate consequences, this model being facilitated *in toto* upon re-presentation of a related CS. As a learned response becomes unrewarding, that part of the model representing its consequences comes to be represented in the form of other memories whose paths of subcortical outflow are to the emergency system. In proportion to the intensity of the drive now *not* rewarded by the CR, presentation of the CS will be followed by a prompt rise in emergency-system activity, touching off some form of general-purpose behavior of the flight or counterattack type, and likewise raising nonspecific input to levels which are de-differentiative, e.g., for the overlying system of neocortical connections by which the miscellaneous basal memories comprising the model are functionally organized. The result is that the organism is set physically in motion, and that with onset of effector-state dominance, the way is cleared, e.g. in neocortex, for a new-learning phase, in which another more effective CR may take shape. This is the variable-behavior phase of extinction reported by Antonitis.*

---

* The so-called brain-washing technique seems aimed at producing and protracting a de-differentiative phase of this type, the object being to make a *tabula rasa* of the subject's mind, upon which more acceptable truths can then be inscribed. If this account of the organization of neocortical functions

The essential feature of a once rewarding response which has become unrewarding is that a corresponding CS, upon presentation, may evoke simultaneous rises in activity of the subcortical reward and pleasure systems. With this, a momentary deadlock (state of mutual inhibition) may be established, during which tonic support of ongoing neocortical activities is reduced. Conceivably this could give rise to the focal slowing reported by Gastaut, and in psychological terms would produce a brief discontinuity in conscious mental processes, followed by an interval of anxiety or fearlike arousal whose internal causes the subject cannot (did not) see. Hence the slang expression for dislike or aversion, "I can't see that," is perhaps in a sense literally correct. In more general terms, any situation which powerfully and simultaneously activates both the reward and punishment systems may produce such a momentary deadlock, resulting in the extreme in unconsciousness. It is my impression that fainting from psychological shock cannot easily be induced in someone already intensely fearful or otherwise agitated, nor in someone profoundly sad, perhaps for the reason that a clear functional imbalance or clear dominance of one major motivational-affective system is in such case pre-established. It is precisely in our normal waking condition, when the activity of both systems is most nearly balanced, that we are most "unguarded" or liable to the type of response just described. Similarly, when we are profoundly disturbed, memories normally invisible because producing such momentary discontinuities in the train of conscious thought may come back with horrible clarity. That is, just when we can least afford the reinforcement of emergency-system activity which it entrains, the "return of the repressed" is most apt to occur— a fact which most psychotherapists know by experience and many neurotics by instinct. In the same way a quarrel may bring to the surface resentments toward friends we never knew we had— possibly because a mechanism essentially similar to repression was operative. To perceive something unpleasant about someone

---

is approximately correct, it is doubtful that that technique cuts as deep as its practitioners hope. For its relation to the three phases of "transmarginal inhibition" of Pavlov, see Sargant, *Battle for the Mind* (New York, Doubleday, 1957).

to whom one is attached may likewise entrain mutually competitive core-activities simultaneously, though the psychological process leading to this result may be quite roundabout and complex. E.g., one's attachment may include intense need. The unpleasant insight may stir up anger. But to express anger would be to threaten one's own security by driving the friend (mate, relative) away. So within a few msec, both the normal-survival (primary rage) and emergency (primary fear) systems are activated.* A brief deadlock results. A skip occurs in the subject's conscious mental processes, and the insight passes all but unseen.† Only later, when an overt quarrel breaks out—i.e., when one's inner balances are decisively upset and rage prevails—do these "repressed" observations come clearly to mind.

It seems probable that elaborated type memories mediate conditioned responses, and that the cortical "strip" regions play an important part in these. During "stimulus generalization," or when posterior intrinsic sectors lying outside the territory of distribution of the specific relay and association nuclei are put functionally out of action by massive nonspecific inputs, our informed responses may be mediated principally in this way, or largely from the specific system proper. This arrangement also favors prompt informed responses of the generic-recognition type. E.g., I step off the curb, see a car speeding toward me, and "automatically" leap back. The response is learned. Certain sights and sounds have long since told me in a general way that I'm in a city, and "car" at a certain distance from me, moving in a certain direction, means "probable collision" (with me). No further particulars are necessary. These perceptual generalizations *qua* elaborated type memories touch off an appropriate (and also somewhat generalized) response "move to safe place"—in the city, the curb.

The implication of the views expressed in earlier chapters is that many functional human mental disorders result from prolongation and exaggeration of subcortical answering-effect trains

---

* And, more specifically, divisions of the latter inhibitory for the former.

† Some of the neurophysiological mechanisms possibly involved are discussed in some detail in Chapter VIII, note 54.

in the primary phase of an emergency response. That is, when output of the inherently more massive acting emergency system is maintained at high levels by a relative predominance of avoidance conditioning, a situation may arise in which the subject or victim manifests a statistically high percentage of anxiety-responses to events in the present, many of whose origins-in-memory are invisible to him. The result may be to impair the elaboration of abstract memory-systems which in effect constitute the rational conscious self and are commensurate with its powers, such as they are, to control subcortical activities equivalent to those of the id. When such a condition is established early in life, it may lead to great difficulties in growing up, both emotionally and intellectually, or to a condition in some ways comparable to that of Thompson and Melzack's Scotties (Chapter II, note 19).

In a later study, I hope to analyze the process of maturation, in particular the period of adolescence, in which a massive reassociation of the basal memories comprising conditioning appears to occur. That is, those which were before associated with the emergency system and prohibitory in function tend predominantly to activate the sexual and ferocity system, now reaching physiological maturity, the result being a protracted acute emotional episode à la Whitehorn. I will attempt also to show how, in neurotics, chronic impairment of the normal elaboration of abstract memory-systems and chronic dominance of "pleasure principle" processes (i.e., of neocortical processes determined from the bottom up) result in the elaboration of a grossly false image of reality, the self included. Experience of the mismatch between parts of this image and fact in turn gives rise to anxiety responses of the orienting reflex type and to a slow enlargement of conditioned avoidance responses. With this there often begins a retreat to a rigidly prescribed way of life which the neurotic finds "safe"—a stratagem also likely to fail, since it reduces that influx of objective knowledge and guards against those acute emotional episodes which between them might be his salvation.

It is perhaps peculiar to man to be able to form an extensive self-image; and to the extent that the memories comprising it can, like any others, become reassociated so as to form part of

Conclusion / 189

the emergency system, the self itself can disappear into the unconscious.* It is essentially this event which the stratagems of the neurotic are aimed at avoiding. Similarly, events which precipitate acute self-disesteem, or suddenly cause much of the self *qua* memory to become functionally related to the emergency system, may produce a crisis of anxiety followed by rebound rage directed against the (physical) self—i.e., self-mutilation or suicide.

Finally, a predominance of avoidance conditioning so great that the de-differentiative effects of the acute emotional episode outrun or preclude adequate reorganization in the aftermath or new-learning phase may lead to breakdown in "reality principle" processes generally and to psychotic regression. In that the frontal intrinsic sectors may reinforce "most motivated" activities as described in the preceding chapter, they may be uniquely accelerative of this sort of functional collapse. It is significant also that most apparently functional mental disorders in man, unlike some of organic basis, are seldom or never genuinely euphoric[19] but suggest gross exaggerations of arousal and inhibitory functions of the emergency system—e.g., protracted states of mental pain or terror, with or without catatonic features, and interspersed with periods of agitation or maniacal hyperactivity suggesting long-deferred answering effects in which ragelike reactions of the normal survival system predominate. Their cardinal feature, aside from these, is disintegration of "reality principle" processes and the waking conscious "I."

It is because, in effect, the neocortex and core compete for control of the thalamus in the way suggested here that the functional system equivalent to the conscious "I" of man is, in a sense, in a perpetual contest with the remainder of the system out of which it arises.† As a principle inferred from experience

---

* That is, the self may come to have double (good-bad) meanings and so become "repressed." "Return of the repressed" self may then, as described, precipitate suicide.

† As suggested earlier, it perhaps cannot arise in cortex of the rhinencephalic type in which olfactory afferents distribute to the tangential layer, or in which layers II and III are comparatively thin and "the afferent plexus approaches the plexiform layer" (Lorente de Nó, *op. cit.*, Chapter IV). Thus the id or instinctive self is not an item of direct conscious knowl-

and represented *qua* abstract memory, this awareness of inner division becomes for man as much an item of knowledge and a determinant of consciously directed actions as any other. From it, however, arises our peculiar sense that the conscious self—in physical fact perhaps a shell a few hundred microns thick and some 2000 square centimeters in area—is enduringly *other* than the memories and feeling-states and bodily processes out of which it so precariously arises. In a very real sense it may be so, reflecting our inability to become "integrated"—which is to say our transitional evolutionary status as creatures neither wholly determined by "pleasure principle" processes nor consistently capable of rational self-determination.

Earlier I quoted Bishop to the effect that the plexiform layer represents the terminal link in a chain of reticular core-systems running the length of the neuraxis. Pribram has suggested that the reticular formation itself may be a mechanism for the formation of "temporary connections." Just as the thalamic reticularis may have become to a considerable extent a neocortical dependency, as described in Chapter VI, the plexiform layer may represent an adaptation of the temporary holding-functions of the RF, subserving labile neocortical activities equivalent to thought. The fact, reported long ago by Cajal, that horizontal cells in the plexiform layer of infants undergo regression, may correspond to a dying away of true reticular functions in this part of the cortex, which thereafter becomes an area of convergence of activities entirely originating elsewhere.* In other words, it would be a mistake to regard the plexiform layer as merely another link in the reticular system. Rather, a phylogenetically old system has here been anatomically drawn out in the form of a thin sheet and interlaced with newer pallial systems in such a way as to give rise to forms of activity and functions themselves new.

---

edge, but one whose properties we must learn almost in the same way that we learn those of external objects. From this, in part, arises our sense of inner division or self-alienation.

* Purpura has questioned whether this regression of Cajal-Retzius cells, said to occur by the fourth or fifth postnatal day, is truly that. Possibly, like those of the external lamina in neonate cerebellum, they migrate inward. (See Ramón y Cajal, *Histologie du Système Nerveux*, Paris, Maloine, 1909, Vol. ii, p. 68.)

Conclusion / 191

IN the Introductory and Chapter I, I have discussed the probable relations of "drives" to basal motives, of homeostatic to motivational-affective functions of the autonomic system, and of the "answering effect" or Sherrington's serial activation principle to the genesis of basal drive and emotional states.

In Chapters III through V I have presented an hypothesis of neocortical memory-functions including the possible areal and laminar (or cytoarchitectural) substrates of these.

In Chapter VI I have presented analyses of certain data relating to functions of the midbrain reticular formation with a view to clarifying the problem of how and where "central integration" may be accomplished.

In Chapter VII and part i of Chapter VIII I have reviewed evidence suggesting the way in which motivational-affective functions may be represented in the rhinencephalon. In part ii of Chapter VIII I have endeavored to suggest how the neocortex, rhinencephalon, and midbrain act as a functional unit, concluding with a discussion of morphological similarities between the neocortex and hippocampal-cingulate complex (or tertiary olfactory system of Pribram and Kruger).

In this chapter I have cited neuropharmacological data which may or may not prove to be consistent with the scheme of structural and functional relationships proposed earlier.

The value of the answering-effect concept as used here is that it suggests experimental predictions as to *sequences* of focal central nervous activity. It seems to me that our greatest gains in understanding may shortly be made in this direction—that is, by studies showing what parts of what subsystems of the CNS are mobilized in what order during the genesis of a particular form of behavior, or at apparent onset of a particular motivational-affective state. Modern techniques of recording from multiple indwelling electrodes make such an approach feasible. What I have sought to do is to provide a tentative rationale for this sort of investigation, in some respects different from those now in use. What current theories of memory may have overlooked is the principle suggested here in the case of extrinsic sector-type memories—namely that "temporary memory" may not be wholly that, or wholly dependent upon reverberatory thalamocortical maintenance. Rather the same extrinsic sector-memory apparatus may continue to exhibit continual progressive changes in the engrams stored, for as long as the organism lives. Whether the (intrinsic sector) thing and abstract memory systems show "saturation" or some degree of functional rigidification with time is another matter. The tendency of human personality to "set" with age suggests that something of the sort may occur. It should also be recalled that our brains evolved at a time in prehistory when human life expectancy was perhaps less than half of what it is in some countries of the West today. There is little evidence that they have increased in size since, and Von Bonin is of the opinion that, judged by cranial capacity, they may somewhat have decreased. In any case, we may now tend to outlive by some decades the better of our mental faculties, although the exchange of plasticity for inner organization which this process often involves is not without advantages for both the individual and his society.

My guess is that this book may contain one or two ideas of value embedded in a matrix of others either incorrect or truistic or both. I shall be happy if it achieves that much. The human brain being constructed as I believe it is, the difficulties of achieving new insight into and new tenable ways of describing natural phenomena are apart from, and much greater than, the problem of achieving skill in intellectual manipulation of the familiar. In each generation a considerable minority of men manage the latter without ever surmounting the former. In this perhaps presumptuous undertaking, I have been motivated by a feeling that self-understanding of a most fundamental biological kind is what we pressingly need, even though, if achievable, it may still not prevent us from exterminating ourselves in the name of survival.* Otherwise, the object of this work is best expressed by something Dr. Pribram said at one of the Macy conferences on the central nervous system: "It comes to a very fundamental

---

* In that we are now faced with the alternatives of mass suicide via the bomb or mass misery through overpopulation, our situation is all too clearly a parable of our evolutionary failure. The "reality principle"—or reason, as it was once called—shows little sign of prevailing over its ancient enemy; and if it does not do so soon, human evolution may be virtually at an end.

point as to what science is all about. We hear that what we ought to be doing . . . is to predict and control. I don't believe that. I would like to understand, and am willing to settle for understanding. Sometimes as result of understanding we can predict and control, but this is not the primary aim of science so far as I am concerned." Stated another way, the mind works best toward purely mental ends; whereas for reasons I hope made plain in this book, introduction of the pragmatic, however indirectly, entrains "pleasure principle" processes; and with them, however subtly, an automatic restriction of thought itself. The ideal of inquiry expressed by Dr. Pribram may thus be more than that. Like the usually corrupted and misunderstood moral ideals of Christianity—ideals which may nonetheless have some foundation in neurophysiological fact—it encourages a type of inner development which may be man's surest, if not his only, route out of the "realistic" animalism which perennially threatens his sanity and now threatens his very existence.

References and Notes

INTRODUCTORY

1. "The acute emotional experience has as its biological function the precipitation of an internal crisis, in which habit is interrupted and the more raw or primitive facilities for biological adjustment are summoned up—not merely sugar for energy production and hastened circulation for increased oxygen use, but also the neural capacities of the organism for forming new associations between reaction and situation, and for reorganizing behavior. These latter are the resources which we recognize as intelligence—the capacity for modifying reaction by experience—a capacity which might lie latent . . . if not activated by emotional experience.

"This idea represents, essentially, an extension of Cannon's emergency hypothesis. . . . In postulating such a function for the acute emotional experience, one must admit that in life its purpose is not always successfully achieved. Inhibitory influences may block the activation of potential resources." (Whitehorn, as quoted in Liddell, *The Biology of Mental Health and Disease,* 506.)

2. Tinbergen, *Study of Instinct,* 105.
3. Beach, *Handbook of Experimental Psychology,* 387, 407.
4. Glover, *Freud or Jung?*, 55, states: "The aim of the infant's sexuality is to obtain genital satisfaction on parental objects. This represents the Oedipus phase which reaches its height between the third and fifth year of life." (See also Waelder, *Basic Theory of Psychoanalysis,* 114.) Glover adds that these strivings may be, indeed mostly are, kept in check, for instance by "the unconscious anxiety of sexual mutilation."

Presumably the latter is not a factor in the lives of young monkeys or apes, which leads one to wonder why, at quite early ages, they don't make determined efforts to copulate with their parents; or if they do, why the fact has not been more frequently reported. From Beach's work it would appear that they don't because they neither innately recognize nor have the behavioral machinery to carry out their sexual aims—these in fact not being aims in the usual sense at all. Are we to assume that the trend in mammalian evolution toward postponement of maturation has gone into reverse in the case of human sexuality? Are we also to assume that the average sheltered middle-class child of three to five is innately aware of the nature of his sexual designs—as must be the case if the Oedipus phase, as Glover describes it, is universal in human young? If so, what evidence have we for these assumptions?

5. Money, *Recent Advances in Biological Psychiatry*, 215 ff. See also Tinbergen, *op. cit.*, 209.

6. For an example from life see Miller, *Handbook of Experimental Psychology*, 451.

7. Lindsley, *ibid.*, 473–480.

8. Pribram and Kruger, *Ann. N.Y. Acad. Sc.*, Vol. 58, Article 2, March 24, 1954, 109–138.

CHAPTER 1

1. Ingram, *Handbook of Physiology*, Sect. 1, *Neurophysiol.*, II, 974.

2. Hoagland, *J. Gen. Physiol.*, 11: 715–738 (1928). Tonic immobility seemed of special interest because of its occurrence in many species including men. Hoagland describes it as "actually a special case of the problem of alternate periods of movement and quiescence of an organism" (*op. cit.*, 717). I would describe it as an arrest of the "answering effect" in the inhibitory phase of intense primary fear, or intense activation of the subcortical emergency system. A more recent study by Moore and Amstey (*Science*, March 2, 1962, 135: 729–730) seems to show that lambs and kids early made aggressive by "capricious" foster mothers (i.e., in which "desire for food dominated the fear response" to the mother) were significantly less susceptible to tonic immobility than normal controls. Here a conditioned tendency toward dominance of the "normal survival" system acted apparently to preclude dominance of the emergency.

Svorad, who studied tonic immobility in the rabbit, concluded that it is a form of paroxysmal inhibition originating subcortically and spreading to neocortex. He believes it to be terminated by the ascending reticular activating system, that system being unaffected throughout. He considers that the appearance of T.I. in man results from a breakdown of higher (e.g., neocortical) functions, with resulting release of this phylogenetically ancient mechanism. (Svorad, *Arch. Neurol. & Psychiat.*, 77: 533–539, May 1957.) The resemblance between tonic immobility and catatonic states has been noted by many.

Hoagland's finding argues that central nervous states may be reinforced, but powerfully resist initiation, by changes in blood-levels of epinephrine. According to Hoch, the same applies in the case of the autonomic system vis-à-vis the brain (cf. Hoch, *Transactions, Second Conference on Neuropharmacology*, 36).

3. Karamyan, *Sechenov J. USSR*, 44, 1958, 285–295. See also Wang Tai-an and Belekhova, *ibid.*, 47, 1961, 12–21. It is interesting that the latter reported something comparable to what I have called the answering effect. "Characteristically, repeated stimulation of the (cervical) sympathetic nerve after a long interval of time (1–1.5 hr.) brought about an opposite effect on the recruiting response; on the first stimulation, inhibition was most commonly observed, while on the second, enhancement took place." This is in line with the view, developed here later, that the centrencephalic-autonomic emergency system has important primary inhibitory effects upon neocortex and upon many mechanisms of the "normal survival" system—e.g., those concerned in feeding and sexuality. The tendency of inhibited systems is then to show escape or post-inhibitory rebound, with corresponding changes in motivational-affective state, as discussed in the text.

4. Marrazzi, *Recent Advances in Biological Psychiatry*, 333–343.

5. Miller, *Handbook of Experimental Psychology*, 454. See also *Problems of Consciousness*, 141–142.

6. Quoted in Hardin, *Biology*, 477.

7. Reference is to Wolff's observations of a patient with gastric fistula and Milhorat and Diethelm's studies of blood changes accompanying emotional states in man (cf. Magda Arnold, *Present-Day Psychology*, 154).

8. Fulton, *Physiology of the Nervous System*, 229. Apropos of the organization of the emergency system, it is also worth noting that in man the only direct preganglionic fibers of the sympathetic system are reportedly those to the adrenal medulla (Hoff, *Textbook of Physiol.*, 233).

9. E.g., goats reportedly show primary tachycardia in the same (fear-provoking) situation which causes bradycardia in dogs and sheep (Liddell, *op. cit.* 145).

10. Maier, *Frustration*; see especially pp. 26–79 regarding the behavior of rats in the "no-solution problem."

11. Cf. Fulton, *Physiol NS*, 547 ff., for a review of Culler and Mettler's and Lebdinskaia and Rosenthal's work with decorticate and decerebrate dogs. See also, Sprague *et al.*, *Science*, 133, Jan. 20, 1961, 165–173.

12. For a splendid description, see Huxley's *Time Must Have a Stop*, p. 227.

13. Tinbergen, *Scientific American*, November, 1954, 154.
14. Rosin and Shulov, *Science*, June, 1961, 133: 1919.
15. Herrick, *The Brain of the Tiger Salamander*, 32–34.
16. Quite lasting decrescendos of hormonal activity can evidently be produced by hippocampal stimulation. E.g., stimulation of the anterior medial hippocampus in monkeys can produce a transient rise in 17–OH–corticosteroids, followed by a fall below normal levels lasting as long as 48 hours (cf. Mason, *Reticular Formation of the Brain*, 656).
17. Stanishevskaya, *Pavlov J. Higher Nerv. Activity*, Vol. 11, No. 1, 1961, 35–36. In what this author describes as cases of "simple" schizophrenia "the vascular component of the orienting-investigatory reflex . . . revealed the presence of pathologically stable 'inextinguishable' undulations in the plethysmogram of the limb vessels during 'spontaneous' records . . . these undulations . . . remained throughout repeated examinations in most of these patients." The author attributes this phenomenon to an "inhibitory state" of the neocortex, resulting in subcortical release of oscillatory processes.

It would evidently be premature to conclude, however, that attentive states involve so great a gain in the variance of unit activity, e.g., in neocortex, that rhythmic activity there and elsewhere tends to be set aside. Freeman (*Science*, June 30, 1961, 133: 2058–2059) reports that in cats "a single shock to prepyriform cortex with implanted electrodes caused a damped sinusoidal oscillation in potential. The root-mean-square amplitudes of potentials evoked by short (115 msec) trains of stimuli, when plotted against the frequency of stimulation, fitted the equation for forced harmonic oscillation when the cat was attentive to stimuli." A rougher fit or none resulted when the cat was seemingly inattentive.

It is nonetheless true that, in neocortex, the transition from sleep to waking appears to involve an increase in the variance of local unit activity, which increase may be accompanied by a fall in the over-all axonal firing-rate. Presentation of stimuli which can be inferred to be foci of attention tends to cause a "major increase" in mean firing-rates. The significance of these findings by Evarts *et al.* (*Science*, March 2, 1962, 133: 726–728) is discussed in a later chapter. The point of importance here is that particularly in "attentive" states, the neocortex may act by feedback to alter or defer sequences of subcortical answering effects arising in the same situation—doing so, e.g., by the imposition of its own inherently more variable patterns of activity upon those of the limbic system and midbrain reticular formation (Section II).

18. The neural mechanisms responsible for answering effects pre-

sent a much more complex problem than the model given in the text suggests. The latter is based on the familiar principle that activation here means inhibition there—or more properly, inhibition at n sites and activation at n' other sites there. Apart from the fact that we know it does occur and does not necessarily depend upon internuncials (cf. Pitts and McCulloch, *Bull. Math. Biophys.*, Vol. 5, 1943, p. 116), inhibition is not yet well understood.

The activating or inhibiting influence of one system upon another evidently may depend upon at least two factors, frequency-specificity and the phase relation or timing of the input with respect to ongoing activities of the receptor system.

The former is illustrated by the fact that stimulation of the anterior lobe vermis of the cerebellum may produce spinal facilitation up to a limiting stimulation rate, and inhibition at higher frequencies (Brookhart, *Handbk. Physiol.*, Sect. 1, *Neurophysiol.*, II, 1260). It is perhaps also exemplified by Purpura's report that "high-frequency reticulocortical stimulation is particularly effective in permitting inhibitory build-up in different cortical organizations" (*International Review of Neurobiology*, I, 1959, p. 142).

The latter is illustrated by Lindsley's studies of the cortical alpha excitability cycle, and by Snider and Sato's of the effects of variously timed auditory and cerebellar stimuli upon activity in auditory areas I and II in Flaxedil-immobilized cats ("Symposium on Dendrites," *EEG Supplement No. 10*, November, 1958, p. 74). When cerebellar stimulation preceded auditory (clicks) by 11–17 msec, depression in the amplitude of cortical response was mostly observed; when the interval was lengthened to 18–26 msec, there resulted mostly facilitation; and at intervals of 32 msec or more, no effect was apparent.

It appears that stimulation of a point on the skin tends to establish a focus of activation surrounded by foci of inhibition, arrival of the corresponding impulse in somatosensory cortex establishing a similar pattern locally (Mountcastle and Powell, *Bull. Johns Hopkins*, Vol. 105, No. 3, September 1959, pp. 108–131). On a still smaller scale, stimulation of the hypogastric nerve (parameters presumably constant) produces a facilitatory-inhibitory sequence, these phases being separable by nicotine (Fulton, *Physiology of the Nervous System*, p. 214) (Monkey).

A particularly interesting behavioral illustration of the answering-effect principle has been given by Liddell, as follows: "We discovered a number of years ago that the simplest procedure for precipitating an 'experimental neurosis' in the sheep or goat was to employ ten-second conditioned signals separated by constant time intervals. When the interval between all signals was two minutes, a type of 'experimental neurosis' resulted which we have characterized as tonic immobility. At the signal the animal reacts with pronounced muscular rigidity, lifting the stiffly extended forelimb from the shoulder instead of flexing it freely in anticipation of the electric shock as the normal does. This neurotic pattern suggests a frozen and distorted startle pattern. . . . With a constant separation of the ten-second signals of five, six, or seven minutes, the neurotic outcome was found to differ radically. Here the animal exhibits in the laboratory a pattern of diffuse nervousness, as shown by repeated movements of the head, repeated tic-like movements of the trained forelimb and rapid irregular respiratory movements.

"Why the experimenter can at will precipitate a neurotic pattern of the frozen-vigilance type or . . . can establish the agitated pattern just described by the simple expedient of spacing the signals farther apart in this rigid temporal pattern . . . we do not know" (*Biology of Mental Health & Disease*, p. 591).

As already suggested, arousal responses often seem to involve a preliminary phase in which each of the major motivational-affective systems is powerfully activated and inhibits parts of the other. Being apparently the more massively acting, the emergency system may then be the more apt to become dominant during the ensuing phase of post-inhibitory rebound, although in this situation, the "informing" action of the neocortex may be crucial in deciding the outcome. (See later chapters here). The function of this preliminary phase may be to insure widespread central nervous mobilization by the mechanism of post-inhibitory rebound. Its role in "repression" is discussed in Chapter IX.

In Dr. Liddell's experiment, renewal of the stimulus at 2–minute intervals appears to prolong this preliminary deadlock phase, whereas increasing the interval to 5–7 minutes evidently permits the emergency system to become clearly dominant. The behavioral paralysis occurring at onset of intense fear may thus correspond to a state in which the normal flux of subcortical answering effects is arrested and its future course made more or less uncertain. The state itself is felt as profoundly threatening because in fact it represents a disruption of a basic pattern of activity of the CNS, and threatens other physiological processes accordingly. Such states may be the essence of psychological conflict in man, in that they represent a likely culmination of intense but factually unresolvable, ambivalences of feeling or intention.

Mere withdrawal from situations causing severe conflict—the stratagem followed by many neurotics—is for reasons just mentioned less likely to produce an aftermath state of pleasure (e.g., relief) than one of anxiety—the probability of the latter being roughly proportional to the intensity of the conflict which preceded it. Since chronic anxiety may impair the neocortical processing of information as described below, a situation may result in which activities equivalent to conscious thought become incapable of altering the daily alternance of conflict and anxiety. Out of this situation grow neurotic automatism and neurotic hopelessness.

In *The Integrative Action of the Nervous System* (Yale edition, p. 223) Sherrington observed that "the waning of a reflex under long maintained excitation is one of the many phenomena that pass in physiology under the name of 'fatigue.' It may be that in this case the so-called fatigue is nothing but a negative induction. Its place of incidence may lie at the synapse. . . . One obvious use attaching to it is the prevention of the too prolonged continuous use of a 'common path' by any one receptor . . . it favours the receptors taking turn about. It helps to insure the serial variety of reaction. The organism, to be successful in a million-sided environment, must in its reactions be manysided."

The same principle we have supposed to apply at the limbic level and to determine not actions directly, but successions of motivational-affective states, out of which actions are likely to arise.

Elsewhere in the same book (p. 213) Sherrington discusses what might be described as spinal answering effects: "I have pointed out . . . the peculiar prominence of 'alternating reflexes' in prolonged spinal reactions. It is significant that they are usually cut short with ease by mere passive mechanical interruption of the alternating movement in progress. It seems that each step of the reflex movement tends to excite, by spinal induction, the step next succeeding itself." An example of the modification of such innate spinal response-trains from higher nervous levels is given (*ibid.*, p. 305).

A principle of some functional importance, discussed here in Section II, is that post-inhibitory rebound, which figures in transfer of dominance from one system or mechanism to another, involves a concealed facilitatory component such that activity of the inhibited system tends, when released, to be at higher than normal levels. Sherrington gives an example of this (post-inhibitory exaggeration of the knee-jerk following stimulation of the hamstring nerve) on p. 213.

Another answering effect of the type involving post-inhibitory rebound is given by Ingram (*op. cit.*, p. 974). Stimulation of the cerebellum (not further specified) produces suppression of the somatic and autonomic manifestations of sham rage in cats, with rebound occurring on cessation of stimulation. The work reviewed was done by Moruzzi, who observed parallel pupillary reactions. (For other examples involving limbic and diencephalic structures, see Section II below.)

The anatomic connections by which autonomic answering effects may be mediated might be divided roughly into two groups, corresponding to Herrick's division of the CNS into cerebrum and rhombic brain, the line of demarcation being "a transverse plane at the posterior border of the midbrain" (*Brain of the Tiger Salamander*, p. 40). This division is in accordance with Ingram's observation that "the more spectacular autonomic mechanisms" are represented "in highly localized fashion" in the medulla, the midbrain containing "relatively few" of these (*op. cit.*, p. 975).

Answering effects occurring at the medullary or segmental level, as well as possibly via the local sympathetic-parasympathetic connections mentioned by Fulton (*Physiol. N.S.*, p. 214), are largely, one supposes, of the type which Ingram describes as functioning "only for the needs of the moment." Those subserving more or less informed intentional or affective states and behavior are perhaps chiefly mediated by the hypothalamus, whose midbrain and limbic connections are discussed at length in Section II. (See also Gurdjian et al., *Trans. Am. Neurol. Assoc.*, 1955, 82–83, who report a communicating branch between the sympathetic chain in the neck and the vagus "is a consistent finding in the Rhesus monkey." Re fibers from X and XI to sympathetic ganglia of the thoracic and abdominal viscera, see Morris and Schaeffer, *Human Anatomy*, 11th ed., p. 1081.)

19. A study of vascular changes and changes in metabolic rate in nembutalized cats, following stimulation of parts of the hypothalamus and of neocortex (monopolar and bipolar electrodes; 10 seconds; 1–4, V, biphasic rectangular pulses, 0.2 msec pulse width at 50 cps), showed slight or nil effects from stimulation of the anterior hypothalamus and sensorimotor cortex. Stimulation of the posterior hypothalamus from the mammillary body to the region of the infundibulum produced an initial "instantaneous" cerebral vasoconstriction and slowing of the blood-flow rate. This was "released" within 5–10 seconds, and followed by cerebral vasodilatation and increased blood flow lasting 1–2 minutes. Oxygen consumption remained above normal 2–3 minutes. Circulatory epinephrine or nor-epinephrine "caused strong vasoconstriction and increase of cerebral vascular resistance" promptly relieved by

posterior hypothalamic stimulation. These authors conclude that the primary vasoconstriction observed with stimulation alone may be adrenergic, the rise in oxygen consumption being independent of (and to an extent antagonized by) vascular changes. These findings argue that in primary fear, humoral vascular effects are exceedingly prompt and may contribute importantly to the mental paralysis characteristic of that state (Geiger, *Trans. Amer. Neurol. Assoc.*, 80, 117–120).

A second study (reported by French *et al., ibid.*, 121–124) showed that out of 13 monkeys, 6, stimulated daily via electrodes implanted in the preoptic (3 animals), mammillary (2), and tuberal (1) regions developed focal lesions of the stomach or duodenum. All placements were near the midline and lesions included peripheral edema, atrophy and dilation of the mucosal glands, and "distention and stasis of the vessels."

There is some question as to the probable autonomic outflow from the areas mentioned, and also as to the hypothalamic structures most directly involved. The "tuberal region" might refer to the diverse nuclear masses, including ventromedial and dorsomedial *nn.*, given under this head by Morris and Schaeffer (*op. cit.*, 1018). Fulton classes the posterior and lateral hypothalamus as chiefly sympathetic in outflow (*Physiol. of the Nervous Sys.*, 246–247), and the tuber and anterior nuclei as parasympathetic. This is not entirely in agreement with Hess, who classes the lateral hypothalamus, including the preoptic area, as parasympathetic (Diencephalon, 162). Hess points out "that similar (parasympathetic) effects can also be elicited occasionally by stimulation of the medial and posterior hypothalamus," with the suggestion that these may be mediated at the medullary level.

An additional complicating factor in interpreting these results is provided by a recent study which shows that in unanesthetized cats, intramuscular epinephrine decreases the force but increases the rate of gastric contraction (Sternbach, *Psychophysiol. Newsletter*, Vol. 8, No. 1, January 1962, 37–44).

Whether the gastrointestinal lesions reported above result directly from activation of the sympathetic-adrenal system, or from direct and indirect (answering effect) activation of the parasympathetic, they do illustrate a point of prime importance—namely, that the vegetative-homeostatic and motivational-affective functions of the autonomic system overlap in such a way that protracted emotional states may tend to produce visceral dysfunction or organic damage. In contrast to the rhombic brain representation of autonomic functions, the hypothalamus seems to be the head ganglion controlling both types of autonomic response.

Many years ago, commenting upon the skeletal as against the visceral expressions of emotion, Sherrington wrote: "The instinctive bodily expressions of emotion [probably arose] . . . as attitudes and movements useful to the animal for defence, escape, seizure, embrace, etc. These as survivals have become symbolic for states of mind. Hence an intelligible nexus between the muscular attitude, pose of feature, etc., and the emotional state of mind. But between the action of the viscera and the psychical state, the nexus is less obvious. This latter connexion adds a difficult corollary to the general problem of [emotion]" (*The Integrative Action of the Nervous System*, 258).

The view outlined in this chapter and the Introductory suggests that with the evolutionary expansion of the forebrain in mammals, some fragmentation of the innate primordial behavioral apparatus occurred, and with it a corresponding expansion of more generalized functions. The latter are chiefly represented by the neopallial memory-apparatus, which is generalized in the sense that, within limits, the functional form it takes depends upon the life-history of the individual; and by adaptation of the primordial olfactory apparatus—notably the secondary and tertiary olfactory systems of Pribram and Kruger—to the production of a variety of motivational-affective states. The latter are generalized in the sense that they no longer strictly or primarily concern olfaction and its corresponding visceral adjustments, but are in various ways modulatory or supportive of neocortical processes which are in turn the seat acquired behavior, including acquired alterations in basal "motivation."

The pathways by which neocortical activity influences and by which it is influenced from, the limbic system are discussed in Section II.

The relevant point here is that many of the systems mediating olfacto-visceral adjustments in lower forms such as *Amblystoma tigrinum* (Herrick) may in higher have become indispensable to a variety of non-olfactory functions as well, including, in the case of the hippocampus, formation of neocortical memories irrespective of their modality or specific behavioral context (cf. Chapter III below). In effect, this mammalian adaptation of the secondary and tertiary olfactory systems is a demonstration of the biological principle of parsimony —since in fact the olfactory system as a whole still retains its olfactory functions. The dual (affective and homeostatic) role of the autonomic system is then the bodily counterpart of the functional duality of the compound olfactory system. In both cases, a saving has been effected by putting old structures to new uses. The occasionally *un*-adaptive

References and Notes / 205

feature of this portmanteau arrangement is that older homeostatic functions may be grossly disrupted by the motivational-affective. The last is especially true in the case of emergency responses, for reasons discussed in the text. From it arises the peculiar fact that an organism may survive actual or theatened stresses originating in its environment, only to succumb to the vegetative consequences of its own "protective" responses. The principle is demonstrated in some detail in the work of Selye (for a brief summary of which see H. Selye, *Biology of Mental Health and Disease*, 595–599). In any case, this account may in part answer the question raised by Sherrington in the passage quoted above. However, the connection between intense emotional disorders and organic damage, e.g., to the stomach or lower intestinal tract, remains I believe to be conclusively demonstrated in man.

20. Welsh, *Quart. Rev. Biol.*, Vol. 13, 2: 123–139, June 1938. Cf. also Vance and Tucker, *Science*, May 4, 1962, 136: 380–381; also Sweeney and Haxo, *ibid.*, 134: 1361–1363.

The persistence of some of these diurnal rhythms—e.g., of color changes when the organism is kept in darkness—is remarkable. For instance, Menke reported that such changes in *Idothea*, an isopod, continued for 60 days (Welsh, *op. cit.*, 127). Twenty-four-hour metabolic cycles have been demonstrated in mammals (e.g., rats and man; see Welsh, *op. cit.*, 136). These cycles can in many cases be inverted, but several attempts to shorten them to 16 hours—e.g., in the deermouse *Peromyscus*—failed (Welsh, *op. cit.*, 134, 136). Similar 24-hour cycles in feeding, general activity, or emergence from puparia have been demonstrated in bees, ants, and *Drosophila* (*ibid.*).

CHAPTER II

1. This conclusion is in accord with Voronin's report that the lower vertebrates are harder to condition and also easier to de-condition than higher. (Cf. Reynolds, *The Central Nervous System and Behavior*, (1959) p. 175. See also Appel, *Science*, Jan. 6, 1961, 133: 36.)

2. Prosser, *Evolution of Central Nervous Control*, 1959, 139.

3. A. J. Marshall, ed., *Biology and Comparative Physiology of Birds*, Vol. II, 15. Cf. also Herrick, *Brain of the Tiger Salamander*, 24, 106. It is worth noting, however, that in the first reference here the authors confirm Cajal's report stating that in some avian striate cortex, up to fifteen layers can be detected, arguing considerable cortical processing of visual data.

4. Sperry's work indicates that in split-brain cats little transfer of visual pattern learning from the side of the uncovered to that of the

covered eye occurs. This can be inferred to mean that neocortical processes on the side of the covered eye are not "informed" or integrated by relay of information from the contralateral hemisphere via the reticular formation (Sperry, in a lecture delivered at Albert Einstein College of Medicine, Yeshiva University, April 28, 1960). Cf. also a similar study by Meikle and Sechzer, *Science*, Nov. 18, 1960, 132: 1496.

5. Sprague *et al.*, *Science*, Jan. 20, 1961, 133: 165–173.

6. Reference is to such evolutionary changes as the differentiation of the colliculi and the emergence, in mammals, of the pons (Herrick, *op. cit.*, 22). However, it is worth noting that structurally the isthmus has regressed in higher forms (*ibid.*, 119).

7. In the dorsal thalamus, the corresponding divisions are the "external portion" (relay and association nuclei) and the "core" (including DM and the anterior, midline and intralaminar nuclei). See Pribram, *Behavior and Evolution*, 147. The significance of these divisions is discussed later here.

8. Tinbergen, *Study of Instinct*, 97.

9. McCulloch, in *Cerebral Mechanisms and Behavior*.

10. Cited by Pauling, *Science*, July 7, 1961, 134: 21.

11. Lorente de Nó, in Fulton, *Physiology of the Nervous System*. The cortical layers referred to are I–IV or what he calls the external lamina.

12. The neuroanatomic and physiological reasons for this statement are given in detail in Chapters IV and V below.

13. E.g., Fulton (*op. cit.*, 426) cites an earlier report that stimulation of optic areas 18 or 19 in man evokes "highly organized visual images"—these not being obtainable from the frontal eyefields.

14. These last being the fiber systems once considered chiefly responsible for the "transcortical reflex" and the "association" of primary sense-data. Cf. Pribram's critique of these "classical" notions, Chapter V below.

15. From the work of Sharpless and Jasper, it appears that some degree of memory-formation may occur in the thalamus; or alternatively, that some assortment and tonotopic distribution of auditory inputs takes place there via innate mechanisms, with the result that after removal of the temporal lobe, the animal can still distinguish pitch but has lost its capacity for more complex forms of auditory discrimination (Sharpless and Jasper, *Brain*, 79, 1956, 655–680. Cf. also Jasper, *Reticular Formation of the Brain*, 321.

16. Mountcastle, *J. Neurophysiol.*, 1957, 20, 408–434; Mountcastle and Powell, *Bull. Johns Hopkins*, Vol. 105, No. 3, September

1959, 108–131; Scheibel and Scheibel, *Ann. N.Y. Acad. Sc.*, Vol. 89, Art. 5, Jan. 28, 1961, 857–865.

17. Reference is to Hydén's work (cited later) as to the possible role of RNA in engram formation and the relation of this, e.g., to the observed "consolidation" time necessary to formation of conditioned reflexes in certain species (Pribram, *Regional Physiology of the Engram*, 6; see also Abt and Essman, *Science*, May 12, 1961, 133: 1477).

18. Sokolov, *Neuronal Models and the Orienting Reflex*, 187 ff. It is important to note that Sokolov distinguishes tonic and phasic forms of the orienting reflex (*op. cit.*, 197), the former of midbrain and the latter of thalamic reticular origin. These two nonspecific systems are discussed at length in Chapter VI below.

19. Thompson and Melzack, *Scientific American*, January 1956, 38–42. Litters of Scotties were divided into experimental and control groups, the former being kept in a nearly "blank isolated environment" for the first seven to ten months of life. These dogs later manifested a pronounced tendency toward exaggerated startle reactions and inappropriate behavior when exposed to test objects such as a slowly swelling balloon. In situations requiring the learning of shock avoidance, they behaved "wildly and aimlessly," and showed up to 50 per cent more errors on maze-running problems than did their littermates, the controls. In other test situations their behavior was also "strikingly unintelligent," and interestingly, they proved less sociable than the controls when put in the same room. "They were apparently a great deal more interested in the inanimate physical aspects of the room"—or it might be more correct to say that they were more generally distracted by surroundings which the controls, by virtue of their better developed memory-systems, could generically "recognize" with ease and without undue de-controlling of core inputs to the neopallium, as described in the text here and later. Testing at intervals over several years led these authors to believe the experimental group never wholly recovered or caught up with the controls.

20. Tinbergen, *op. cit.*, 62.

21. Gerard, *Scientific American*, Sept. 1953, 121–122.

22. E.G., see Pribram, "On the Neurology of Thinking," *Beh. Science*, Vol. 4, No. 4, October 1959, 274. In another paper entitled "Regional Physiology of the CNS, The Search for the Engram," 16, he remarks that the networks in which engrams take shape "appear to be indistinguishable from those that process directly the inputs to and outputs from, the brain." As is clear, especially in Chapters IV and V, that is precisely the view developed here.

23. McCulloch, *Finality and Form*, 60–62. See also *ibid*. 55, for some calculations made by Von Foerster from the half-life of the memory-trace of the "voltage of the potential barrier and hence the wave length which turns out to be in the near infra-red. This value and the characteristic half-life of half a day, and the number of traces and potential carriers of traces [i.e., the cortical neuronal population] seem to us entirely in keeping with the notion that the actual carriers are protein molecules which alone have the property of making others in their own image." The foregoing would appear to anticipate Hydén's RNA hypothesis mentioned in note 17 above.

24. *Ibid.*, 55.

25. Penfield mentions the rarity with which he has obtained "experiential" responses from stimulating in the temporal lobe. The tendency of epileptics to show "experiential" responses may be related to the highly preferential pathways of cortico-subcortical outflow which repeated seizures, initiated from the same site, might be expected to produce. As discussed later, such pathways may involve both short and long feedback loops, it being via these that the remainder of the "mosaic" comprising the memories in neocortex (and producing the "experiential" response) are activated.

26. See for instance Teuber, *Evolution of Central Nervous Control* 157–194.

27. Sholl, *Organization of the Cerebral Cortex.*

28. Reference is to Sperry's split-brain studies, note 4 above; and also to the finding that in precentral cortex an "irritative" focus may produce give rise to a mirror focus contralaterally (Pribram, note 23 above, 2nd ref.).

29. Lorente de Nó, quoted, Chapter V, p. 75 below.

30. Mountcastle, note 16 above, 1st ref. In cat somatosensory cortex he states that "our observations indicate that some neurons closely adjacent . . . are activated reciprocally by reciprocal movements of the joints." This is essentially similar to the arrangement of motor representation found elsewhere in the CNS, and reflects the essentially effector character of the whole. This point is discussed in Chapter VI, specifically in relation to reticular motor representation, reversed patterns of flexion and extension being obtainable by shifting the stimulus-point from the medial to lateral RF. Ultimately, all neocortical "answering effects" of the kind described in the text serve the same purpose as Sherrington's negative spinal induction, namely to promote the "serial variety" of behavior (see Chapter I, note 18).

31. Scoville and Milner, *J. Neurol., Neurosurg., & Psychiat.,*

February 1957, 20: 11–21. See also *Trans.*, Amer. Neurol. Assoc., 80: 42–48, 1955.

CHAPTER III

1. See Chapter IV, note 16.
2. Morillo, *EEG clin. Neurophysiol.*, 13: 9–20, 1961. Morillo's data are discussed in some detail in Chapter V.
3. In the *Handbook of Physiology; Neurophysiol.* Vol. III, 1960, 1738, MacLean points out that "conceptualized thought can give rise to emotion and . . . emotion can give rise to conceptualized thought. . . . This is a fundamental consideration . . . because the preservation of an environmental event in the form of an idea can perpetuate the emotion associated with that event and thereby lead to a vicious circle."

The tendency for memories to form in consequence of an emotional or "drive" state, and to be maintained or reinforced by such states, is suggested by the so-called Zeigarnik effect or our tendency to recall (facts related to) uncompleted tasks more clearly than completed ones. This is said not to apply in the case of "stressful" emotions—e.g., if the task involves a threatening situation or is in some way damaging to self-esteem—in which case repression may occur (A. A. Roback, ed., *Present Day Psychology*, 129). The mechanism of repression is discussed later here.

4. McCulloch, *Finality and Form*, 53.
5. Scheibel and Scheibel, in *Reticular Formation of the Brain*, 53. See also *idem. Ann.* N.Y. Acad. Sc., Vol. 89, Art 5, Jan. 28, 1961, 857–865.
6. Speaking of the temporal lobe stimulation studies of Penfield and Jasper, Pribram (*Behavior and Evolution*, 153) notes that "in practically all cases memories in only one modality are elicited in any one patient from any reasonably circumscribed locus."
7. *Present Day Psychology*, 127.
8. Sherrington, *The Integrative Action of the Nervous System*, 223.
9. It has been reported in the literature that both the neocortex and hippocampus are highly sensitive to anoxia. Metabolic rates at various levels in neocortex are discussed in Chapter V; and the hippocampus, as the precursor of all pallial systems, in Chapter VIII.
10. Cf. Miller, Galanter and Pribram, *Plans and the Structure of Behavior*, 129 and *passim*.
11. Much evidence suggests that "extinction" of a conditioned

response does not involve functional dissolution, e.g., of the neo-cortico-subcortical paths concerned, but rather results from selective suspension of activity over those paths (cf. Gastaut, in *Recticular Formation of the Brain*, 571). Recurrence of the situation establishing the CR to begin with then tends to restore the latter with comparative ease. As suggested later here CR formation may entail establishment of "traces" or "closure" at several central nervous levels; while for reasons discussed in Chapters IV and V, such traces may be both maximally detailed and maximally enduring in neocortex. This means that "extinction" may occur at subcortical levels, and consist in a switching of neocortico-subcortical outflows to other pathways. Appel has presented evidence that avoidance responses persist longer in "higher" forms (squirrel monkey) than in "lower" (rat, pigeon) (*Science*, Jan. 6, 1961, 133: 36). John has shown that a conditioned avoidance response in the cat could, after extinction, be reactivated by amphetamine in neocortex but that "subcortical responses . . . were not brought back." (How this was demonstrated he does not say.) (*Transactions*, First Conference on the CNS, Macy Foundation, 1959, 347). Evidence that neocortical responses alone do not provide the basis for conditioned responses is presented by Chow, Dement and John, (*J. Neurophysiol.*, 20 [1957] 482). That "switching" of neocortico-subcortical outflow to different paths may occur and that it may involve overriding action, e.g., of the normal survival "pleasure" system upon the emergency system during extinction of an avoidance CR, is suggested by Wolpe, who reports that in a conditioned shock-avoidance response in cats, autonomic and other signs do not extinguish, but can be eliminated by "counterposing other emotional responses that are antagonistic to the anxiety" (*Science*, May 19, 1961, 133: 1651–1652).

Presumably psychoanalysis undertakes to establish this "counterposing" of other emotional responses, in effect by recovery and re-association of "the repressed." In the case of unpleasant thing memories early established (e.g., in the first decade) it is a question how effective this technique is likely to be. Data from narcosynthetic studies suggest that recently acquired "traumata" (avoidance conditioning, as in battle) can be re-experienced harmlessly in the present, leading to extinction, whereas long-established avoidance CR's cannot. Freud's early experience in the use of hypnosis on hysterics may have led him to the conclusion that *all* conditioning—save for certain exceptions he made later—was extinguishable, a conclusion which much subsequent neurophysiological and psychological study has I think, failed to bear out. On this point see Percival Bailey, *Perspectives in Biology and*

Medicine, Vol. IV, Winter 1961, 243. Psychoanalysis itself has thus, on the whole, failed to be more than a protracted (and often exorbitantly expensive) palliative technique whose practitioners have shown a marked resistance to collecting and publishing statistics on their therapeutic results. (The interested reader can consult Dr. Warren McCulloch, who recently attempted to collect such data). One follow-up study in this field (*Current Approaches to Psychoanalysis*, 1960, 151 ff.) does not indicate results proportionate to the time and money usually invested in this sort of therapy, nor anything that could be called a cure in the usual medical sense. (See also Regnér, *Acta Psychiat, et Neurol.* Scandinav., 34: 110–125, 1959.)

12. Cf. Hernstein, *Science*, June 30, 1961, 133: 2068–2069.
13. Bailey and Von Bonin, *The Isocortex of Man*, 68.
14. Bishop *et al.*, *EEG clin. Neurophysiol.*, 1961, 13: 40–41.
15. An exception must evidently be made in the case of birds, in which the striatum is greatly developed and the mammalian specific system lacking. The fact that visual cortex in some birds has been found to have the fifteen layers originally reported by Ramón y Cajal suggests that they must have an "influx of precise information" adequate to this elaborate receptor apparatus (A. J. Marshall, ed. *Biol. and Compar. Morphology of Birds*, Vol. II, 1961, 15).
16. Sherrington, as cited in a later chapter, mentions that in mammalian evolution the rhinencephalon shows but little change. In human brain the cortical neuronal population has been estimated at between 5×10^9 and 10^{10} (Agduhr; McCulloch; cf. Sholl, Chapter II, note 27). Some idea of the probable size of core neuronal populations is given by Green and Maxwell's recent estimate of that of the rabbit hippocampus, namely 2 to 5×10^6 per hippocampus (*EEG clin. Neurophysiol.*, 1961, 13: 839).
17. Cf. Magoun *et al.*, *Transactions*, Second Conference on the CNS, Macy Foundation, 1960, 40 *et seq.* The illustration from Bailey and Von Bonin mentioned in the text is deceptive in that, of course, much koniocortex is buried.
18. Lorente de Nó, *op. cit.*, Chapter IV, note 1.

CHAPTER IV

1. Fulton, *Physiol. Nervous System*, 288–320.
2. Bailey and Von Bonin, *The Isocortex of Man*.
3. Sholl, *Organization of the Cerebral Cortex*.
4. In a review of present theories as to the nature of synaptic transmission, Bodian (*Science*, August 3, 1962, 137, 323–326) makes

the point that the perikaryon "is primarily the trophic center of the nerve cell and that its position is therefore irrelevant as far as the major 'neural' or electrochemical functions of the neuron are concerned." He adds that there is no contradiction in the fact that synaptic junctions are found on the somata of many neurons, when "it is recognized that the membrane of the cell body is the part which is involved in transmission." See also Droz and Leblond, "Migration of Proteins along the Axons of the Sciatic Nerve," *Science*, September 28, 1962, 137: 1047–1048; and the work of De Robertis, cited in Chapter IX below).

5. The following is taken from a letter recently sent to a neurophysiologist of my acquaintance. While it repeats certain points made *passim* here, I have included it because it states quite clearly the postulated memory-functions of large-celled bands in neocortex and reasons underlying the postulated memory-functions of large-celled bands in neocortex and elsewhere. The passage follows:

"The assumption I have gone on is that Grundfest and Purpura are probably correct. I.e., as Bishop has suggested, the axon is probably a later adaptation, favoring rapid communication with minimal loss of informational content, between membrane systems showing graded activity only. According to Grundfest & Co., this applies to axon terminals as well as to postsynaptic membrane. (Cf. Ward, *Internat. Rev. Neurobiol.* III, 148.) De Robertis' work on 'synaptic vesicles' presumably transported down the axoplasm and released at the terminals, is consistent with their views. It also suggests why tonic and phasic effects, particularly at high general levels of excitation, tend to go together. [See Chapter IX, note 2 here.]

"Begging many questions the above leaves unanswered, I have supposed there is some relation, evidently complex and fluid rather than simple and fixed, between graded activity and the action potential. For instance Baumgarten, Green, and Mancia (*EEG clin. Neurophysiol.*, 1962, 14: 621–634) report that firing of axons in the bulb is in general correlated with the "negative-going phase" of the wave. Secondly, I have supposed that the interposition of the axonal apparatus between graded membranes acting as in Tetrahymena geleii S (in which ciliar movements are blocked by DFP or eserine) has been important in the development of memory-functions since it has made for a type of strictly conditional patterned activity, and so for such conditional psychological processes as recognition of *that* person, object, etc. (I'm leaving redundancy out of account here, though it obviously plays a considerable part in compensating, e.g., for local variations in unit excitability.)

"The conservation of such patterned activity I have inferred to depend largely upon preferential changes in postsynaptic membrane. Once an axon is fired, one can imagine that very similar events occur in all of its terminals. Across the synapse, not so. Whatever occurs at each of the terminals may impinge upon membrane of different sorts and in different states of excitability. What results from repeated firing of a given group of axons in a given spatio-temporal order is a set of changes in postsynaptic membrane not strictly predictable but only tending to conserve a corresponding order in the neurons next downstream. These changes may involve RNA as Hydén has suggested, or may occur at a higher level and be enzyme-induced, as Smith has recently proposed (*Science*, Nov. 23, 1962, 138: 889).

"A given assembly of cortical neurons (each receiving 8000 or so end-feet as mentioned by Ward, *loc. cit.*, and capable of influencing approximately 4000 other neurons, according to Sholl) can presumably realize a large but finite number of action-patterns. Memories are simply those patterns which, through repetition and consequent postsynaptic membrane changes, have become most probable for the assembly. At those levels of neocortex where the concentration of afferents is greatest and cell-sizes are smallest, I wonder if the combinative potential of the assembly isn't realized to such a degree that all "memories" are, practically speaking, equi-probable? Given adequate tonic maintenance and a minimum of patterned inputs, the output of the assembly would then not be biased in favor of certain patterns; that is, it would tend toward randomness. One can imagine that extrinsic sectors in particular are in this sense input-dependent. Ergo drastic reduction in sensory input should tend to randomize neocortical activity, and the resulting disorganization of cortico-subcortical outputs should result in some release of subcortical mechanisms. Hence perhaps, the automatisms shown by Sprague *et al.*'s bilaterally lemniscal cats; or the disorganization of conscious thought and the mounting agitation (RF release?) reported by some subjects as occurring in sensory deprivation. (*Sensory Deprivation*, Solomon *et al.*, eds., Harvard University Press, 1961.)

"Both the distribution of input fibers and the laminar concentrations of ATP and phosphocreatine found by Vladimirov *et al.* in various areas of rat neocortex, suggest that the highest turnover rates are to be found in the external lamina or I–IV; whereas V–VI (cf. Lorente de Nó, in Fulton's *Physiol. of the N.S.*) can be inferred to be chiefly in receipt of the resultants of that activity, and to show, on the average, lower turnover rates, as measured either by gross metabolic indices (Vladimirov *et al.*, *Regional Neurochemistry*, Pergamon, 1961, 126) or by the variance of unit activity. . . .

"Because of their relatively large dendritic fields, I have supposed that bands of larger cells—for instance the pyramids of IIIc and V which occur in most generalized eulaminate cortex in Bailey and Von Bonin's sections—serve as a collecting apparatus by which activity involving far larger numbers of smaller cells, is averaged out into sequences of simpler, less frequent action-patterns. IIIc and V may consequently mediate a two-stage sorting of inputs (e.g. to IV–lower III), in that part of what reaches V has already been sorted in III. . . .

"However, if the properties of neurons do not significantly change with their size, there is no reason to suppose that patterns realized in any large-celled collecting apparatus will persist indefinitely. Patterns say in V, might form somewhat more slowly than corresponding patterns in II–III (where in fact higher concentrations of ATP and phosphocreatine have been found); but the lag would theoretically have fixed maxima, and all assemblies might be expected in time to reach the state of equi-probability described above.

"The fact is, though, that certain memories do exhibit indefinite persistence, and don't seem to be obliterated by the high sensory input rates that go with a busy variegated life. Since Neolithic times, our life-expectancy in some quarters has perhaps more than doubled, yet most of us no matter how active, retain into remote old age memories formed in our early impressionable years.

"I wonder if the explanation may not be that larger cells, such as Bailey and Von Bonin's 39×24 μ pyramids, exhibit what might be called functional inertia, or a reluctance proportioned to their size, to respond to patterned inputs with corresponding changes in postsynaptic membrane. This amounts to postulating a decrease in metabolic efficiency with increasing cell size. The impressionability of the young and the tendency of something like imprinting to occur during critical growth periods in many species (Scott, *Science,* Nov. 30, 1962, 949–958) may, in this sense, be metabolic. Similarly, as we age, learning or altering our points of view becomes increasingly difficult, and new knowledge, more perishable. Of the 10 "photos" our minds can take per second, a small percentage "develops" (outlasts the half day normal half-life) and a still smaller percentage becomes permanent. With time, and with suitable allowances for episodic variation (e.g. due to intense motives or emotions), these percentages probably diminish slowly from early maturity on. Hence the events of our middle years fade more readily from mind than do those of childhood or youth. Hence too—as psychoanalysis has found—the inextinguishability of conditioned responses early formed, or the transience of most later counter-conditioning.

"In short the neocortex may be so organized that the combinative potential of its smaller-celled assemblies (e.g., in extrinsic sectors) is quite fully realized, whereas in larger-celled assemblies this process never goes to completion. The paradox is that the former process is in theory anti-entropic in that, as Herrick puts it, it represents "an increase of heterogeneity and complexity," but if fully realized might result in behavioral randomness and incoherence, or in stimulus-bound behavior. The latter process—the early binding of certain experience as maximally enduring and physiologically influential memories—represents a certain constraint on this anti-entropic trend, but also acts to conserve a continuity of organized central nervous activity during periods of reduced input or between behavioral occasions [i.e. what I have here called "intrinsic" activities of neocortex]. Moreover a function of large-celled bands may be to simplify, as well as conserving *qua* memory, effector outputs, thus guaranteeing that these are in fact practicable. [See Chapter VIII, part ii, below.] Hence the Betz cell layer in motor area 4. Some years ago Dusser de Barenne and Murphy reported that apparent retention of motor "memories" was not abolished by electrocoagulation of I–IV, but was by electrocoagulation which included V. (*J. Neurophysiol.*, 1941, 4, 147–152.)

"Applying these notions to the olfactory bulb, I would suspect that the tufted and mitral cell layers (the former in part commissurally) effect a roughly two-stage sorting of the input. That is, these layers may have memory-functions, the sorting of the input being a matter of congruences, if any, with pre-established action-patterns. The inner granular layer responds both to these processed inputs and to fibers, e.g. from the midbrain RF (as reported by Green, though not this specific terminal distribution), and projects outward so as to "partition" inputs in the light of information pre-recorded both in the bulb proper and elsewhere in the CNS.

"The two 'virtual generators' of slow potential activity which Von Baumgarten *et al.*, *op. cit.*, described in the bulb, then correspond to the regions in which traffic in general is most diverse—namely the granular layer, where centrifugal and centripetal influences converge (need neuroanatomic evidence on this point) and in the outermost regions of the bulb where inputs are in the pre-processed (pre-simplified) stage. This conclusion is exactly the opposite of that reached by Haines *et al.* (*Ann. N.Y. Acad. Sc.*, Vol. 58, Art. 2, March 24, 1954, 165) who inferred memory-functions for the granular layer.

"The central nervous processing of information is, I believe, simply an elaboration of the one just described. . . . The question is what warrant is there for the assumption that with an increase in size, neurons exhibit the (probably nonlinear) increase in 'functional inertia' necessary to this theory of memory."

Studies of cellular respiration might shed some light on the last question. The linear increase in conduction velocities in myelinated peripheral fibers with increases in fiber diameter (internal to sheathing), being accomplished at a considerable cost in structural outlay, tells little or nothing about how properties of postsynaptic membrane may change as the size of neurons is increased.

6. Pribram, *Behavioral Science,* Vol. 4, No. 4, October 1959, 274.

7. Fulton, *op. cit.,* note 1, 596.

8. Nauta, personal communication.

9. Scheibel and Scheibel, in *Reticular Formation of the Brain,* 52–53.

10. MacLean (*The Central Nervous System and Behavior,* 61–62) suggests that the septal Islands of Calleja may have secretory functions, stimulation in this region having been found to produce ovulation in rabbits. This supposition has, I believe, not yet been confirmed, and may not be necessary to explain the observed effect (which can also be obtained by stimulation of the amygdala). See later chapters here on the organization of the rhinencephalon.

11. Cf. Petsche *et al., EEG clin. Neurophysiol.,* 1962, 14, 202–211.

12. Cf. Marrazzi, Chapter I, note 4; also Lindsley, in *The Reticular Formation of the Brain,* 513 ff.

13. Vladimirov *et al., Regional Neurochemistry,* 126–134.

14. This slight rise in concentrations of phosphocreatine and ATP in VI vis-à-vis V may reflect "granular layer" functions of VI. As suggested by the distribution of nonspecific afferents (principally to I and VI; Lorente de Nó) and association fibers (to II, III, and VI; *ibid.*) and the origins of the latter (III and V; Von Bonin), the internal lamina as a whole may be concerned in the receipt of memory data, relayed both from overlying III and from III and V elsewhere. The effect of nonspecific inputs may be greater upon VI than, say, upon II, via the plexiform layer, since in the former case, axosomatic synapses may be involved, whereas in the latter, the mode of synapse is axodendritic. Owing to its inputs and fine-structure, VI may show an appreciably slighter tendency toward formation of enduring firing-orders than does V. These "granular layer" functions of VI may be of importance in conserving a degree of functional flexibility in the basal memory apparatus, permitting for instance the use of most or all of the n vertical columns comprising a given thing memory, in other combina-

tions with other columns, in this way permutatively increasing the total engram capacity of the cortex concerned. (See note 18, below.)

15. In *Beyond the Pleasure Principle* Freud says that the "system pcpt–Cs" (or roughly, the perceptive waking-conscious system) must "lie on the borderline between outside and inside; it must be turned outward toward the external world and must envelop the other psychical systems. . . . Becoming conscious and leaving a memory trace are processes incompatible with each other within one and the same system. Thus . . . the excitatory process becomes conscious in the system Cs., but leaves no permanent trace behind there: the excitation is transmitted to the systems lying next within and . . . it is in them that its traces are left. . . . We lay down the proposition that consciousness arises instead of a memory trace."

In the same passage, Freud tentatively locates "the 'seat' of consciousness in the cerebral cortex—the outermost enveloping layer of the central organ."

Neurophysiologically, it is impossible to describe the latter as "lying on the borderline between inside and outside," since neocortex is clearly a terminal receptor station for sensory inputs subject to peripheral and spinal "gating" by efferents from a number of neuraxial levels. Moreover, fractionation of neocortex, as here, suggests that those maximally labile upper-layer activities perhaps equivalent to the waking conscious "I" may be affected by sensory inputs not directly but via IIIc, which means in effect by resultants of those inputs with pre-established "memories" or most probable firing-orders in IIIc. Hence my statement that at maturity we may perceive external reality through a screen of pre-existing type memories.

16. Cf. Fulton, *op. cit.*, 277, figure showing temporal areas not receiving projections of the pulvinar in macaques. Yakovlev has made much of the fact that certain neocortical areas in man may be "a-thalamic," hence not stimulus-bound, hence the seat of "higher" functions (see *CNS and Behavior*, 1958, 405). In a letter dated January 5, 1960, Dr. Yakovlev informed the writer that "during the past several years a systematic study of secondary and retrograde degenerations in the thalamus following surgical lesions or after circumscribed infarcts of the cerebral cortex has led me to propose that in the case of man, the cerebral cortex has taken a different evolutionary path in the organization of thalamo-cortical connections than the cortex of the other primates. . . . The human material, of the type as above indicated, failed to show us any retrograde degenerative changes in the thalamus when lesions were confined to Flechsig's terminal zones which

cytoarchitecturally correspond to eulaminate homotypical cortical area. The negative evidence for the frontal eulaminate . . . areas (10, 9, 46, of Brodmann) is consistent and rather clear. Here the lobotomy material was sufficiently ample and readily available. We are currently in the process of gathering and studying specimens with vascular cortical lesions in parietal and temporal terminal zones."

This finding raises some difficulties. Both it and Dr. Yakovlev's conclusions from it are in contradiction to Papez' report on the nonspecific system in man, suggesting that the reticular nucleus reaches virtually all neocortical areas (*EEG clin. Neurophysiol.*, 1956, 8: 117–128); and to Purpura's concerning rostral cortical projections of anteroventral portions of the intralaminar group, and posterior cortical projections of dorsolateral portions (*International Rev. Neurobiol.*, 1959, 127; see also Jasper, original reference, and Jasper, *Handbook Physiol.*, Section 1, *Neurophysiol.* II, Amer. Physiol. Soc., 1960, 1307 ff.). If frontal intrinsic cortex has "higher" functions because "a-thalamic" the pronounced influence of nonspecific inputs here, noted by Jasper, can only be accounted for by transcortical conduction (e.g., via association fibers) and the bulk of present evidence is that these play a supportive but not an indispensable or primary role in intracortical communication. (On this point, see previous reference, Vol. III, 1695; see also Pribram, cited later here.)

17. I.e., while the heritability of stupidity is unquestionable, it is also probable, as suggested later, that great relative enlargement of a group of thing memories comprising a particular motivational-affective "constellation" may act to unbalance subcortical functions. Especially when this imbalance is in favor of emergency system overactivity, the resulting changes in nonspecific input may be such as to interfere with the elaboration of abstract memory systems or the growth of the rational conscious self. In this way stupidity, though not native, may be acquired.

18. A bit of evidence in favor of the fact that the internal lamina generally embodies memories with "effector" functions vis-à-vis either the spinal motor or motivational core systems (depending upon the type of cortex considered) is reported in a paper by Murphy and Dusser de Barenne (*J. Neurophysiol.*, 1941, 4, 147–152). These authors state that "while an animal whose 'motor' cortex has been destroyed only to the extent of the four outer layers exhibits at most a very slight and transitory motor impairment, that in which thermocoagulation . . . has included the layer of large and giant pyramidal cells evidences typical and long-lasting motor deficit, as may be seen in the protocols outlined above."

This raises the question of the afferent supply of the motor cortex of those animals in which layers I–IV have been destroyed, and here again we seem to fall back upon the nonspecific system, and the mode of distribution of its fibers as reported by Lorente de Nó.

Finally, the structure of layer VI is of interest, in particular as it bears on the question of how "abstract" memory-systems come into being. Lorente de Nó (*op. cit.*) describes three principal cell types in this layer; long spindles with collateral dendrites in VI and apical, in I; medium spindles with dendritic shafts ending in IV; and short spindles with shafts ending in V. He reports that VI is a source of association fibers distributing to II, III, and VI elsewhere, while callosal fibers arise chiefly in the short pyramids of Vc and VIa. As noted earlier, he describes I and VI as the chief recipients of nonspecific fibers, in the former terminating axodendritically and in the latter, in part perhaps, axosomatically.

By analogy with II vis-à-vis the plexiform layer, the most direct local influence upon VI may be exerted by V, via apical dendrites of the short spindles. What VI relays elsewhere may be a resultant of this predominant influence and lesser influences arising principally in IV and the plexiform layer. On relay these are not distributed directly to V but pass, e.g., via II and III. If one assumes close communication between layers for instance in the receptor columns here, the arrangement just described might serve as a means by which basal memories represented at site A were compared with those at B, C, etc., "congruences" if any surviving, e.g. at the level of III.

CHAPTER V

1. Bailey and Von Bonin pointed out that the existence of these circuits remains to be demonstrated in man though they have been shown to exist in other mammals (e.g., projections from area 19 chiefly to the pulvinar, have been reported in the monkey [Fulton, *op. cit.*, 278]). In rabbits and monkeys, projections from auditory cortex to the medial geniculate have been reported by several authors. In macaques, fibers have been traced from area 4 to anterior parts of the lateral and ventral nuclei. Hirasawa and Kato demonstrated fibers from the frontal eyefields, and Murphy and Gellhorn from orbital cortex, to *dorsomedialis*. It is interesting that whereas the pulvinar appears to project to areas 18 and 22 (Fulton, *op. cit.*, 275) striato-geniculate fibers may arise largely in 19. In a recent conversation, Dr. L. Hausman stated the belief that there is sufficient indirect evidence today to justify the assumption that similar cortico-thalamic pathways exist in man. (See also note 10.)

2. Sperry, *Science,* June 2, 1961, 133: 1749–1757. From this review it is evident that hemispheric transfer of visual information (intensity-values and crude patterns perhaps excepted) does not occur via the midbrain.

3. Sperry, *Handbook of Experimental Psychology,* 267, reports: "The central nervous tracts tend to become myelinated in a definite sequence that shows considerable constancy in all mammals and follows roughly the order in which the tracts were developed phylogenetically." Sperry adds that "function may further myelination as well as conversely."

4. Bailey and Von Bonin, *op. cit.* The evidence for an orbital-tempero-polar connection via the uncinate fasciculus seems to these authors sufficient, as is that for the arcuate fasciculus, which has a similar distribution but also apparently reaches tempero-parietal cortex. The evidence for a fronto-occipital bundle is chiefly derived from the study of malformed human brains, but is supported by a study of Chusid, Sugar, and French. The distribution of the cingulum to the subiculum and cornu ammonis is questioned by these authors, who favor Elze's view that the precuneus receives most of its fibers. In the case of the inferior longitudinal fasciculus, it is not clear whether, in the *strata sagittalia* in the lateral wall of the posterior horn of the lateral ventricle, optic radiation and association fibers are both present. "Physiological neuronography proves, in any event, that there are association fibers in the inferior longitudinal fasciculus and shows that some of these fibers are . . . long, although never as long as the whole bundle." These authors believe it probable this bundle may "subserve some of the higher visual functions." It may form part of the multiple convergence mechanism described herein later, by which thing memories necessary to visual discriminations come into being—the capacity for such discriminations being greatly diminished by bilateral inferotemporal resection in monkeys (see Pribram, cited below).

In addition, Bailey and Von Bonin describe several dorsoventral bundles in occipital and parietal cortex whose existence has been confirmed anatomically and by strychnine neuronography (*op. cit.,* 234–238).

Concerning the cingulum, see the latter part of note 54, Chapter VIII.

5. Pribram, in *Biological and Biochemical Bases of Behavior,* 166–167.

6. Teuber, *Handbook Physiol., Neurophysiol.,* III, 1653. In humans with "large subtotal" occipital lesions, vision is initially lost and then

recovered in stages reminiscent of those observed in patients who, blind from birth, have had sight "restored" surgically (cf. Young, *Doubt and Certainty in Science,* Oxford, 1950, 61–63). The suggestion in both cases is that visual perception sharpens as type memories take shape. In the lesioned patients this is presumably a reorganization occurring in the remnant of striate cortex; in the blind from birth, the whole visual type-memory system has to be elaborated, including those periextrinsic formations I have supposed equivalent to perceptual generalizations. Such patients are in fact slow to generalize in this way, requiring many exposures to triangular shapes to recognize this common feature of them. Learning to see in this full sense reportedly requires about two years—or about the time Nielsen has reported as necessary to effect "transfer," by retraining, from the damaged dominant to the nondominant hemisphere in the case of speech deficits. (*Trans. Amer. Neurol. Assoc.,* 80, 1955, 143–148.)

The important point here is that in the occipitally lesioned patients, little or no intrathalamic distribution of visual information, e.g., from LG to the pulvinar prior to extrinsic sector relay, can be inferred to have occurred.

7. Jasper, *op. cit.*, note 6, Vol. II, 1315.

8. The question of the latency of reticular responses vis-à-vis those of the specific system appears still to be somewhat in doubt. The supposition that nonspecific inputs resulting from collateral sensory inputs to the midbrain may lag some msec behind receipt of the same data in neocortex has direct and indirect (e.g., cytoarchitectural) evidence in favor of it (see Morillo paper cited below). There may nonetheless exist a fast, possibly extrathalamic, fiber system originating in the RF, related to fast retisculospinal fiber systems and higher (mammalian) homologues of the basal optic system described in *Amblystoma* by Herrick. These are discussed later in the text. See, for instance, Chapter VI, note 54.

9. Morillo, *EEG clin. Neurophysiol.,* Feb. 1961, 13: 9–20. These results were obtained from nembutalized or *cerveau isolé* cats, and so perhaps should be taken with caution. Purpura has reported that a thalamocortical response of 2 msec latency was increased to 15 msec under moderate i.v. pentothal (cf. also Arduini, in *Reticular Formation of the Brain,* 343).

10. The term "partitioning" is, I believe, Pribram's. In 1903 Ramón y Cajal suggested that corticothalamic paths might serve selectively to partition inputs at the diencephalic level (cf. Lindsley, *Handbook Physiol., Neurophysiol.,* III, 1561, 1592).

11. These functions are shown by split-brain studies (reference 2, above) and by the fact that an irritative focus in one hemisphere reportedly may cause a mirror focus in the contralateral hemisphere (Pribram, *Regional Physiology of the CNS, The Search for the Engram,* 5). In the macaque and chimpanzee, the anterior commissure appears to connect the second temporal gyri (Bailey and Von Bonin, Chapter IV, ref. 2). These authors also report a study which showed that lesions in one hemisphere produced (evidently transcallosal) retrograde degeneration in layers III, V, and VI contralaterally (*op. cit.,* 240). This finding—like the data from split-brain studies—suggests that it is primarily the *memory* apparatus which projects interhemispherically. That is, it is not the moment-to-moment labile activity of a given hemisphere which tends to be duplicated in the opposite one, but rather the more invariant patterns sorted from and surviving that activity, as described here. The lack of commissural connections between the first and third temporal convolutions (Bailey and Von Bonin, *ibid.*), may, by failing to establish directly parallel processes of memory-formation, favor hemispheric dominance in language representation.

12. It seems probable that the type of signal or patterned action representing information in the tactile modality differs considerably from that representing auditory or visual data, with the result that there tends to be segregated columnar representation of each of these, e.g., in temporal intrinsic cortex (cf. Chapter III, note 6). However, it is worth noting that the Scheibels (Chapter III, note 5) describe their nonspecific columns as overlapping, an arrangement which might favor conjoint activation of memories representative of data in more than one modality.

13. Lindsley, in *Reticular Formation of the Brain,* 520 ff.

14. Papez, *op. cit.,* Chapter IV, note 16. Papez favors the reticular nucleus as the probable major path of entry of nonspecific inputs. Other authors assign a major role to CM or VA (cf. Jasper, *op. cit.,* or Lindsley, *op. cit.,* 1566).

15. Livingston, *op. cit.,* note 13, 182.

16. It is possible that certain of the activities equivalent to thought—i.e., reflection or problem-solving without direct reference to immediate sense-data—involve a "sweeping" or scanning process in which focal activity proceeds from periextrinsic to intrinsic sectors, this process being the equivalent of proceeding from a generalized notion of a given problem (as represented in elaborated type memories) to the particulars and particular principles concerned in its solution

(these represented as thing and abstract memories). In other words, the sequence of neocortical events in thought may be the same essentially as those in perception. For this reason damage to cortical areas which form important links, e.g., in the cortico-thalamo-cortical chain involved, may produce deficiencies of performance not attributable to memory-loss but to disruption of the sequence in which orderly mobilization of memory-data occurs. Examples are the agraphia and acalculia which accompany damage to the angular gyrus in the region of the second occipital convolution in the dominant hemisphere (Gerstmann's syndrome; cf. *Neurol.*, Dec. 1957, 7: 866–869). It is reported that "psychic blindness" accompanies parastriate damage. In the latter case, as confirmed by electrical stimulation studies, "the patient may be able to see perfectly, but he has no understanding of what he sees" (Herrick, *The Evolution of Human Nature*, 425). Acalculia in Gerstmann's syndrome has been related to the early use of the fingers in arithmetic. Defects in thinking which involves visual imagery may not accompany parastriate damage because such thinking might involve other periextrinsic-intrinsic sector routes (e.g., the auditory) terminally activating visual components of the thing memories concerned. Alternatively it is possible that *actions*, or cortico-thalamo-cortical activation of precruciate and other effector cortex (and also of subcortical motor mechanisms), may be mediated from cortical regions adjoining or including the cortical "strip" areas—in accordance with the idea developed here later that receptor-effector system outputs necessarily require a degree of presimplification, if they are to result in practicable "instructions" to the motor apparatus. Such simplification might be accomplished by having receptor system "instructions" pass through the elaborated type memory apparatus at exit.

17. E.g., Nauta reports that "the medial lemniscus represents an almost entirely direct projection from the nuclei of the dorsal funiculus to the ventral thalamic nucleus with only a minor offset to the paramedian region of the pontine protuberance" (*op. cit.*, 25). With due allowance for restriction by feedback of sensory inputs at lower levels, this arrangement would seem to guarantee a degree of input to the thalamus not entraining extensive parallel changes in the core.

18. Williams, *Brain*, March 1956, 79: 29–67. In contrast, cf. Gibbs, *Biol. Ment. Health & Disease*, 454; also Wyke, *Ann. Royal Coll. Surgeons*, Eng., Feb. 1958, 22: 117–138.

19. Walter, *The Living Brain*, 108 ff.

20. Whitehead (*Essays in Science and Philosophy*, 200) defines mathematics as "the science concerned with the logical deduction of

consequences from the general premises of all reasoning," pointing out that "the traditional field of mathematics in the province of discrete and continuous number can only be separated from the general abstract theory of classes and relations by a wavering and indeterminate line." (However, see Henkin, *Science,* Nov. 16, 1962, 138: 788–794.)

The terms "pure fact" and "pure reason," used here, are meant only comparatively, since extrarational bias can be, and probably often is, a factor in determining the facts selected by scientists for study, and the particular line of reasoning followed in interpreting them. As I hope to show in a later book, such biases are often, if not usually, common to the trend of thought of an age. In the case of our own, the trend toward a logical positivistic interpretation of phenomena is of a piece, I believe, with many superficially dissimilar trends in our arts, politics, and social customs, all of them less "realistic" and more indicative of a basic regressive psychological change than we presently appear to realize.

Finally, it is not necessary to add that abstract thinking is not more effective simply *because* abstract. Even when least interfered with by core-processes representative of "drives" or basal wishes, the imitations-of-reality achieved in neocortex may either be in error outright or else logically faultless but without equivalents in external fact. That they also on occasion anticipate the workings of external reality with marvelous acuity should be no cause for surprise; millions of years of evolutionary improvement have led up to that result, and even today it is distinctly the exception among us. Our most successful scientific hypotheses are no more than approximations, doomed without exception to be superseded. Most of us have real competence or insight in only a few directions; and for the most part we are objective and sustainedly curious only to the extent that our creature needs in some way require us to be so. In proportion as our interest is restricted in this way, we are apt to have a few opinions which are really tenable and a great many which are arbitrary and demonstrably absurd. This is to say that, while abstract memories cumulatively confer a certain logic upon thought and at maturity may be increased and altered in form through conscious effort, the logic they embody is frequently tainted and at its best does not present us with conclusions which are necessarily verifiable propositions as to the nature of reality external to mind itself.

21. Witness the visual images which can be evoked by stimulating in this cortex (Von Bonin, *Essay on the Cerebral Cortex,* Thomas, 1950, 76).

22. This in contrast to the conceptual *Gestalten* represented by intrinsic sector abstract memories. Concerning figure-ground, see Koffka, *Classics in Psychology*, 1128 ff.

23. Chaplin and Krawiec, *Systems and Theories of Psychology*, 132–133.

24. Cf. Grundfest, in *Reticular Formation of the Brain*, 482–483. A similar point was raised at the Symposium on Dendrites in Santa Fé (see Supplement 10, *EEG clin. Neurophysiol.*, November, 1958).

25. Cf. Goldstine, *Science*, July 8, 1960, 133: 91. See also Cowan, *Information Theory in Biology* (unpub. paper presented at the Conference on Biomathematics, Cullowhee, North Carolina, August 16, 1961). Cowan's paper discusses the problem of constructing reliable machines from unreliable components, the model employed being a net of formal neurons. Apropos of the latter, he concludes: "Points to note are (a) multiple diversity of the network . . . each component computes a mixture of many of the precursive functions, and any one precursive function is computed by many components. For large enough n, such components may in fact compute an arbitrary mixture of precursive functions; (b) the heterogeneity of the network . . . this follows immediately from the previous remark; (c) the efficiency of the network . . . much smaller component redundancies are needed, than in comparable networks of Von Neumann." Unless I have misunderstood him, Cowan's work shows that the *modus operandi* of the neocortex suggested here is not logically untenable.

26. Patton, in J. Fulton, ed., *Textbook of Physiology*, 384.

27. In the rhesus monkey, the divergence is as follows; approximately 88,000 cells in the cochlear nuclei, 392,000 in the inferior colliculi, 433,000 in the medial geniculate body and on the order of 10^7 in auditory cortex (Glees, *Experimental Neurology*, 432).

28. *Op. cit.*, note 27, 462.

29. Smith, *Science*, Nov. 23, 1962, 138: 889.

30. *Op. cit.*, note 27, 448. The phrase "private line" (of cones to optic nerve) was used by Ruch, *op. cit.*, note 26, 455.

31. Cf. Nakahama, *Internat. Rev. Neurobiol.* III, 187 ff.

32. These authors (D. H. Hubel and T. N. Wiesel, *J. Physiol.*, 1962, 160: 106–154) demonstrate that the "simple" receptive fields of striate neurons take a greater variety of forms, in respect of the arrangement of their component "on" and "off" regions in the retina, than do those of lateral geniculate units. (*Op. cit.*, 111, Text-fig. 2.) They propose a model showing how convergence of lateral geniculate fibers upon a single striate neuron may give rise to the "simple" re-

ceptive field of the latter—e.g., by a topographic mode of projection such that n lateral geniculate receptive fields of simple circular type, lying along a straight line in the retina, comprise the elongated "simple" field of the striate unit. (*Op. cit.*, 142.)

Approximately 23 per cent of a total of 303 striate neurons tested showed what they describe as "complex" receptive fields. "Unlike cells with simple fields, these responded to variously shaped stationary or moving forms in a way that could not be predicted from maps made with small circular spots. . . . When separate 'on' and 'off' regions could be discerned, the principles of summation and mutual antagonism, so helpful in interpreting simple fields, did not generally hold." They remark that "it does . . . seem probable that simple receptive fields represent an early stage in cortical integration and the complex ones a later stage. Regardless of the details of the process, it is also likely that a complex field is built up from simpler ones with common axis orientations. . . . We may tentatively look upon each [vertical] column as a functional unit of cortex, within which simple fields are elaborated and then in turn synthesized into complex fields. The large variety of simple and complex fields to be found in a single column . . . suggests that the connections between cells in a column are highly specific. . . . The presence of an occasional cell with a very large complex field . . . makes one wonder whether columns with similar receptive-field orientations may not possess some interconnections." (I have postulated intercolumnar communication as playing a major role in the elaboration of extrinsic sector data elsewhere. If it also figures in "complex" field elaboration in striate cortex, the fact should be reflected in unit response-latencies.)

In their text-figure 20 (*op. cit.*, 143) Hubel and Wiesel show a second schematic model according to which fibers of several striate neurons having "simple" fields converge upon a single cortical neuron, thus giving rise to the latter's "complex" receptive field. The model involves a restriction in that, generalizing from their experimental data, they postulate that "a complex field is built up from simpler ones with common axis orientations." (This point raises an important question, into which I have gone below.)

"Cells with simple fields tend to respond only when the stimulus is both oriented and positioned properly. In contrast, the neurons to which they supposedly project are concerned predominantly with stimulus orientation and are far less critical as regards stimulus placement. Their responsiveness to the abstraction which we call orientation is thus generalized over a considerable retinal area. . . . It is clear that a given form in the visual field will, by virtue of its borders, excite a combination of cells with complex fields. If we displace the form it will activate many of the same cells, as long as the change is not enough to remove it completely from their receptive fields. Now we may imagine that these particular cells project to a single cell of a still higher order: such a cell will then be very likely to respond to the form (provided the synapses are excitatory) and there will be considerable latitude in the position of the retinal image. Such a mechanism will also permit other transformations of the image, such as a change in size associated with displacement of the form toward, or away from, the eye."

The mechanisms just discussed imply that, to perceive angles readily, for instance, the organism must have variously oriented retinal simple fields, with no particular axis-orientations predominating. This appears to be the case in cats and adult humans, but not in children under four or in the octopus. (See N. S. Sutherland, *Science*, Jan. 18, 1963, 139: 209–210.) Cells having second-order complex fields, conserving information as to form without regard to retinal position, may be found in periextrinsic areas (e.g., 18–19) and may embody what I have called elaborated type memories.

The important question mentioned above concerns the degree to which retinal-field representation in the lateral geniculate and striate cortex is dependent upon projection systems laid down at birth and susceptible of little or no later modification. The relatively standardized form of geniculate retinal fields, and the miscellaneous (often overlapping) forms taken by striate "simple" fields (see Hubel and Wiesel, *op. cit.*, 111, text-fig. 2, and 137, text-fig. 16), suggest that the former are the result of an inherited, functionally rigid projection scheme. The latter, by contrast, may result from a system of projections so arranged that despite their orderly, genetically determined mode of distribution, a considerable latitude exists as to the size and position of the retinal fields which particular simple-field neurons in a particular striate vertical column may come to represent at maturity of the organism. Further analysis of this point suggests how it may be possible for brains to fractionate their own inputs in a way which permits to the central processing of information many more degrees of freedom than can be inferred for the peripheral receptors or for relay systems, e.g., of the diencephalon.

In the course of one stepwise cortical penetration, Hubel and Wiesel (*op. cit.*, 136, text-fig. 15) found three neurons at the top of the cortex and one at the bottom, having "complex" fields, the eight neurons tested at intermediate levels (layers IV and lower III) all having "simple" fields. Except for that of the bottommost unit (apparently in V), all fields represented in the column had a common axis of orientation in the retina, but otherwise showed differences in shape and position which were not discernibly systematic. The authors describe this as "a consistent and somewhat surprising finding," adding that "within a column defined by a common field-axis orientation, there was no apparent progression in field positions along the retina as the electrode advanced. . . . If there was any detailed topographical representation within columns, it was obscured by the superimposed, apparently random staggering of field positions."

In Chapter IV above, learning or the formation of preferential action-patterns was postulated chiefly to involve changes in postsynaptic membrane which caused the cell to become selectively responsive to a certain fraction of its (total possible) inputs. The question not raised until now is whether such cellular biases may not be both positive (in favor of the preferred inputs) and negative (exclusive of others); that is, whether the RNA mechanism proposed by Hydén may not mediate two sorts of membrane change: 1) changes at n sites, favoring depolarization via these; and 2) changes in the remainder of postsynaptic membrane, increasing its resistance to depolarization, thus in effect raising the threshold of the cell to activation by nonpreferred inputs. (Such a mechanism can be conceived as protective, in that it would tend to prevent the overdriving of units which might result from acquisition of positive biases only.)

Perhaps particularly in the case of larger cortical cells (because of the factor of "functional inertia"—see Chapter IV, note 5), this biasing mechanism may serve to set limits, far below the theoretical maximum, to the combinative potential of a given cell or assembly, thereby giving rise to the phenomenon of memory—which is to say, the persistence of certain acquired action patterns, to the partial or total exclusion of others of which the cell or assembly is in theory capable.

Much of neocortex may be, in this sense, a nonbiased system at the outset of life and may become an increasingly biased one as the organism is exposed to experience. Before extensive biasing, units or aggregates may be significantly more drivable or subject to diffuse activation (and the systems they comprise more liable to functional confusion; in this connection, see the findings of Thompson and Melzack, Chapter II, note 19, and of Melzack, Chapter VIII, note 41). Depending upon factors such as cell size and location, biasing once established may be subject to change as result of input conditions. E.g., a certain minimal frequency of repetition of the preferred input may be necessary not only to establish but to maintain the cellular bias guaranteeing maximal preferred and minimal nonpreferred responses. When, as in deafferentation, this condition is no longer met, partial return of the cell or aggregate to the prebiased condition may result—a mechanism conceivably figuring in denervation sensitization and in the failure of organized neocortical activity evidently occurring in cats following bilateral lemniscal section (Chapter VI, note 34). In Section II, below, it is suggested that high levels of nonspecific input may be de-differentiative of neocortical action-patterns, acting in particular to obliterate those biases which, because of their recency and inadequate reinforcement, may be regarded as "temporary connections" similar to those formed in the midbrain RF itself* (Scheibel and Scheibel)—it being in this way that the neocortex is kept, in part, an "open" system, subject to new bias-formation in the declining phase of reticular activation. Stated another way, it is as result of intermittent core intervention that manifold routes for the neocortical "irradiation" of sensory data new to the organism are kept in being and that the capacity for new learning (biasing conserving certain of these novel inputs) is maintained.

In this and the preceding chapter, it was proposed that the distribution of incoming sensory information—particularly that new to the organism—is divergent and involves a determinacy gradient such that at each stage in the relay—e.g., from extrinsic to periextrinsic to posterior intrinsic sectors—the form and loci of events become less predictable. In the case of striate cortex, the gradient can be extended to include the lateral geniculate and retina such that, for a given visual input, the order of predictability of events is: retina>lateral geniculate>striate cortex.

This decrease in determinacy may be accomplished through stepwise increases in the redundancy of distribution of the input, as follows. Assume, for the moment, that all simple-field cells in a given striate vertical column receive geniculate fibers corresponding to the same (or to nearly congruent) blocs of linearly aligned retinal fields (Hubel and Wiesel, *op. cit.*, text-figs. 2 and 19). However, each of these cells is somewhat differently situated than the others (see their text-fig. 15), so that on any given occasion, or over the succession of occasions comprising the life history of the organism, its excitability level and concurrent inputs from other sources are also likely to differ from those

---

* And also similar to what we call thoughts or ideas.

of the other simple-field cells in the same column. The result is that with the passage of time each tends to become biased somewhat differently, the only remaining feature common to the retinal fields of all being the one guaranteed by the systematic, if also redundant,* distribution of geniculate fibers to striate vertical columns. That distribution is evidently such that only fibers corresponding to (roughly circular) geniculate receptive fields lying in the same or parallel straight lines reach the same vertical column—an "orientation-pure" arrangement possibly analogous to the "submodality-pure" type of representation found by Mountcastle in columns of cat somatosensory cortex. In consequence, though the simple fields of neurons in a striate column may come to differ greatly in shape and position, as result of differential biasing, they necessarily retain a common axis of orientation.

This essentially probabilistic biasing mechanism might explain why Hubel and Wiesel consistently found a common axis of simple-field orientation within a given column, but also a "random staggering of field positions" rather than the orderly layer-by-layer representation of adjacent or overlapping simple fields they appear to have expected. It also suggests why the diverging, redundant distribution of incoming sense data in the CNS is not apt to lead to a mere blurring or loss of informational content, but to just the opposite result—namely, the breaking up of relatively stereotyped message units into larger numbers of more heterogeneous units, many of which hold certain informational elements in common. The result of this process is greatly to increase the number of ways in which, depending upon the context of inner and outer circumstances, an organism can fractionate its exteroceptive inputs and put them to behavioral use.† The first stages of this process, in neocortex, are those described by Hubel and Wiesel, in the case of simple and first- and second-order complex fields; its final stages are perhaps those described in the text, in the case of posterior intrinsic sector "thing" and "abstract" memories. The experimental prediction which follows is that, early in the life of the organism, there must be a stage at which the simple fields represented in a given striate column show less differentiation than was found by

---

* I.e., systematic by columns, redundant within columns. Apropos of redundancy of another sort, it is interesting that their work confirms earlier reports by Talbot and Marshall, and Talbot, as to the existence of a laterally placed Visual Area II, in the cat (*op. cit.*, 134).

† On the effector side, compare the way in which, during maturation, certain basic "total patterns" (Herrick) become differentiated so as to form a repertoire of more precisely adapted actions.

References and Notes / 231

Hubel and Wiesel. For instance, in immature cats, or in mature ones which had from birth been subjected to radical sensory restriction and chronic (e.g., anesthetic) immobilization, the simple retinal fields of cells in a given column should be more uniform and perhaps more nearly congruent.

On neuroanatomic grounds, I have inferred that the convergence of influences and average transaction rates must be maximal in layers I–II of neocortex, and also high in V (because of the distribution of descending fibers to this layer, reported by Lorente de Nó). By implication, concentrations of striate cells having complex fields should be maximal at these levels. As can be seen from the accompanying diagram, adapted from Hubel and Wiesel's data, that seems to be the case. Similarly, because of the concentration of specific afferents usually found in IV and lower III in extrinsic sectors, one would predict a high proportion in III, and a still higher one in IV, of cells having simple fields. The data cited also bear out this prediction. While the small percentage of simple-field cells found in II may be due to a few higher-level terminations of geniculo-striate fibers, the substantial percentages of these cells found in the internal lamina are more difficult to account for. Although there are known differences between the cat and primate visual systems (e.g., at the level of the lateral geniculate; cf. Glees, *Experimental Neurology*, 455) these authors believe, on the basis of preliminary work with the spider monkey, that such differences may not be major ones. The question of the meaning of the distribution of simple-field cells in considerable numbers, in layers V and VI of cat striate, must therefore, pro tem, be left open.

It will be recalled that in the text, type memories were defined as continually changing residues of perceptual experience, involving extrinsic and periextrinsic sectors (here 17, and 18–19). The question is whether in the mature organism such changes occur at the unit level, as result of the rebiasing of individual neurons; or whether they are essentially recombinative, resulting from continual reshuffling of the simple-field components constituting complex fields, or of components of the latter type, entering into the formation of second-order complex fields. In turn, this comes down to a question of whether, in the mature organism, both new additions to memory and forgetting are truly that, or simply result from the use of fixed, early established ultimate components (e.g., striate simple fields) in new combinations, as dictated by the flux of inner and outer events. In other words, if neurons are biasable, as defined above, to what extent may such biases a) preclude nonpreferred modes of response of the unit and b) resist alteration, e.g., upon repeated exposure to one or more nonpreferred inputs.

One of Hubel and Wiesel's findings is relevant in this connection. Recording from single striate units for periods of one to two hours, or in some cases for as long as nine hours, they detected no changes in the shape or position of either simple or complex retinal fields. While this result may be attributable to the state of extreme immobilization in which these animals were kept during the experiment, one cannot dismiss the possibility that it is not an artefact. More experimental evidence on this point might go far toward solving the problem of how memory- and data-processing functions are organized in the neocortex.

Suppose, for example, that the experiment proposed above, disclosed that in fact immature animals showed more nearly uniform simple fields in given striate columns, and that with maturation these fields differentiated so as to exhibit the "apparently random staggering of field positions" found by these authors in adult cats. If then subsequent recordings—e.g., made intermittently over periods of days or weeks, between which the animals were permitted a nearly normal existence —revealed little or no further changes in the retinal fields of these cells, we might be safe in concluding first that neurons are biasable, as suggested here, and second that such biases, once established, may not significantly change and may effectively exclude nonpreferred inputs.

Assuming that this finding holds for all parts of neocortex—since we have no present reason for supposing that the properties of cortical neurons differ significantly from area to area—we might then be forced to conclude that during maturation all parts of neocortex, even if at different rates, become highly inflexible in respect to the spatiotemporal configuration of inputs necessary to "fire" a given unit or assembly. Quite possibly incorrectly, I believe that a brain constructed in this way—of neurons whose biases, once acquired, are uniformly inalterable and absolutely exclusive of nonpreferred inputs—would lack many of the properties of real brains.* It would neither forget

---

* E.g., the account of the orienting reflex given here presupposes that considerable numbers of neocortical neurons remain rebiasable, with the result that inputs in some respect "new" tend not to be precluded but in fact to be more widely distributed than familiar ones. The result is then a net gain in facilitatory and inhibitory outputs of neocortex to the midbrain RF, and a tendency on the part of the latter system—the more prone to massive action of the two—to show "escape"; i.e., to override higher-level restraint and bring on general activation. If neurons in neocortex do

to the extent that real brains seem to do, nor show their (admittedly reduced) capacity to continue learning into late maturity or old age—in man, up to ages about twice his probable life expectancy at the time in prehistory when human brains reached their present level of evolutionary development.

My own hunch—and it is no more than that—is that neurons are biasable but that, depending upon the size and locus of the unit, these biases may be more or less alterable and may render the unit more or less responsive to nonpreferred inputs. For example, in extrinsic cortex, a unit of layer II and one of IV may be comparable in size and in the gross amount of axonal activity each shows over the same time interval. What will perhaps differ is the variance of activity of each, reflecting the relative diversity of inputs to each. If the layer-IV cell is of the simple-field and that of II of the complex-field type (see diagram), the probability is that biasing of the former may become the more inalterable and the more exclusive of even transient responses to nonpreferred inputs.* This view predicts that careful, protracted studies of unit activity in a given striate vertical column will disclose differences in the alterability of the observed retinal fields, these differences correlating with the size and position of the units tested, as suggested by the account of neocortical memory- and data-processing functions given here. Except that it raises the question of memory, and so ultimately of the flexibility of the processes concerned, that account seems consistent with the present findings of Hubel and Wiesel, and also with earlier theoretical work of Pitts and McCulloch ("How We Know Universals," *Bull. Math. Biophysics*, 1947, 9: 127–147), the latter involving the principle, as stated elsewhere by McCulloch, that "any object, or universal, is invariant under some groups of transformations and consequently the net need only compute a sufficient number of averages" (McCulloch, *General Semantics Bulletin*, Nos. 26, 27, 1960, 12–13). What McCulloch gives is the form of the computation. What I have tried to suggest is the arrangement of neocortical components by which it is accomplished.

---

not remain rebiasable, some other mechanism must underlie the OR in mature organisms.

* Note that, according to Lorente de Nó, IV receives few collaterals of descending fibers, and mainly specific afferents, among input fibers. The restriction on forms of input to striate vertical columns is discussed above. And finally, visual experience itself involves much repetition. All these are factors conducive to the formation of minimally alterable, maximally exclusive biases in layer IV striate simple-field cells. Type memories may thus not exhibit much change at this level in mature animals.

234 / THE PHYSICAL FOUNDATIONS OF THE PSYCHE

Solid bars = units having "simple" receptive fields.
Dashed bars = units having "complex" receptive fields.

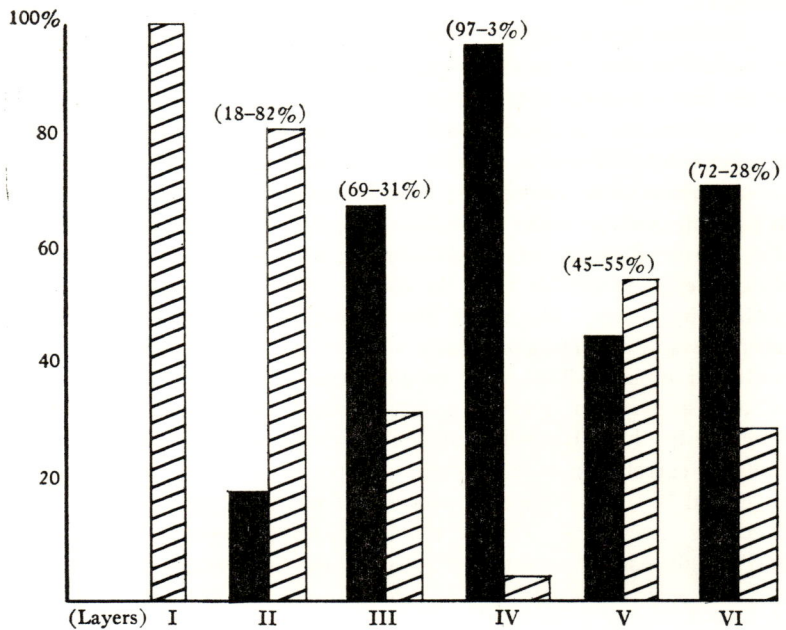

Laminar distribution of neurons in cat striate having "simple" and "complex" receptive fields; expressed as the approximate percentage of each found among the total of units tested in each layer. Adapted from Hubel and Wiesel, *J. Physiol.* (1962), 160: 106–154. See their text-figure 18, *op. cit.*, 139.

CHAPTER VI

1. Livingston's remark on the brain possibly localizing its own functions is cited here earlier (Chapter V, note 15). In *Diencephalon*, 48, Hess refers to the "burning problem" of defining a center. Lashley's well-known theory of the "equipotentiality" of all parts of neocortex in respect to the elaboration of behavior was based upon studies of the rat. Because neocortex in that animal is largely sensori-motor, "most of the nervous elements of the associational systems [are]

mingled with those of the projection systems" (Herrick, *Evol. of Human Nature*, 425). Lashley's views consequently go too far in the other direction. As evidence relating to the various aphasias and agnosias shows, they are clearly inapplicable in the case of human brain.

2. Jasper, in *Reticular Formation of the Brain*, 506.
3. *EEG clin. Neurophysiol.*, 1, 455.
4. Kety, *Science*, Dec. 22, 1960, 132: 1865.
5. Pribram, personal communication; see also Pribram, Miller, and Galanter, *Plans and the Structure of Behavior*, 177 ff.
6. Chapter IV, note 9. See also *Ann. N. Y. Acad. Sc.*, Vol. 89, Art. 5, Jan. 28, 1961, 857–865.
7. *Op. cit.*, note 2 above, 69–109.
8. *Ibid.*, 491 ff.
9. *Ibid.*, 507.
10. *Trans.* 2nd Conf. CNS, 37.
11. *Op. cit.*, note 2 above, 263 ff.
12. Kuypers *et al.*, *Science*, July 1, 1960, 132: 38–40.
13. *Op. cit.*, note 2 above, 16–17.
14. *EEG clin. Neurophysiol.*, 1956, 8: 117–128. See also Scheibel and Scheibel, *op. cit.*, note 2, 51, 62.
15. *Internat'l Rev. Neurobiol.*, Vol. 1, 127.
16. Cf. Lindsley *et al.*, *EEG clin. Neurophysiol.*, 2, 483–498.
17. *Op. cit.*, note 2 above, 594.
18. *Science*, Nov. 25, 1960, 132: 1551.
19. *Trans.* 2nd Conf. CNS, 67.
20. Impairment is of feeding behavior (*Science*, March 24, 1961, 133: 887–888). Medial "satiety" and far-lateral "feeding" centers have since proved "punishing" and "rewarding" upon stimulation. Cf. *Science*, Sept. 11, 1961, 135: 374–375 and 375–376. See also *ibid.*, Nov. 16, 1962, 138: 822–823.
21. *Op. cit.*, note 2 above, p. 669.
22. *Internat'l Rev. Neurobiol.*, Vol. 1, 30.
23. Fulton, *Physiol. of the Nervous System*, 308.
24. *Organization of the Cerebral Cortex*, 11–80.
25. Cf. *Ann. Rev. of Psych.*, 1960, 8–9.
26. *Op. cit.*, note 2 above, 413 ff.
27. *Trans.* 2nd Conf. CNS, 207 ff.
28. *Op. cit.*, note 2 above, 565.

29. *Arch. ital. biol.*, 1959, 97: 357.
30. *Science*, August 1960, 132: 547–548.
31. Personal communication.
32. Cf. Chapter II, note 4.
33. *Ibid.*
34. *Science*, Jan. 20, 1961, 133: 165–173.
35. *Op. cit.*, note 2 above, 321–322.
36. *Internat'l Rev. Neurobiol.*, Vol. 1, 142.
37. Jouvet, *Symposium on the Nature of Sleep*, 88; see also Jouvet et al., *EEG clin. Neurophysiol.*, 1962, 14: 138–149.
38. Cf. Davidson, *Science*, July 13, 1962, 137: 125–126; see also Michael, *Science*, Apr. 27, 1962, 136: 322–323.
39. *Op. cit.*, note 2 above, 263 ff.
40. Demetrescu and Demetrescu (*EEG clin. Neurophysiol.*, 1962, 14: 602–620) report that in *encéphale isolé* cats with lesions of the central grey, high-rate (100–200/sec) stimulation of the dorsal pontine RF produced facilitation, and of the ventral pontine RF, inhibition, of evoked cortical potentials (optic tract, optic radiation, or LG stimulation). In animals without central grey lesions, stimulation of the ventral pontine RF "usually produced either no effect or only a slight facilitation." In similar preparations (*encéphale isolé*, intact central grey) acetylcholine injections in the dorsal pontine RF produced facilitation, and in the ventral pontine RF, inhibition, of evoked cortical potentials. These authors postulate a tonic activating system (posterior hypothalamus–central grey–RF) counterbalanced by, or counterbalancing, an ascending inhibitory system involving the ventral pontine RF. These data are perhaps relevant to Olds' finding (discussed in Chapter VII) of a dorsomedial "punishment" and a ventral "reward" system in the tegmentum of the rat.

Ward's suggestion that some reticular synapses (or nuclei) may be cholinergic and some adrenergic is apparently borne out by a recent report by Courville *et al.* (*Science*, Nov. 30, 1962, 138: 973–975). These authors present evidence in favor of the conclusion that the pontine and bulbar RF contain adrenergic and cholinergic subsystems which are respectively facilitatory and inhibitory of cortically evoked potentials (unanesthetized *encéphale isolé* cats, immobilized with gallamine; optic chiasm stimulation).

Rhythmic movements are perhaps more characteristic of the core "pleasure" systems and depend upon the inhibitory constraint which the latter exert upon central excitatory states leading to action. (Thus with increases in emergency-system support of "pleasure" system activity, rhythmic activity, as in sexual intercourse, increases in frequency *crescendo* to an arhythmic or spasmlike climax, something quite similar occurring in other forms of motor behavior during rapidly intensifying fear or rage.) If the ventral tegmentum has inhibitory functions similar to those of the ventral pontine RF, the tremor reported by Ward as following ventral tegmental lesions may result from impairment of this inhibitory control, or from periodic escape of systems whose outflows determine tonus of the skeletal musculature (e.g., RF→gamma motor system). That phasic rhythmic movements may originate in the cholinergic midbrain system (e.g., as a well-organized release or answering-effect phenomenon) is suggested by his report that rhythmic movements elicited by RF stimulation are suppressed by anticholinergic drugs.

The outflows which result from interaction of these more rostrally situated systems then impinge upon the spinal apparatus which itself is evidently not a passive system, but an oscillatory one organized upon similar though simpler lines and displaying, at least in some species, a type of innate rhythmic activity. The existence of such rhythmic activity in the cord is shown by the work of Weiss with deafferented tadpoles, of Adrian with the beetle *Dytiscus*, and of Von Holst with the annelid worm *Lumbricus*. (For these and other references, see Tinbergen, *The Study of Instinct*, 68; see also Chapter VIII, note 1).

41. French, *Handbook Physiol., Neurophysiol.*, Vol. II, 1293.
42. Jung and Hassler, *ibid.*, 900.
43. Herrick, *The Brain of the Tiger Salamander*, 99.
44. Bishop, *op. cit.*, note 2 above, 414.
45. Jasper, *op. cit.*, note 41 above, 1318.
46. Purpura, *Neuropharmacology*, III 300 ff.
47. Scheibel and Scheibel, *Ann. N. Y. Acad. Sc.*, Vol. 89, Art. 5, Jan. 28, 1961, 863.
48. Lindsley, *op. cit.*, note 41 above, Vol. III, 1566.
49. Schlag and Herzet, *Science*, Nov. 24, 1961, 134: 1691–1692.
50. Steiner and Himwich, *Science*, June 8, 1962, 136: 873–874.
51. Hassler, *EEG clin. Neurophysiol.*, 14, 1962, 422–423.
52. Sherwood, *Neuropharmacology*, II 85–179. Also Nachmansohn, *Science*, Dec. 15, 1961, 134: 1962–1968.
53. Cf. Hernández-Peón *et al.*, *The Efferent Control of Afferent Signals Entering the Central Nervous System*, *op. cit.*, note 47 above, 866–882. See also Hagbarth and Kerr, *J. Neurophysiol.*, 17, 295. Re reticular fibers to the bulb in rabbits, see Green, *Science*, Nov. 3, 1961, 134: 1429.

54. However, Dr. Warren McCulloch has pointed out to me that there exists in man a fast visual path, capable of activating the frontal eyefields and reticulospinal fiber systems in advance of activation of occipital cortex by the same inputs. In this connection, it should be added that Herrick (*op. cit.*, 38–39, 221) describes a short and perhaps maximally rapid visual path to the superficial peduncular neuropil in *Amblystoma*, to which he tentatively ascribes an inhibitory action such as figures in the "regarding reaction"—i.e., a response similar to "freezing" in fear. He adds that the basal optic tract is present in all vertebrates "from cyclostomes to man. It is evidently of major importance though little attention has been given to it." Conceivably the extrathalamic reticular fibers passing rostralward via the zona incerta (Scheibel and Scheibel, *op. cit.*) form part of this system; hence the rapid activation of area 8 mentioned by McCulloch. (Cf. also Lindsley, *op. cit.*, note 41 above, Vol. III, 1567.)

55. A study of the effects of "mild" reticular stimulation on striate cortical activity in New Zealand white rabbits in darkness and during exposure to light showed some cells "off" during light exposure and "on" during darkness, and some selectively responsive to movement in the visual field, as reported earlier by Hubel in the cat. Those cells "on" to light showed reticular activation, those "off," reticular inhibition, the suggestion being that at this level of reticulocortical input the chief effect in extrinsic cortex is a sharpening or intensification of *foci* of activity determined by the specific projection system. This author adds that "no correlation was found between cortical depth and types of response to either light or . . . [reticular] stimulation." Like Mountcastle's vertical column studies, cited earlier, this one fails to confirm the columnar distribution of activity which this theory predicts. However, since the neocortex during waking is in semicontinuous activity, the decisive test will be that suggested earlier here—namely, analysis of variance of unit activity continuously recorded for relatively long periods at several cortical depths in a number of cortical areas.

56. Arduini, *op. cit.*, note 2 above, 343.

57. Jasper, *ibid.*, 325. See also Glees, *Experimental Neurology*, 363.

58. Grastyán reports that stimulating in the region of the fornix in cats produced no direct motor effects, but caused intense fixation upon anything moving in the animal's visual field at the time—to the point that it would sometimes "lose its balance or be forced into unusual postures" (*op. cit.*, note 10 above, 119–120). This reaction

appeared to be accompanied by hyperorality, i.e., seizing and chewing the moving object even if inedible. Similar sensory fixation reactions were released in the phalanger following bilateral destruction of entorhinalis (Adey *et al.*, *Brain,* 79, 414–439).

59. Pribram, *Ann. Rev. Psych.,* Vol. 11, 1960, 14. Sperry's review of the evidence from split-brain studies (*Science,* June 2, 1961, 133: 1749–1757) appears to support this conclusion. It argues further that phasic outputs of the neocortex cannot effectually impose corresponding form (hence informational content) upon reticular activity, e.g. at the collicular level. Consequently such phasic components as nonspecific inputs do have may in large part be imposed upon them as result of the interaction of the neocortex with the thalamic reticularis.

60. What is obviously least clear from this account is the role of neurohumors in establishing the tonic influence of one subsystem of the CNS over others. It is odd, for example, that apparently adrenergic parts of the ascending RF are facilitatory for neocortex, whereas cholinergic parts are inhibitory (Courville *et al.*, note 40), the neocortex under other experimental conditions showing cholinergic activation (Steiner and Himwich; Monnier and Romanowski, Chapter IX, note 9). See also Chapter IX for a brief résumé of other neuropharmacological data whose significance is equally elusive, at least to me.

Concerning the mechanism of ventral pontine inhibition of neocortical activity, possibly via the caudate and ventralis anterior, see Chapter VIII, note 54.

CHAPTER VII

1. MacLean, *2nd Conf. CNS and Behavior,* 34.
2. Morris and Schaeffer, *Human Anatomy,* 1040.
3. Papez, in *Reticular Formation of the Brain,* 593.
4. Regarding medial hypothalamic satiety and lateral hypothalamic feeding centers, see Anand *et al., EEG clin. Neurophysiol.,* 13, 54–59, 1961; see also Morgane, *Science,* March 24, 1961, 133: 887–888.
5. French, *op. cit.,* note 3, 491 ff.
6. Green, *et al., EEG clin. Neurophysiol.,* 1961, 13, 837–879 (four papers).
7. Petsche *et al., ibid.,* 14, 202–211.
8. Nauta in *op. cit.,* note 3, 26; see also 601 (Papez).
9. Adey, in *op. cit.,* note 3, 629; see also *Internat'l Rev. Neurobiol.,* I, 28.
10. Sherrington, *Encyclopaedia Britannica,* 11th edition, Vol. 4, 407.

11. Herrick, *Brain of the Tiger Salamander*, 328.
12. Herrick, *Evolution of Human Nature*, 372.
13. Fulton, *Physiol.* 263. Cf. also Herrick, *op. cit.*, 104.
14. Bureš, in *op. cit.*, note 1 above, 231.
15. Olds, in *op. cit.*, note 1 above, 65–67.
16. See Lilly, in *op. cit.*, note 3 above, 711. Also MacLean, *op. cit.*, 83, on the fact that in higher mammals and man the distance between "motivational active" points in the CNS increases.
17. It is interesting, apropos of the connection between rhythmic movement and pleasure-system dominance (Chapter VI, note 40), that Lilly's monkeys would stimulate in lower brainstem regions producing intense tremor.
18. Glickman and Feldman, *EEG clin. Neurophysiol.*, 13, 1961, 703–709.
19. Cf. Fulton, *Frontal Lobotomy and Affective Behavior*, Ch. 2 and *passim*.
20. Lilly, in *op. cit.*, note 3 above, 709. See also *op. cit.*, note 1, 40, 79–80, 119, 149, 174, and 188. Olds (*ibid.*, 121) says: "When we stimulate in the septal area we have found . . . the animal gives no response to a painful stimulus while . . . [this area] is being electrically stimulated, but upon discontinuation of the current, he gives an exaggerated response to the noxious stimulus." Grastyán (*ibid.*) reports that discontinuation of hippocampal stimulation may activate a feeding response, but that this sort of rebound activation "occurs more often in an avoidance situation."
21. Adey, 2nd reference, note 9 above, 30.
22. Saul and Sawyer, *EEG clin. Neurophysiol.*, 13, 1961, 307. In New Zealand rabbits, ovulation was induced by brief seizure-producing electrical stimulation of the medial amygdala, stimulation of the lateral nuclei not producing this result. At higher intensities in the latter area, prolonged after-discharge and "psychomotor fits" resulted. I have cited evidence later that mounting reactions can also be obtained from stimulation in the amygdaloid region.

It should be noted, however, that ovulation obtained in this way may be a rebound effect, whereas the feeding and defensive autonomic and skeletal motor behavior obtained by MacLean and others may represent primary functions of this structure. The signficance of these effector functions of the amygdala is discussed below.

23. Gloor, *Handbook Physiol., Neurophysiol.*, II, 1416. See also Kaada, and Pampiglione and Falconer, *ibid.*
24. MacLean, *op. cit.*, note 1, 291. What Galambos said, to be

precise, was: "One guesses that much of the built-in or innate aspect of behavior is related to activity in the limbic midbrain circuit. One supposes that the reticular system has to do with attentive aspects." Since he doesn't specify exactly where in this circuit the "innate aspect" may be built in, I may be misinterpreting him.

25. Adey, 2nd ref., note 9 above, reports that hippocampal seizures (cat, guinea pig)propagate to the midbrain reticular formation and medial geniculates. The ventral hippocampus (cat) reportedly projects to the ventromedial hypothalamic nucleus and mammillary body, the dorsal hippocampus projecting less massively to the mammillary body alone. There also appear to be differences in the projections of the ventral and dorsal hippocampus to the entorhinal area. Single shocks to the fornix (1st ref., note 9 above, 625) evoke responses in both hippocampus and entorhinal area; whereas stimulation of the latter evokes responses in the hippocampus but not in the fornix. So long as induced discharges do not spread beyond the hippocampus, animals give no sign of motor or sensory impairment. Other reports indicate that during hippocampal seizure, functional decortication may occur "without appreciable involvement of the neocortex" (Fulton, *Textbook of Physiology,* 262). However, it appears from other studies (Adey, *op. cit.*) that hippocampal stimulation (cat) may result in general cortical activation, whereas cingulate stimulation does not. Also hippocampal seizures may spread to the cingulate, but the reverse is said not to occur.

Amygdaloid seizures spread to the ventromedial nucleus and, less directly, to the mammillary body. Gloor reports that in cats amygdaloid seizures propagate to the septum, hypothalamus, subthalamus, and thalamus, after-discharges extending into the lower midbrain tegmentum and dying out at the pontobulbar level (*Arch. Neurol., & Psychiat.,* 77, March 1957, 247–258). The loss of contact with the environment accompanying amygdaloid stimulation in man is perhaps in part attributable to thalamic invasion by impulses from the amygdala, e.g., via the posterior hypothalamus and the tract of Clark and Boggon to dorsomedialis. A similar mechanism may figure in the "depersonalization" sometimes accompanying intense fear. However, it should be noted that amygdaloid seizure in cats does not appear to involve frontal cortex but does involve the insula and cortical areas homologous to anterior and mesial temporal areas in man (Gloor, *op. cit.*). A similar propagation-pattern has, I believe, been observed in man. Bureš (in *op. cit.,* note 1, 223–224) reports that spreading depression induced by aqueous KCl in the hippocampus does not abolish the neocortical arousal response.

In the case of neocortex, Poggio *et al.* (*Neurol.*, 6, Sept. 1956, 616–626) describe three main routes of subcortical propagation of seizural activity. Seizures arising in frontal granular cortex chiefly involve the caudate (whose "emergency" functions are discussed here in Chapter VIII); those arising in more central regions, the thalamus and putamen; and those in the temporal lobe, the amygdala, hippocampus, and their respective projection areas.

26. "Emotionally significant" memories were found to evoke high-voltage regular wave-trains in the amygdaloid and rostral hippocampal region (Heath *et al., J. Nerv. & Ment. Dis.*, 122, November 1955, 433–440).

27. Gastaut, in *op. cit.*, note 3 above, 569. See also Morrell, in *op. cit.*, note 1 above, 291. Both concern the cessation of "closure" in the RF with extinction, and the former presents the hypothesis of reticular "closure."

28. Cf. Gastaut, *loc. cit.*, Voronin, Chapter II, note 1; see also John, Chapter III, note 11.

29. By W. McCulloch.

30. Cf. Green, *Science*, Nov. 3, 1961, 134: 1429.

31. Pechtel and Masserman, *Ann. N.Y. Acad. Sc.*, Vol. 58, Art. 2, March 24, 1954, 256–260. These authors report that "aversive reactions to a specific odor tend to generalize to related odors and to become more intense and persistent than parallel reactions in other sense-modalities." During extinction of the primary olfactory phobic response, this generalized reaction diminished somewhat. "However these three odors [used as CS's] were never again perceived with complete equanimity; instead the animals remained overly sensitive to all olfactory experiences and were likely to be suspicious of places with unaccustomed odors and to refuse strangely scented food without attempting to taste it."

CHAPTER VIII—part i

1. In *The Evolution of Human Nature*, 244, Herrick wrote: "In my description of the generalized brain of a salamander . . . it is shown that although the sense organs and their peripheral nerves are highly specialized, the muscular system is at a relatively low level of differentiation. . . . Even the locomotion of [fully grown salamanders] when they walk on land is fishlike, for all movements of the limbs are co-ordinated with rhythmic contractions of the body musculature. In short, the sensory analyzers are much more elaborately developed than are the motor analyzers."

2. Cf. Schusterman, *Science*, August 10, 1962, 137: 422–433.
3. Marrazzi, Chapter I, note 4. Elsewhere Marrazzi has noted that equivalent concentrations of norepinephrine are less inhibitory for nerve than is epinephrine (*Neuropharmocology*, III, 1957, 135). However, in concentrations producing comparable b.p. rises, norepinephrine appears to cause smaller increases in cerebral blood turnover (Ingvar, in *Reticular Formation of the Brain*, 400). Ingvar also cites evidence supporting the conclusion that cortical vasomotor tone does not rely entirely upon vasomotor innervation (*ibid.*, 392).
4. Davis, *Trans. N. Y. Acad. Sci.*, 19, 1957, 731–739.
5. Fox and O'Brien, *Science*, August 10, 1962, 137: 423–425.
6. MacLean, in *CNS and Behavior*, 1959, 41, 44, 48.
7. Chapter VII, note 18.
8. Heath, *Internat. Rev. Neurobiol.*, *Vol. 1*, 300.
9. Grastyán, *CNS and Behavior*, 1959, 119 ff.
10. Schreiner and Kling, *Am. J. Physiol.*, 184, March 1956, 486–490. See also *op. cit.*, note 9, 87, 89, 92–93.
11. Schreiner and Kling, *loc. cit.* See also Gloor, in *Handbook Physiol. Neurophysiol. II.*, 1412.
12. Macaques; Pribram, *Current Trends in Psychology*, 135–139.
13. Adey, *Internat. Rev. Neurobiol.*, I, 30. The relation of these effects to some of those accompanying anterior temporal lobe seizures in man is obvious. It is interesting that in some patients removal of the temporal pole, including first, second, and third temporal gyri and the uncus hippocampal gyrus and amygdala on the side of the observed focus, may not preclude psychomotor "fits" presumably originally arising in these structures. See Morris, *AMA. Arch. Neurol. and Psychiat.*, 76, November 1956, 479–496. It is also interesting that a species difference exists between man and the rat, in that the latter will self-stimulate at high rates in the amygdaloid area (Gloor, *op. cit.*, 1406).
14. Kaada, *op. cit.*, note 11 above, 1367–1368.
15. Wyke, *Ann. Royal Coll. Surgeons*, Feb. 1958, 22: 117–138.
16. Fulton, *Frontal Lobotomy and Affective Behavior*, 86–87.
17. Delgado, *EEG clin. Neurophysiol.*, 14, 1962, 419–430. In this study subcortical stimulation in monkeys was correlated with social behavior. The results are interesting. Stimulation of the amygdala evoked mounting reactions: of the central grey—increased aggressiveness toward objects or other monkeys; of the head of the caudate—inhibition of aggressiveness with "loss of territoriality and aggressiveness"; and of *ventralis anterior*—avoidance of obstacles and other

animals, and hiding. The role of the striatum in the creation of motivational-affective states is discussed below.

18. Saul and Sawyer, *EEG clin. Neurophysiol*, 13, 1961, 307.

19. Brutkowski and Mempel. *Science*, Dec. 22, 1961, 134: 2040–2041.

20. Fulton, *op. cit.*, 128.

21. I.e., the principal structure in man is *n. anteroventralis* projecting to posterior granular area 23. Cf. Fulton, *Physiology of the Nervous System*, 269; Pribram, *Behavior and Evolution*, 149.

22. Papez, in *Reticular Formation of the Brain*, 601. Apropos of the role of the mammillary body in sleep, Hernández-Peón (*EEG clin. Neurophysiol.*, 14, 1962, 423) has suggested it may be inhibitory for the midbrain RF during sleep (possibly a frequency-specific phenomenon). Nauta believes a hypothalamic sleep center is to be found in the preoptic and suprachiasmatic regions, a "wakefulness" center lying in the mammillary body with some opposition between the two (Lindsley, *Handbook Physiol., Neurophysiol.* III 1558). This arrangement suggests high- and low-energy subdivisions within the "reward" system which are internally competitive and (respectively) facilitatory or inhibitory for the dynamogenic emergency system, e.g., of the midbrain. Similarly, in the secondary olfactory (emergency) system, there appear to be high- and low-energy divisions (these terms referring to the rates of energy expenditure each tends to establish in the organism), the posterior hypothalamus and parts of the amygdala constituting the former; orbital 13 and 14, and possibly the ventromedial nucleus and anterior midline region of the hypothalamus constituting the latter and having important inhibitory functions vis-à-vis the pleasure system. Evidence cited later, in addition to that presented in Delgado's study (*loc. cit.*) suggests that the striatum may have mixed functions although caudate inhibition, e.g., of neocortical activity, may be important in the development of emergency states, or in those constraints imposed upon behavior by learned or innate fear-responses. (Concerning the probable role of the ventromedial hypothalamic nucleus in catatonia, see *Yearbook Neurol., Psychiat., and Neurosurg.*, 1956–1957, 252.) In animals, stimulation of the anterior lobe of the cerebellum has been reported to produce marked following in activity of the ventromedial nucleus (increases in frequency and voltage) accompanied by sympathetic signs, the converse of this relation or cerebellar "following" of ventromedial stimulation also having been observed. Similar changes were not observed, under these experimental conditions, in the lateral hypothalamus (Ingram, *Handbook Physiol., Neurophysiol.*, II, 974).

23. MacLean, in *op. cit.*, note 9, 55. Certain recent evidence suggests rhinencephalic routes which may figure in what I have called answering effects, or the mobilization of one motivational-affective system in such a way as functionally to support or supersede the other (or both, in that order). Adey (*op. cit.*), reports that transection of the anterior dorsal hippocampus "markedly retards" avoidance conditioning in rats; also that ventral temporal resections in the baboon, involving entorhinalis and partially destroying the hippocampus, but "largely sparing the amygdala on one or both sides" greatly diminished apparent fear-responses without impairing appropriate avoidance behavior. In the same paper he points out that (in the cat) while the ventral hippocampus projects to the mammillary body and ventromedial hypothalamic nucleus, the dorsal hippocampus projects only (and less massively) to the mammillary body. Andy and Mukawa (*EEG clin. Neurophysiol.*, April 1961, 13: 317) report that (also in cats) amygdaloid and ventral hippocampal seizures propagate to the same septal region; whereas dorsal hippocampal seizures appear to follow a somewhat different path and activate other septal nuclei (e.g., *n septalis dorsalis*).

I would interpret these results as follows. Structures of the anterior dorsal hippocampus may figure prominently in answering effects following upon activation of emergency functions mediated via the amygdala (or conversely may activate the emergency system; see MacLean, cited above). For this reason projections of the anterior dorsal hippocampus reach the mammillary body—a part of the dynamogenic "pleasure" system apparatus—and also septal nuclei perhaps selectively concerned in the genesis of "normal survival" states (in this case, e.g., rebound rage).

Conversely, structures of the ventral hippocampus may be chiefly concerned in answering effects following upon activation of parts of the "pleasure" system—e.g., mobilization of the emergency system in support of sexual excitement or primary rage, and including some inhibitory restriction of these in the light of conditioned avoidance responses. For this reason, fibers from the ventral hippocampus reach not only the mammillary body but also the ventromedial hypothalamic nucleus (perhaps mediating fearlike inhibition; see preceding note) and the same septal regions as are reached by projections of the amygdala.

In connection with the foregoing, it is interesting that the British neurosurgeon Turner has reportedly diminished the proclivity toward irrational rages in certain patients by section of amygdaloid-hippocampal fibers (McCulloch, in *Lectures on Experimental Psychiatry,*

315). Also, in contrast to the autonomic system, in which the emergency (sympathetic) branch appears to be the more organized for massive action, the rhinencephalic "pleasure" system may predominate over the emergency in this respect, if susceptibility to seizure is a reliable index. A study of rhinencephalic seizure duration in cats (Andy and Webster, *EEG clin. Neurophysiol.*, April 1961, 13: 312) shows that average after-discharge duration was greatest for the hippocampus (27.6 sec.) as was seizure variability (33 per cent)—the latter point being of importance, as it may reflect the greater tendency of "receptor" systems to less predictable or strictly determinate modes of action (cf. Chapter V, above). In order of descending magnitude, average seizure durations and range of seizure variability for various rhinencephalic structures were as follows: hippocampus, septum, amygdala, and gyrus cinguli.

24. Pampiglione and Falconer, *Handbook of Physiol.*, *Neurophysiol II*, 1391.

25. Adey, *op. cit.*

26. Mason, in *Reticular Formation of the Brain*, 655.

27. *Ibid.* This phenomenon suggests an interesting parallel with the so-called Kamin effect. Kamin noted that during avoidance conditioning rats showed a decline in avoidance behavior roughly for the first hour of testing and an increase over the next twenty-four hours—the former attributed to "freezing" (*J. Comp. & Physiol. Psych.*, 50, 1957, 457). Together with the data reviewed in note 23 above, this suggests that the pleasure system may play a major part in fear-freezing responses, and may do so, e.g., via ventral hippocampal-ventromedial nucleus projections activating the "low-energy" or inhibitory portions of the emergency system (note 22, above). Thus, fearlike inhibitory responses may in part owe their tenacity to the greater tendency of the rhinencephalic pleasure (vis-à-vis the emergency) system to prolonged quasi-seizural activity (note 23). In turn, a predominance of avoidance conditioning, for instance in man, will mean that neocortical-rhinencephalic outflows will predominantly activate the emergency system over pathways including the ones just mentioned. The net effect may be indirectly to cause some impairment of neocortical activity, e.g., via the midbrain, in fear-states of whatever intensity, though the extent and type of impairment will differ with intensity. There is experimental evidence that such impairment occurs. Denny and Thomas, in a follow-up study using rats and varying the length and height of the Skinner box, found that "learning, despite greater motivation for learning, tends to be poorer [the greater the

References and Notes / 247

punishment]." They also report that fearlike "freezing" is greater in female rats—perhaps reflecting a lesser tendency in these to ferocity or facilitatory rage-rebound responses (*Science,* Sept. 2, 1960, 132: 620).

28. Fulton, *op. cit.*, note 21, 450.
29. Fulton, *op. cit.*, note 16, 87.
30. Pribram, *op. cit.*, note 21, 147 ff.
31. Pribram, *Behavioral Science,* Vol. 4, No. 4, Oct. 1959, 265–287. See also Jacobsen, *J. Comp. Neurol.*, Vol. 52, No. 2, April 15, 1931, 271–340.
32. Cf. Fulton, *op. cit.*, note 16. See also *Textbook of Physiol.*, 499, and various follow-up studies on lobotomized or leucotomized patients, notably Freeman, *South. Med. Jour.*, June 1958, 51: 739–745; also Freeman, *Dis. Nerv. System*, Jan. 1958, 19: 11–15; and McCausland and Wickware, *Canad. M. A. J.*, 79, 168, 1958. See also Paillard, in *Handbook Physiol., Neurophysiol.*, Vol. III, 1689 ff. In the case of gestures the organization of which may be affected by damage to the second parietal convolution, near the extremity of the Sylvian fissure, this author quotes Lhermitte to the effect that those gestures most affected are those which are most symbolic or, in a biologic sense, least pragmatic (drive- or affect-related). "The movement which is impaired may be carried out in perfectly adapted fashion when the patient is under the influence of an emotional experience" (Paillard, *op. cit.*, 1692). The contrast between this type of apraxia, which damages behavior at its neocortical receptor system source, and the type resulting from frontal lesions, e.g., to Broca's area, underscores the point that the frontal organization of actions may in part be under control of motivational core-processes and in part under control of neocortical "reality principle" processes, the latter type of control being selectively impaired by certain types of posterior sector damage.

CHAPTER VIII—part ii

33. Thompson, *Science,* Nov. 25, 1960, 132: 1551.
34. Cf. Lindsley, in *Handbook Physiol., Neurophysiol*, Vol. III, 1556.
35. Mirsky and Cardon, *EEG clin. Neurophysiol.*, 14, 1962, 1–10.
36. Cf. MacLean, in *op. cit.*, note 34, 1730.
37. Pribram reviews studies by Adey, Freeman, and Doty bearing on the question of whether engram formation takes place in parts of the rhinencephalon during conditioning, the suggestion being that it does

(*Regional Physiology of the CNS*, 3.); MacLean (*op. cit.*) believes that rhinencephalic memories may be of a qualitative kind. Pechtel and Masserman's study (Chapter VII, note 30) suggests that olfactory memories are quite enduring.

38. Reference is to the distribution of sense-data apparently directly to "motor" neocortex, including those auditory projections mentioned by Nakahama (Nakahama, *Internat. Rev. Neurobiol.*, III, 187). It is possible that the two motor-sensory and sensori-motor systems discussed in this paper represent core-mediated and neocortically mediated effector functions of the neopallium, with cross-connections, e.g., via the thalamus, serving to adjust or synchronize these.

39. E.g., M. and D. Demetrescu present evidence for what they call a "diffuse ascending inhibitory influence" mediated in extrinsic neocortical sectors by the caudate (*EEG clin. Neurophysiol.*, 14, 1962, 37–52). Previously Heuser et al. (*ibid.*, 13, 1961, 821) demonstrated that the path responsible passed via *ventralis anterior,* and observed desynchronization at the vertex following "high frequency" caudate stimulation in intact animals (cat). While there are some electrocortical similarities between the results of caudate and midbrain reticular stimulation (Fox and O'Brien, *op. cit.*) the caudate may more specifically be involved in mobilization of the neocortical effector apparatus or in conjoint extrapyramidal-pyramidal activity. Possibly this last is related to the phenomenon observed by Rusinov (*CNS and Behavior*, II, 249 ff.), namely desynchronization of the EEG of the vertex in man, a response found to be independent of the SGR.

40. Hernández-Peón et al., *Ann. N. Y. Acad., Sc.*, Vol. 89, Art. 5, Jan. 28, 1961, 866–880. Elsewhere this author demonstrated depression or abolition of secondary evoked potentials in *n. gracilis* when dorsal column stimulation was accompanied by stimulation of the midbrain RF. Following destruction of the midbrain tegmentum, enhancement of the secondary potentials evoked by trigeminal nerve stimulation was observed (cf. Lindsley, *op. cit.*, 1587). In the first paper above, alerting of the animal (cat) produced mixed peripheral effects (enhancement of olfactory bulb activity and of potentials evoked from the trigeminal; diminution of auditory potentials) while during presumed attention reduction of the last two occurred. Recordings were made from implanted bipolar electrodes in the bulb, optic tract, and dorsal cochlear and Vth sensory nuclei.

41. Steiner, *EEG clin. Neurophysiol.*, 14, 1962, 233–243. In this study aimed at showing a parallel relation between "drive-level" and "level of awareness," this investigator produced acute thirst by

salt-loading albino rats which then "displayed a hyperactivity which reached frantic bizarre proportions. . . . Response patterns were repetitious and seemed to bear no relationship to the external events. The animal looked as if he were searching or trying to escape but he did not appear to be utilizing the information gained from his activity." Gratification of thirst promptly abolished these signs.

Another series of experiments demonstrates how a deficiency in the neocortical processing of sense-data can lead to (what I would interpret as) a comparable decontrolling of core-activities, with somewhat similar behavioral results. A group of beagles raised in a visually "restricted" environment were later matched against controls in CR formation to visual cues. The experimental group showed significantly higher errors, which the experimenter attributed in part to the "exceptionally high level of emotional excitement—including 'whirling fits' similar to a seizure." (Melzack, *Science*, Sept. 21, 1962, 137: 978–979.)

42. Gibbs, *Biology of Mental Health and Disease*, 454.

43. See S. B. Wortis, *Yearbook Neurol., Psychiat., and Neurosurg.*, 1956–1957, 253.

44. Evarts *et al.*, *Science*, March 2, 1962, 135: 726–728.

45. Purpura, *Internat. Rev. Neurobiol.*, 1, 1959, 142.

46. E.g., Matsumoto (*EEG clin. Neurophysiol.*, 13, 1961, 538–552) reports that in the cat cerebellar rhythmic activity at 20–40/sec could be evoked by stimulation of the ascending reticular activating system, the frontal areas being those in neocortex from which the same response could be evoked at the lowest threshold. Cf. also Fulton, *Frontal Lobotomy and Affective Behavior*, 102 ff.

47. Teuber, *Evolution of Nervous Control from Primitive Organisms to Man*, 157 ff.

48. Akert *et al.*, *Science*, Dec. 30, 1960, 132: 1944.

49. A hippocampal theta response rather than desynchronization reportedly occurs concurrently with stimulation of the midbrain tegmentum. Cf. Green, in *Reticular Formation of the Brain*, 614.

50. Olds, in *CNS and Behavior*, II, 141–144. This finding, however, might be interpreted several ways, since stimulation of the anterior thalamus produced effects similar to hippocampal stimulation. That is, frontal activation, with corresponding posterior sector effects as described here, may have acted to block new learning during stimulation. Pribram (*op. cit.*) reports that "mild" frontal stimulation in monkeys impairs learning, and more intense, both learning and performance of the already learned; the former perhaps mimics the frontal

influence of the anterior nuclei and cingulate, the latter, that of dorsomedialis.

51. Akert *et al.*, *Brain*, Vol. 84, part III, 1961, 480–498.

52. Hughes and Mazurowski, *EEG clin. Neurophysiol.*, 1962, 14, 477–485.

53. Many of Freud's notions of psychic mechanisms, including that of sublimation, appear to date back to his Project of 1895, in some ways a remarkably prescient work which has recently been reviewed by Karl Pribram (*The Neuropsychology of Sigmund Freud*). Freud's concept of sublimation seemed to involve the idea that when sexual activity proper was repressed, a "lateral" displacement of related central nervous activity occurred, resulting in substitute activities, e.g., intellectual effort. See Pribram *op. cit.*, 21, on Freud's view of the nature of defenses.

Since, however, central nervous activities equivalent to thought may be favored by a more or less balanced action of the subcortical emergency and normal survival* systems, and since an imbalance in favor of excessive emergency-system activity may be the more destructive of thought,† it is doubtful if prolonged sexual deprivation is conducive to "creative" or intellectual achievement. The notion that the latter can be substituted for the former may, in other words, be incorrect, except in the crude sense that *any* form of activity may temporarily diminish the central excitatory state of frustration as described here. Conversely, sexual activity, when not so violent as to be exhausting, often seems to favor an expansiveness conducive to those very activities which Freud conceived as "sublimated" forms of sexuality. In other words, our sexual and our "creative" pursuits are competitive chiefly in a practical sense, but are neurophysiologically complementary in that the central nervous conditions accompanying the one are frequently optimal for the other. Thus rage may drive men to write letters to a newspaper, or love make poets of the unpoetic; but anxiety or fear seldom have "creative" consequences.

I find it interesting that the argument presented in this book leads to an account of primary and secondary (psychological) processes essentially like Freud's. The mechanism of repression proposed below in Chapter IX and the abstract memory systems discussed in Chapters III–V suggest an hypothesis of dreams also like Freud's. The "dream work" may basically resemble forms of conscious rationalization originating in parts of our recalled experience which are repressed.

---

* Or regulatory and constitutive, respectively.

† Or "regulate" it down to a bare minimum.

Processes of both these kinds involve logical transformations of (equivalent to transitions from) memory data which themselves fail to become "conscious" or clearly recalled elements of the sequence.

Whereas in waking, such transformational sequences may have the complexity and coherence characteristic of "reality principle" processes and may involve both first- and second-order abstract memories (cf. Chapter V), in sleep the subsidence of neocortical activity, as it may particularly affect the external lamina (cf. Vladimirov *et al.*, cited in Chapter IV), may cause those processes to become more disjointed or logically primitive. That is, they are then chiefly "pleasure principle" processes, paralleling subcortical answering effect trains and proceeding from the bottom of the cortex up. Participation of the external lamina may be minimal and may largely involve first-order abstract memories —i.e., intracortical communication of a relatively simple linear type. First-order abstract memories, in other words, mediate what Miller, Galanter and Pribram, in *Plans and the Structure of Behavior*, describe as Markov processes or a "nonanticipatory grammar"; whereas second-order abstract memories provide a continually changing repertoire of potential master plans, equivalent to an anticipatory grammar. As a whole, these memory-systems thus embody three layers of logic—the given logic of experienced fact as thing memory; a logic of simple relations, such as partial formal resemblance, between otherwise unrelated facts, embodied in first order abstract memories; and a logic as it were of probable future spatio-temporal complexes of fact, or events, embodied as second-order abstract memories. Through the last, certain external cues in effect evoke central nervous events equivalent to predictions. The behavioral sequences prefacilitated, e.g., in the motor and related frontal intrinsic areas are the organism's "plans" corresponding to these predictions.

First-order abstract memories may be regarded as multiple-distribution points through any one of which a thing memory may facilitate a number of others—the number finally activated depending upon convergence effects where n ($=$ more than 1) thing memories are originally involved. This mechanism might account for what Freud calls displacement and condensation in dreams and for his observation that there is no element in a dream "whence the chains of association do not lead in two or more directions" (*Dream Psychology*, 25). That dream sequences are mediated in parallel with subcortical answering effect trains is perhaps reflected in his remark that in dreams "it is almost the rule that one train of thought is followed by its contradictory" (ibid., 40).

Like fantasy or reveries, dreams presumably arise out of core-states surviving from the just preceding active period, and represent neocortical consequences of core-release.* Freud (*op. cit.*, 35, 51) notes that dreams are "linked up with our impressions of the day" and also are "uncreative." Like most fantasies, a dream "judges nothing, decides nothing." As the abstract memory system is the last to come into being in the course of individual development, it is possibly logical to expect, as he reports, that the dreams of children, up to about age six, tend to be of an easily readable wish-fulfillment type. The same is of course true of many adult dreams in which the element of "conflict" or repression is lacking. (E.g., a hungry man dreams of food.)

Two other points are of interest here. One is that linear associational processes dependent upon what I have called first-order abstract memories may in fact involve "elaborated" type memories (cf. Chapters IV–V above), and hence periextrinsic sectors mobilized by cortico-thalamo-cortical relay from posterior intrinsic areas. In dream symbolism, "snake" is often said to represent "penis." Memories corresponding to particular snakes or penises (posterior intrinsic sectors) may then each have more generalized equivalents (periextrinsic sectors), and finally a common ancestor (also periextrinsic, possibly parakoniose, cortex) embodying certain (e.g., visual structural) features common to both snakes and penises. This last typelike memory-formation presumably lies along the route of cortical "irradiation" (extrinsic→ periextrinsic→intrinsic) by which sense-data originally giving rise to these two groups of memories were distributed. By retraverse of these routes, the memory "penis" activates the common generalized protoform and the latter "snake" (e.g., intrinsic→periextrinsic→intrinsic). In a dream involving sexual strivings which are "forbidden"—i.e., which simultaneously activate an avoidance CR and so the core emergency system—"penis" tends to be repressed (see Chapter IX); while what does reach "consciousness" as the manifest content of the dream is "snake," an item of recall with "bad" meanings for many people, and here highly probable because 1) structurally similar to penis and 2) tending to establish circular interaction with the core avoidance system. (It is interesting that chimpanzees and monkeys evidently have an innate fear of snakes which is abolished by the Klüver-Bucy procedure. Whether this innate reaction survives in man is, I believe, not known.)

In any case, this account might explain why "first-order abstract memories" continue to function in sleep while second-order do not. For

---

* From neocortical feedback control.

References and Notes / 253

if the former are in fact elaborated type memories, they may, like thing memories, chiefly have representation in the internal lamina, postulated here to be less affected by the decline in cortical metabolic rates occurring at onset of sleep. If periextrinsic sector memories play the part suggested in the linear organization of thought or of spoken or written speech—and if this mode of organization is a prerequisite of non-linear organizational processes originating in the "second-order abstract" memory-systems, and in effect redirecting linear processes according to various controlling schemata—then it becomes easier to understand the uniquely disorganizing effects produced by certain limited cortical lesions—e.g., in the region of the angular gyrus transitional to the second occipital convolution (Gerstmann's syndrome; cf. *Neurol.*, Dec. 1957, 7, 866–869).

The second point concerns the rhombencephalic state of sleep described by Jouvet. Elsewhere (Chapter VI, note 40) I have cited work by Demetrescu and Demetrescu, showing that in the cat there is a system in the dorsal pontine RF which is facilitatory, and in the ventral pontine RF one which is inhibitory for neocortex, the latter system being antagonized by the more rostrally lying activating complex of the midbrain. Onset of sleep appears to involve rostralmost portions of the CNS first. Thus with the subsidence of neocortical activity in drowsiness, surviving focal activity, e.g., in the midbrain, may tend to show release and augmentation sufficient on occasion to cause rearousal of neocortical activity and reversal of the drift into sleep. A mechanism of this kind may figure in the insomnia of the disturbed.

With the deepening of sleep, the same release occurring earlier in the midbrain, with subsidence of neocortical activity, may occur in the pontine RF with subsidence of activity at the midbrain level. The rise in GSR accompanying Jouvet's stage of sleep in man (Hawkins et al., *Science,* April 27, 1962, 136: 321–322) as well as the marked loss of muscle tonus suggest quiescence of the midbrain RF; while simultaneous cortical desynchronization (*ibid.*) suggests a rise in the activity of the dorsal (facilitatory) pontine RF.

54. In cats, single shocks to the head of the caudate have been found to evoke a short latency potential and a longer latency (150–250 msec) spindle-train. Spindling was most readily obtained in ipsilateral precruciate cortex. Spindles were also obtainable from many thalamic sites, from the globus pallidus and contralateral caudate, *n. entopeduncularis*, and septum. Spindling could not be evoked in the medial or basolateral amygdala in "several hypothalamic sites" or in the mid-

brain RF. Spindle thresholds rose and durations fell in proportion to the degree of neocortical desynchronization observed at the time. Spontaneous spindling differs from that evoked from the caudate in that it appears in auditory or occipital cortices but not in precruciate, and in that stimulation of the midbrain RF blocks it but may not block caudate-evoked spindling. For example, mesencephalic reticular stimulation sufficient to block a recruiting response obtained by 6/sec stimulation of CM failed to block caudate spindles. However, increasing the intensity of midbrain stimulation shortens and finally abolishes caudate spindles, unless the intensity of caudate shocks is also increased. Neither hippocampal theta activity nor seizure influences precruciate spindling. Electrocoagulation of ventralis anterior will block spindling ipsi- but not contralaterally. Destruction of VA bilaterally abolishes spindling. "These facts indicate not only that the ventral anterior nucleus (and reticular nucleus) is essential for spindling, but also that it is the only necessary thalamic nucleus" (Buchwald *et al.*, *EEG clin. Neurophysiol.*, 1961, 13: 509–538).

The effects obtained in the monkey by stimulation of the head of the caudate suggest that this structure (and ventralis anterior) may be concerned in the inhibition which occurs at onset of fear or intense alerting. See note 17 above; see also Van Buren, *EEG clin. Neurophysiol.*, 1962, 14: 586, who obtained loss of consciousness, interruption of speech, and on repeated stimulation, persisting "mild confusion" following stimuli delivered to the head of the caudate or deep frontal white substance in humans.

It is tempting to suppose that this caudate–VA mechanism is related to the neocortical and rhinencephalic "strip" regions, and together with these mediates the responses described by French (in *Reticular Formation of the Brain*, 496). Arrest of activity followed by orientative behavior or (at higher stimulus-intensities) alerting "tainted with emotional coloring" and followed by hiding behavior, can be obtained from stimulating cortical "strip" regions. (Delgado *et al.* obtained "hiding" reactions by stimulating VA in monkeys; note 17 above). Stimulated at still greater intensities, the "strip" regions evoke "a frenzy of terror." French describes these strip regions as reaching the midbrain via the septum. They may also reach ventralis anterior, e.g., by the corticofugal routes mentioned by Jasper. It is clear also that the effects obtained from them are specific to their rates of input. The same seems to apply to the caudate-ventralis anterior system.

In the last paper of their series, Buchwald *et al.* reported the effects of various rates of stimulation of the head of the caudate, upon cats lever-pressing to obtain a reward of cream. At rates of 1 pulse/5 sec. to 5 pulses/sec., 0.1 msec pulse-duration, 50 V. (bilaterally), a "relaxed" cat resulted. Lever-pressing slackened and stopped. Below the lower rate (threshold for spindling) no result was observed. At 5/sec, lever-pressing sometimes stopped abruptly. At 20/sec, 0.1 msec duration, 30 V, "freezing," occasionally with slow neck and trunk torsion, occurred. At 300/sec., 0.01 msec pulse duration, 70 V "no overt motor manifestations were observed. In alert hungry cats this high frequency never increased the rate of bar-pressing." (The same result was obtained from ventralis anterior.)

This last finding, contrary to Fox and O'Brien (note 5), clearly differentiates the caudate–VA system from the midbrain RF. One wonders if this rate of input is inhibitory for the caudate and VA, and comes into play as rises in midbrain reticular activity begin greatly to exceed the level necessary, e.g., to block caudate spindling.

In other words, the caudate and ventralis anterior may figure in the momentary "deadlocks" which occur when activity of the receptor-pleasure and effector-punishment systems is simultaneously accelerated. The influence of the former (e.g., posterior neocortex→ thalamus) activates the caudate spindling mechanism, particularly evident in precruciate motor cortex, as noted by Buchwald *et al.*, and may produce "freezing" at intensity levels equivalent to the stimulation rate producing this effect in cats. This mechanism conceivably figures in the "regarding reaction" or the pause-permitting-orientation postulated here as mediated by receptor system inhibition of effector systems. The results obtained by caudate stimulation in man (Van Buren), because involving frontal cortex, may have caused speech disorganization and likewise an abrupt cessation of frontal-midbrain output, hence in tonic maintenance of neocortical activity, hence a "skip" in consciousness. This is perhaps an exaggerated form of the mechanism of repression proposed in Chapter IX below. The orientative reactions produced by stimulation of the cortical "strip" regions at low intensity (French) suggest implication of the caudate and ventralis anterior, as does the "freezing" occurring at higher intensitites. At still higher, the midbrain RF apparently predominates, with appearance of overt panic activity. This perhaps corresponds to the high-frequency caudate or VA stimulation at which Buchwald *et al.* obtained no behavioral result—i.e., the level of input at which the inhibitory functions of these structures are either inhibited or otherwise set aside by the tonic activating system. Behaviorally and psychologically, this corresponds to the phase in which "regarding" or fearlike freezing reactions are superseded by rises in activity of the dynamogenic emergency system of the core, with a resulting transfer of dominance from the receptor to the effector systems, the sequels to which are discussed in the text.

Some of the influence which the neocortex brings to bear upon the caudate–VA mechanism may be exerted by long corticofugal pathways. The neocortex may thus, as suggested earlier, compete functionally at the lower brainstem level with the reticular formation, in effect for control of its own modulatory inputs. Evidence is cited above in favor of the existence of a ventral pontine division of the RF which is inhibitory for neocortex and antagonized by a more rostrally situated facilitatory system comprising the posterior hypothalamus, periaqueductal grey and reticular activating substance lying e.g. "between the post-collicular and the pre-trigeminal planes" (Demetrescu and Demetrescu, *op. cit.*, below).

The latter authors (*EEG clin. Neurophysiol.*, 1962, 14: 602–620) cite evidence that in the cat, after central grey lesions, arousal can still be obtained by stimulation of the dorsal RF, commenting that here the basal activating apparatus appears to be still intact, while "the tonic driving influences are lacking." They point out that the "results of Jouvet *et al*. . . . and those of Rossi et al. [are] evidence for the existence of a region in the lower brainstem, especially at the pontine level, responsible for deep sleep." They conclude that "the ascending inhibitory system, including an area of the [ventral] pontine RF and the caudate nucleus, balances the ascending activating system, including the activating RF, its hypothetical driving-structures (posterior hypothalamus and central gray) and the thalamic unspecific system."

It is interesting that Arnold's frontopontine bundle reportedly arises in the motor and premotor areas (Brodmann 4 and 6; cf. Fulton, *Physiol. N.S.*, 327), Türck's bundle arising in the inferior and middle temporal gyri (*ibid.*; macaques). One wonders if the former reaches the ventral pontine inhibitory system described by Demetrescu and Demetrescu and thereby figures in the diminishment of central activation which often accompanies overt action, or the decelerative new-learning phase of behavior described in this chapter.

Finally, apropos of possible receptor functions (including effector system "antagonism") of cingulate area 23, discussed in the text, Ralston obtained bilateral synchronized spikes and 8–12/sec spindling from a unilateral mid-cingulate site in cats (*EEG clin. Neurophysiol.*, 1961, 13: 591–598). Middle suprasylvian gyrus showed spindles but little or no preliminary spiking. With a right mid-cingulate focus, most pronounced spike-and-spindling activity appeared to be obtained in the right anterior sigmoid gyrus. Destruction of the massa intermedia and mesial thalamus abolished these cingulate cortical effects (whereas "irritative lesions" of the massa intermedia "may duplicate the bilateral spindle synchrony seen with a unilateral cingulate lesion").

An anatomical point of interest, in relation to the reported distribution of the cingulum reported by Bailey and Von Bonin (*op. cit.* above, Chapter IV), is implied by Ralston's finding that when the cingulum was interrupted both anterior and posterior to the midcingulate focus "the synchrony and transmission of spiking ceased." When section was made only anteriorly or posteriorly, this effect was not obtained. The suggestion is that the cingulate-thalamic pathway here involved is not a simple one.

CHAPTER IX

1. Cf. Grundfest, in *Reticular Formation of the Brain*, 483-484. Also *Evolution of Nervous Control*, 43–86.
2. De Robertis, *Regional Neurochemistry*, 248–258.
3. Nozdrachev, *Physiol. Jour.*, U.S.S.R., Vol. 47, No. 1, 1961, 87–92.
4. Knapp and Domino, *EEG clin. Neurophysiol.*, 1961, 13: 144.
5. Costa *et al.*, *Science*, June 9, 1961, 133: 1822–1823.
6. Stein and Seifter, *ibid.*, July 28, 1961, 134: 286–287.
7. Barbeau, *ibid.*, 133, May 26, 1961, 1706–1707.
8. Marrazzi, *Trans 2nd Conf. Neuropharmacology*, 135.
9. Monnier and Romanowski, *EEG clin. Neurophysiol.*, 14, 1962, 486–500.
10. Sadowski and Longo, *ibid.*, 14, 1962, 465–476.
11. Wada, *Science*, Nov. 24, 1961, 134: 1688–1689.
12. Von Euler and Lishajko, *Science*, Aug. 5, 1960, 132: 351.
13. McGeer, *American Scientist*, June 1962, 322–338.
14. Heath's proposal that this disease involves a basic defect of pleasure (i.e., pleasure-system activities) with distinctive septal electrographic signs is entirely in accord with the ideas developed here (*Int. Rev. Neurobiol.*, 300–328). However, the taraxein hypothesis put forward by his group does not seem to have been confirmed by others' results. A recent paper by Seijun Tatetsu of the University of Kumamoto, Japan, read at Albany Medical College, November 2, 1961, presented striking evidence of widespread neuronal changes in brains of schizophrenics examined post mortem (in each case as compared

with parallel observations made upon brains of psychiatrically normal controls of approximately the same age). Tatetsu used Bielschowski's method on extremely thin sections (approx. 5 micra), keeping sections in 2 per cent Ag nitrate one to four months. Whether this one will go the way of other such promising reports remains to be seen. If these results prove duplicable and differential for schizophrenia, the problem remains as to whether the observed neuronal changes represent a heritable anomaly, or are of functional origin, or whether a (possibly heritable) metabolic defect such as that suggested by Heath above leads to dysfunction and thence to progessive organic changes worsening the former. I am obliged to Dr. Lewis Stevenson for calling my attention to Dr. Tatetsu's report.

15. In this connection, see three papers by Bishop and co-workers (M. Clare and W. Landau), *EEG clin. Neurophysiol.*, 13, 1961, 21–33, 34–42, 43–53. In this study, Bishop noted that augmenting responses were obtained most readily in the cat near the lateral geniculate "or in the optic radiation dorsal and anterior to the nucleus," adding that "it is therefore difficult to escape the [conclusion] that the augmenting phenomenon is correlated with stimulation of slowly conducting corticipetal fibers passing near to but not from the lateral geniculate nucleus and mingling with radiation fibers to cortex." Augmenting waves showed mutual occlusion with recruiting waves elicited by stimulation of the medial thalamus.

16. Fuster, *Science*, June 23, 1961, 133: 2011–2012.

17. Ward, *Internat. Rev. Neurobiol.*, III, 1961, 137–183. Ward cites the posible importance of this mechanism in epilepsy, pointing out, however, as others have done, the sometimes odd lack of correlation between EEG and behavioral changes, a similar lack of strict correlation existing between slow potential waves and unit activity.

18. Conceivable as due to a driving of the systems concerned beyond their capacity for patterned action. The difficulty, of course, lies in defining what is a pattern, and so what isn't. However, the fact that the projection system of the thalamic reticularis may, as Jasper has suggested, be more loosely organized may be a factor working against too strict point-to-point intracortical communication and so against functional rigidity in processes equivalent to thought. This system may, in other words, introduce a factor of "useful noise," whose advantages in theoretical computers have recently been mentioned by Fogel (*Ann. N.Y. Acad. Sc.*, Vol. 89, Art. 5, June 28, 1961, 732 ff). Increases in this noise, of midbrain origin, may then cause it to be obliterative rather than useful.

19. Campbell (*Manic-Depressive Disease*) states on the basis of clinical experience that euphoric phases of this disorder always show a negative cast. He stresses importance of autonomic disturbances in manic-depressives (p. 56). One wonders if the heritable feature of this disorder may not consist in structural or other (e.g., neurohumoral) anomalies such that small imbalances resulting from normally tolerable amounts of avoidance conditioning give rise to chronically exaggerated answering-effect sequences. If so, limited rhinencephalic intervention— e.g., in the hippocampal-amygdaloid region— might produce far better results in such patients than it has done in psychotics of other types.

Bibliography

Books of Single or Joint Authorship

BAILEY, P., AND VON BONIN, G. *The Isocortex of Man.* University of Illinois Press, 1951.

CAMPBELL, J. D. *Manic-Depressive Disease.* Lippincott, 1953.

CHAPLIN, J. P., AND KRAWIEC, T. S. *Systems and Theories of Psychology.* Holt, Rinehart & Winston, 1960.

FREUD, S. *Beyond the Pleasure Principle.* Liveright, 1950.

———. *Dream Psychology,* McCann, 1921.

FULTON, J. F. *Physiology of the Nervous System.* 3rd edition, Oxford, 1949.

———. *Frontal Lobotomy and Affective Behavior.* Norton, 1951.

GLEES, P. *Experimental Neurology.* Oxford, 1961.

GLOVER, E. *Freud or Jung?* Meridian Books, 1956.

HERRICK, C. J. *The Brain of the Tiger Salamander.* University of Chicago Press, 1948.

———. *The Evolution of Human Nature.* University of Texas Press, 1956.

HESS, W. R. *Diencephalon.* Grune and Stratton, 1954.

MAIER, N. R. F. *Frustration.* McGraw-Hill, 1949.

MCCULLOCH, W. *Finality and Form.* C. C. Thomas, 1952.

MILLER, G. A.; GALANTER, E.; AND PRIBRAM, K. H. *Plans and the Structure of Behavior.* Holt, Rinehart & Winston, 1960.

RAMÓN Y CAJAL, S. *Histologie du Système Nerveux,* Paris, Maloine, 1909 (2 vols).

SHERRINGTON, C. S. *The Integrative Action of the Nervous System.* Yale, 1906; Yale paperbound, 1961.

SHOLL, D. A. *The Organization of the Cerebral Cortex.* Wiley, 1956.

TINBERGEN, N. *The Study of Instinct.* Oxford, 1951.

WALTER, W. G. *The Living Brain.* Norton, 1953.

WHITEHEAD, A. N. *Essays in Science and Philosophy.* Philosophical Library, 1948.

Collections of Papers in Book Form

Behavior and Evolution. Anne Roe and George G. Simson, eds. Yale, 1958.

Biological and Biochemical Bases of Behavior. H. F. Harlow and C. N. Woolsey, eds. University of Wisconsin Press, 1958.

Biology and Comparative Physiology of Birds, Vol. II. A. J. Marshall, ed. Academic Press, 1961.
Biology of Mental Health and Disease. 27th Annual Conference of the Milbank Memorial Fund. Hoeber, 1952.
Central Nervous System and Behavior. Transactions, 2nd and 3rd Conferences, Josiah Macy Jr. Foundation, 1959, 1960.
Classics in Psychology. T. Shipley, ed. Philosophical Library, 1961.
Current Approaches to Psychoanalysis. P. H. Hoch and J. Zubin, eds. Grune & Stratton, 1960.
Current Trends in Psychology. University of Pittsburgh Press, 1955.
Evolution of Nervous Control. A. D. Bass, ed. American Association for the Advancement of Science, 1959.
Handbook of Experimental Psychology. S. S. Stevens, ed. Wiley, 1951.
Handbook of Physiology, Section 1: Neurophysiology, Vols. II and III. John Field and H. W. Magoun, eds. American Physiological Society, 1960.
Human Anatomy, 11th edn. J. P. Schaeffer, ed. McGraw-Hill, 1953.
Lectures on Experimental Psychiatry. University of Pittsburgh Press, 1961.
Neuropharmacology. Transactions, 2nd and 3rd Conferences, Josiah Macy, Jr., Foundation, 1956, 1957.
Present Day Psychology. A. A. Roback, ed. Philosophical Library, 1955.
Problems of Consciousness. H. A. Abramson, ed. 2nd Conference, Josiah Macy, Jr., Foundation, 1951.
Recent Advances in Biological Psychiatry. J. Wortis, ed. Grune & Stratton, 1960.
Regional Neurochemistry. S. S. Kety and J. Elkes, eds. Pergamon, 1961.
Reticular Formation of the Brain. H. H. Jasper, L. D. Proctor, R. S. Knighton, W. C. Noshay, and R. T. Costello, eds. Little, Brown, 1958.
Sensory Deprivation. P. Solomon et al., eds. Harvard, 1961.

Author Index

NOTE: In this section of the Index, figures set in italics refer to the "References and Notes" section of this volume.

A

Abt, J. P., *207*
Adey, W. R., 99, 122, 147, *239, 240, 241, 243, 245*
Akert, K., 168, 172, 179, *249, 250*
Allison, T., 74
Amassian, V. E., 98, 100
Amstey, M. S., *196*
Anand, B. K., *239*
Andy, O. J., *245, 246*
Antonitis, J. J., 161, 185
Appel, J. B., *205, 210*
Arduini, A., 116, *221, 238*
Arnold, M., 67, *197*
Ayala, G. F., 112

B

Bagehot, W., 86
Bailey, P., 40, 51, 54, 56-60, 67, 70, 71, 88, 89, 94, 113, 154, *210, 211, 214, 219, 220, 222, 257*
Barbeau, A., *257*
Baumgarten, R. v., *212, 215*
Beach, F. A., 5, 6, *195*
Belekhova, M. G., 17, *197*
Bernard, C., 17
Betz, W., 59
Bishop, G. H., 99, 110-111, 113, 178, 190, *211, 237, 258*
Bodian, D., *211-212*
Bonin, G. v., 40, 51, 54, 56-60, 62, 67, 70, 71, 88, 89, 94, 113, 192, *211, 214, 216, 219, 220, 222, 224, 257*
Bonvallet, M., 116 fn.
Brookhart, J. M., *197*
Brutkowski, S., *244*
Buchwald, N. A., 120 fn., *254-255*
Bureš, J., 100, 124, *240, 241*
Burns, B. D., 105

C

Campbell, J. D., *259*
Cardon, P. V., 155, *247*
Chambers, W. W., 26, 102, 107
Chaplin, J. P., *225*
Chow, K. L., *210*
Clare, M., *258*
Clark, W. E. le Gros, 124
Costa, E., 180, 181, *257*
Courville, J., *236*
Cowan, J., *225*

D

Davidson, J. M., *236*
Davis, E. W., 154
Davis, R. C., 141, *243*
Delgado, J. M. R., 23, *243, 254*
Dement, W. C., *210*
Demetrescu, Mihai, 129, 163 fn.
Demetrescu, Mihai, and Demetrescu, Maria, 155 fn., *236, 248, 256*
Denny, M. R., *246-247*
De Robertis, E. P. D., 178, *212, 257*
Descartes, R., 97
Domino, E. F., 180, *257*
Droz, B., *212*
Dusser de Barenne, J. G., *215, 218*

E

Economo, C. v., 59
Essman, W. B., *207*
Euler, U. S. v., 181, *257*
Evarts, E. V., 162, *198, 249*

F

Falconer, M. A., *240, 246*
Feindel, W., 99
Feldman, S. M., 128, *240*
Finer, B. L., 157 fn.

Flechsig, P., 70, 71, 86
Fogel, L. J., *258*
Fox, S. S., 142, *243*, *255*
Freeman, W., *247*
Freeman, W. J., *198*
French, J. D., 98, 108, 118 fn., 121, *203*, *237*, *239*, *254*
Freud, S., 49, 64, 176, *210*, *217*, *250-252*
Fulton, J. F., 54, 71, 148-149, 150, 160, *197*, *199*, *202*, *203*, *206*, *211*, *216*, *217*, *219*, *235*, *240*, *241*, *243*, *244*, *247*, *249*
Fuster, J. M., 116, 183, *258*

G

Galambos, R., 134, *240-241*
Galanter, E., *209*, *251*
Gastaut, H., 9, 26, 100, 134, 185, 186, *210*, *242*
Geiger, A., *203*
Gerard, R. W., 35, *207*
Gibbs, F. A., *223*, *249*
Glees, P., 58, 93, 104 fn., 119 fn., 122 fn., *225*, *231*, *238*
Glickman, S. E., 128, *240*
Gloor, P., 132, 133, 173, *240*, *241*, *243*
Glover, E., *195*
Goldstine, H. H., *225*
Grastyán, E., *238*, *240*, *243*
Green, J. D., *211*, *212*, *215*, *237*, *239*, *242*, *249*
Grundfest, H., 178, *212*, *225*, *257*
Gurdjian, E. S., *202*

H

Hagbarth, K.-E., 157 fn., *237*
Hainer, R. M., *215*
Hassler, R., 108, 113, *237*
Hausman, L., *219*
Hawkins, D. R., *253*
Haxo, F. T., *205*
Heath, R. G., 134, 182, *242*, *243*, *257-258*
Henkin, L., *224*
Hernández-Peón, R., 72, *237*, *244*, *248*
Hernstein, R. J., *211*

Herrick, C. J., 22, 110, 113, 120 fn. 121, 123-124, 133, 134, 136-137, 142-144, 152-153, 154-155, 157, 173, *198*, *202*, *205*, *215*, *221*, *223*, *235*, *237*, *238*, *240*, *242*
Herzet, J.-P., *237*
Hess, W. R., 97, 130, 155, *203*, *234*
Heuser, G., *248*
Himwich, H. E., 112, 119 fn., *237*
Hoagland, H., 17, *196*
Hoch, P. H., *197*
Hoff, H. E., *197*
Hubel, D. H., 93 fn., *225-234*
Hugelin, A., 116 fn.
Hughes, J. R., 176, *250*
Hunsperger, R. W., 155
Hydén, H., *207*, *208*, *213*, *228*

I

Ingram, W. R., 16-17, 158, *196*, *202*, *244*
Ingvar, D. H., *243*
Ironside, R., 69

J

Jabbur, S. J., 100
Jacobsen, C. F., *247*
Jasper, H. H., 72, 77, 103, 111, 112-114, 116-117, 118, 182, *206*, *218*, *221*, *222*, *235*, *237*, *238*, *254*, *258*
John, E. R., *210*
Jouvet, M., 104, *236*
Jung, R., 108, *237*

K

Kaada, B. R., 144, 147, *243*
Kamin, L. J., *246*
Karamyan, A. I., 17, *197*
Kerr, D. I. B., *237*
Kety, S., 97, *235*
Kleyntjens, F., 108
Kling, A., *243*
Knapp, D. E., 180, *257*
Koffka, K., *225*
Krasne, F. B., 130 fn.
Krätzig, H., 34
Krawiec, T. S., *225*
Kruger, L., 10, 120, *196*

Author Index / 265

Kuypers, H. G. J. M., 98, 101, 108, 109, *235*

L

Landau, W., *258*
Lashley, K. S., 97, *234-235*
Leblond, C. P., *212*
Lewin, K., 161 fn.
Liddell, H. S., *195, 197, 199-200*
Lilly, J. C., 128, 130, *240*
Lindsley, D. B., 8, 76, 111-112, *196, 199, 216, 221, 222, 235, 237, 238, 244, 247, 248*
Lishajko, F., 181, *257*
Livingston, R. B., 77, 97, *222, 234*
Lloyd, D. P. C., 108
Longo, V. G., 130, *257*
Lorente de Nó, R., 36, 54, 55, 60, 61, 62, 74, 75, 88, 99, 166, 183, 189 fn., *206, 208, 211, 213, 216, 219, 231, 233*

M

McCulloch, W., 28, 35, 40, 43, 72, *199, 206, 208, 209, 211, 233, 238, 242, 245*
McGeer, P. L., 181, *257*
MacKay, D. M., 35
MacLean, P. D., 98, 120, 121, 124, 135, 144, 173, 175, *209, 216, 240, 243, 245, 248*
Magoun, H. W., 97, *211*
Maier, N. R. F., 21, 161, *197*
Mancia, M., *212*
Margules, D. L., 126 fn.
Marrazzi, A. S., 17, *197, 216, 243, 257*
Marshall, W. H., *230*
Mason, J. W., *198, 246*
Masserman, J. H., 137, *242, 248*
Matsumoto, H., *249*
Maxwell, D. S., *211*
Mazurowski, J. A., 176, *250*
Meikle, T. H. Jr., 101, *206*
Melzack, R., 34, 119 fn., *207, 249*
Mempel, E., *244*
Meyer, A., and Meyer, M. (and Glees, P.), 58
Michael, R. P., *236*

Miller, G. A., *209, 251*
Miller, N. E., *196, 197*
Milner, B., 39, 44, *208*
Mirsky, A. F., 155, *247*
Money, J., *196*
Monnier, M., 112, 180, *257*
Moore, A. U., *196*
Morgane, P. J., 99, *239*
Morillo, A., 73-74, *209, 221*
Morrell, F., *242*
Morris, H. (and Schaeffer, J.P.), *202, 203, 239*
Moruzzi, G., 97, 100, *202*
Mountcastle, V. B., 33, 36, 37, 44, 55, 93, *199, 206, 208*
Mukawa, J., *245*
Murphy, J. P., *215, 218*

N

Nachmansohn, D., 115, *237*
Nakahama, H., 93, *225, 248*
Nauta, W. J. H., 58, 74, 98, 121, 122-123, *216, 223, 239, 244*
Neumann, J. v., 68
Ngowyang, G., 59
Nielsen, J. M., *221*
Nozdrachev, A. E., 180, *257*

O

O'Brien, J. H., 142, *243, 255*
Olds, J., 9, 23, 99, 125, 126 fn., 130, 154, 155, 169, *240, 249*
Orbeli, L. A., 17

P

Paillard, J., 107 fn., *247*
Pampiglione, G., *240, 246*
Papez, J. W., 77, 98, 110, 121, 153, *218, 222, 239, 244*
Patton, H. D., *225*
Pauling, L., *206*
Pechtel, C., 137, 147, *242, 248*
Penfield, W., 35, 77, 97, 99, *208*
Petsche, H., 121, 123, *216, 239*
Pitts, W., *199, 233*
Poggio, G. F., *242*
Powell, T. P. S., *199, 206*
Pribram, K., 10, 35, 60, 70-71, 76, 91, 99, 120, 147, 151, 168, 175,

179, 190, 192-193, *196, 206, 207, 209, 216, 220, 221, 222, 235, 239, 243, 247, 248, 249-250, 251*
Prosser, C. L., *205*
Purpura, D. P., 98, 103, 111, 156 fn., 178, 182, 185, 190 fn., *199, 212, 218, 221, 237, 249*

R

Ralston, B. L., *256*
Ramón y Cajal, S., 99, 190, *205, 211, 221*
Redding, F., 170 fn.
Regnér, E. G., *211*
Reynolds, O. E., *205*
Ricci, G. F., 116-117
Romanowski, W., 112, 180, *257*
Rosin, R., 22, *198*
Ruch, T. C., *225*
Rusinov, V. S., *248*

S

Sadowski, B., 180, *257*
Sargant, W., 186
Sato, K., *199*
Saul, G. D., *240, 244*
Sawyer, C. H., *240, 244*
Schaeffer, J. P., *202, 203, 239*
Scheibel, A., and Scheibel, M., 33, 36, 44, 98, 99, 111, 156 fn., 157, *207, 209, 216, 222, 235, 237, 238*
Schlag, J. D., 112, 113, 115, *237*
Schreiner, L., *243*
Schusterman, R., *243*
Scott, J. P., *214*
Scoville, W. B., 39, 44, *208*
Seifter, J., 180, *257*
Selye, H., *205*
Sharpless, S. K., 112, *206*
Sherrington, C. S., 46, 123, 171, 173, *201, 204-205, 209, 211*
Sherwood, S., 115, *237*
Sholl, D. A., 36, 54, 55, 99, *208, 211, 213, 235*
Shulov, A., 22, *198*
Siegfried, J., 170 fn.
Smith, C. E., *213, 235*
Snider, R. S., *199*
Sokolov, E. N., 34, *207*

Sperry, R. W., 26, 71, 101, 106, 138, *205-206, 208, 220, 239*
Sprague, J. M., 21, 26, 101-103, 107, 118, 135, *197, 206, 213*
Stanishevskaya, N. N., *198*
Stein, L., 180, *257*
Steiner, W. G., 112, *237, 248*
Stellar, E., 26, 102
Stériade, M., 129, 163 fn.
Sternbach, R. A., *203*
Stevenson, L., *258*
Sutherland, N. S., *227*
Sutro, L., 72
Svorad, D., *196*
Sweeney, B. M., *205*

T

Talbot, S. A., *230*
Tatetsu, S., *257-258*
Teuber, H.-L., 168, *208, 220, 249*
Thomas, J. O., *246-247*
Thompson, R., 99, 154, 155, 158-159, 179, *247*
Thompson, W. R., 34, *207*
Tinbergen, N., 5, 6, 15 fn., 22, *195, 196, 198, 206, 207, 237*
Towe, A. L., 100
Tucker, V. A., *205*

V

Van Buren, J. M., *254*
Van Meter, W. G., 112
Villablanca, J., 105
Vladimirov, G. E., 63, 68, 184, *213, 216*
Voronin, L. G., 135

W

Wada, J., 98, 181, *257*
Waelder, R., *195*
Waller, H. J., 98, 100
Walter, W. G., 83, *223*
Wang Tai-an, 17, *197*
Ward, A., 98, 107-108, *212, 213, 236, 258*
Webster, C. L., *246*
Welsh, J. H., 24, *205*
Whitehead, A. N., *223-224*
Whitehorn, J. C., 38, 51, *195*

Whitlock, D. G., 58, 74
Wiesel, T., 93 fn., *225-234*
Williams, D., 80, *223*
Wolpe, J., *210*
Wyke, B. D., *223, 243*

Y

Yakovlev, P. I., *217-218*
Young, J. Z., *221*

Subject Index

A

"Abstract" memories, 57, 58, 65-6, 70, 72, 83-4, 87, 89, 139, 156 fn., 163, 165, 184, 251-2: as anti-entropic, 90: as comprising meta-informational system, 48-9, 139: and conceptual Gestalten, 225: and dreams, 250-53: first-order, and elaborated "type" memories, 252-3: and functions of cortical layer VI, 219: as mediating logical transformations of basal memory data, 85: and rational-conscious self, 188, 218: as residues of "thought," 48: and thought-processes, 223, 224

Acalculia, 223

Acetylcholine, 180, 181, 236: alerting, 112; blocked by atropine, 112 fn., 180

Acetylcholinesterase, *see* Cholinesterase

Actions, organization of, in frontal cortex, 247

Activation, nonspecific, 59, 141 fn., 155 fn.: accelerative and decelerative phases of, 163: and hippocampus, 170 fn.: inhibitory component in, 103: neocortical control of, 160: phasic and tonic forms, 111, 113: as reducing prebehavioral delay, 158: tonic neurohumoral, 239; as demonstrated by cross-perfusion, 111, 178-9

Acute emotional experience (episode), 38, 51, 163, 195: and adolescence, 188: de-differentiative effects of, 189

Adenosine triphosphate (ATP), laminar distribution of, in rat neocortex, 63-4, 68, 90, 213, 216

Adolescence, reorganization of basal memory-systems in, 188

Agraphia, 223

Aggressiveness, effect of cingulate lesions on, 147: and central grey, 243

Alerting, and cortical "strip" regions, 254: and gating of sensory inputs, 248: and "regarding reaction," 174

Allocortex, 50, 60, 120, 137

Alpha (activity, neocortex), excitability cycle, 133, 199: scanning function, 83-4

Amblystoma tigrinum, 204: basal optic system, 221, 238: brain of, 124, 133, 142-4: disparity in development of receptor and effector divisions of CNS, 139, 242: forebrain motor and sensory areas, 142-4: interpeduncular system, 152: reticular formation, 110: three principal fields in brain of, 153

γ-Aminobutyric acid, 17, 180, 181

Ammon's formation, 120

d-Amphetamine, alerting, 112: and

268 / THE PHYSICAL FOUNDATIONS OF THE PSYCHE

food-getting behavior, 126, 146, 180-1: and reactivation of avoidance conditioning, 210
Amygdala, 69, 79, 80, 108, 120 fn., 121, 130, 152, 170, 173, 243, 245: basolateral nuclei, 120; hyperphagia and, 122; caudate spindling, 253: emergency functions, 143-4, 240, 244: and "emotionally charged" memories, 242: and mounting reactions, 145, 243: and neocortical inhibition, 151: and ovulation, 216, 240: projections of medial forebrain bundle to, 123: and psychomotor seizures, 240: route of propagation of seizures of, 241, 245; loss of contact with environment in, 241: self-stimulation in, 243: seizure-proneness of, 246: sexual, feeding, and defense responses represented in, 132, 144, 146, 173: stimulation of, and 17-hydroxy-corticosteroid levels, 150: and temporal lobe seizures, 242
Amygdalectomy, effects of, 144
Amygdaloid complex, centrencephalic projections of, 99: and frontal cortex, 164: and *gyrus cinguli*, 147: stimulation of, and behavior, 169-170
Analogical reflex, 38
Answering effect, 19-24, 36, 46, 115, 117, 118 fn., 128, 158, 167, 171, 181, 191, 200, 240, 245: on cessation of brain-stimulation, 131: distortions of, and psychic disorders, 148, 167, 187-8: and "functional unanimity," 171: mechanisms involved in, 198-202: and spinal induction, 171, 201, 208: and tonic immobility, 196: trains of, in rhinencephalon, 133, 145, 150, 201; role in dreams, 251
Anterior commissure, 222
Anterior horn, termination of medullary tegmental fibers in, 101
Anterior lobe (cerebellum), effect of ipsi- and contralateral stimulation, and stimulation of the vermis, on muscle-spindle discharge, 104 fn.: frequency-specificity of inhibitory and facilitatory effects, obtained from vermis, 104 fn.
Anterior perforated substance, 121: nucleus basalis, 121, 152
Anxiety, effect of chronic, on thought, 201: in neurotics, 188, 201: and repression, 186: and rigor in thought, 177
Apes, prepuberal sexual behavior in, 5
Arcuate fasciculus, 220
Arousal, 34, 111, 112, 118, 128-9, 141, 142, 156, 174, 183, 184, 256: "attending" phase, 163: and cerebellum, 169: facilitatory aftereffect, 163 fn.: from lateral tegmentum, 125: neocortical, and hippocampal spreading depression, 241: onset phase, 200
Ascending inhibitory system (ventral pontine reticular formation, caudate, ventralis anterior), 256
Association cortex, 51, 74, 77, 182 (*see also* Cerebral cortex, intrinsic sectors)
Association fiber systems, 32, 36, 69-70, 75, 80, 86-7, 216, 218: cortical layers of origin, 219: dorsoventral bundles, 220: laminar distribution, 219
Association nuclei (thalamus), 44, 60, 65, 71, 73, 78, 118, 151, 182, 206
Associational processes, intermodal, as figuring in memory-formation, 31-2: linear, in dreams, 252: older neurophysiological view of, 70: "subjective," 85
Associationism, doctrine of, 35
Atropine blocking of cholinergic activation, neocortex, 180
Attention, 26, 43, 57, 72, 92, 174: caudate and ventralis anterior in, 174 fn.: competitive processes underlying, 73: and frontal intrinsic cortex, 168: and gating of sensory inputs, 248: mechanisms involved

Subject Index / 269

in perceptual, 117, 146: orgasm and, 146: and variance of unit activity, 198 (*see also* Partitioning)

Auditory pathway, divergence of inputs in, 225

Augmenting responses (neocortex), origins, 258: and recruitment, 258

Autonomic system, 144, 197, 246, 259: contrecoup in, 19: "defense" responses of, as damaging, 139 fn.: functional relations between two main branches of, 16, 174: homeostatic and motivational-affective functions of, 18, 202, 203, 204-5: medullary reflexes, 158, 202 (*see also* Parasympathetic and Sympathetic systems)

Averages, nerve-nets as computers of, 233

Avoidance (learned), 185: and anterior temporal cortex, 172: and anterodorsal hippocampus, 145: and caudate, 243-4: effect of predominance of, 188, 246: effect of sympathectomy and parasympathectomy on, 17: and frustration, 161: and interpeduncular system, 98-9, 154 ff.: persistence of auditory, visual, and olfactory, in monkeys, 137, 242: persistence in higher and lower evolutionary forms, 210

Axon, all-or-none activity, as quantum of action of nerve-nets, 178: as special adaptation of nerve, 178, 212

Axonal action-patterns (firing orders), 83, 163, 178, 184: half-life of neocortical, 39: inherited, and innate behavior, 25: lability of frontal intrinsic, 164: and memory, 33, 36-7, 46, 61-2, 64, 67, 93-4, 178, 212

B

Beagles, effect of early visual restriction on, 249

Behavior, adaptive, and frontal ablation, 138; and temporal lobe lesions, 138: answering effect and "serial variety" of, 171, 201, 208: collapse of adaptive, following bilateral lemniscal section (cat), 102: conditioned and rational, compared, 50, 52-3: deficits in, in mammals, following decortication, 25: differentiation of, from primitive "total patterns," 230 fn.: effect of cingulate ablation on maternal, 147: effect of medially and laterally placed reticular lesions on, 101-2: emotion and memory in, 6, 10: in fear, as forced, 174: and frontal intrinsic cortex, 167-9: increased variability, during "extinction," 161: innate, and cortical structure, 60-1; in higher forms, 204; and rhinencephalon, 134: learned, and neocortex, 204; and rhinencephalon, 134: neocortical "models" of, 165-6, 168: new-learning phase of, 163, 185, 189: orientative and cortical "strip" regions, 254: primitivization, in fear or rage, 75 fn.: rostral migration of centers controlling, 109, 135, 158: sexual, 5; and rhinencephalon, 144-5: two basic forms of instinctive, 16; and compound olfactory system, 173: unpredictability, and neocortical potential, 171

Betz cells, 59, 63: effects of thermocoagulation, Betz cell layer, motor cortex, 215

Biasing, of neurons, 288 ff.

Bradycardia, 20-1: at onset of arousal, 141, 174: in primary fear, 197

Brain, capacity, and life-expectancy of pre-civilized man, 192, 233: course followed by evolution of, 133: evolutionary evagination of dorsal pallium, 124: neuronal population of human, 35, 211: segregation of receptor and effector functions in, 176

Brain-washing, 185 fn.

Broca's speech area, 247

Bufotenine, 17
Bundle, corticopontine, of Arnold, 71 fn., 108, 256: of Türck, 71 fn., 108, 256

C

Calleja, islands of, 60: in septum, 216
Cajal-Retzius cells, 190 fn.
Catatonia, 115: and tonic immobility, 196: and ventromedial n., hypothalamus, 244
Catecholamines, 180, 181
Caudate, and conditioned alimentary behavior (cat), 254-5: and cortical desynchronization, 142: and inhibition of aggressiveness, 243; of neocortex, 142 fn., 176 fn., 239, 244, 248, 254: and "regarding reaction," 174 fn.: role in "freezing," 255: and seizures, frontal granular cortex, 242: spindling, 120 fn., 253-4: stimulation of, in man, 254: and ventral pontine inhibitory system, 256
Central grey, and aggressiveness, 243: and tonic activating system, 236
Central integration, 54, 97, 118: collapse of, in bilateral lemniscal cats, 118-19: decortication and, 100: midbrain reticular formation as seat of, 101, 103: as a synergy, 119
Central nervous system (CNS), circular interactions in, 155, 166: degrees of freedom attainable by receptor and effector divisions of, 139: development of receptor and effector functions in salamander, 242: as effector apparatus, 106, 138, 208: effector and receptor divisions, and motivational-affective functions, 142 ff., 172-3: feedback action of effector on receptor divisions, 140, 161 fn.: influence of receptor on effector divisions, 139, 141: intelligence as receptor system activity, 139-40: order of myelination in mammalian, 220: phylogenetically older divisions as mediating emergency responses, 174
Centralis lateralis (thal.), 73, 74, 112
Centralis medialis (thal.), 112
Centrum medianum (thal.), 222
Cerebellum, 104, 108, 153: anterior lobe, and ventromedial n., hypothalamus, 244: effect of stimulation, on evoked potentials, auditory cortex, 199; on sham rage, 202: facilitatory and inhibitory effects from anterior lobe vermis, 199: migration of cells of external lamina in neonate, 190 fn.: "slow" response to reticular arousal, 169, 249
Cerebral cortex, 183, 185: agranular, 58, 60, 165: angular gyrus, 223, 253: area *agranularis gigantopyramidalis,* 59: area 18 (parastriate), p. 31: areas 18–19, pp. 206, 231: area 19, projections to the pulvinar, 219: area 22 (temporal), 31: auditory, neuronal population, monkey, 225: composed of vertical internuncial chains, 88: dysgranular, 140, 165: external lamina (I-IV), 40, 48, 61, 86, 163, 172, 206, 251: metabolic rates and variance of unit activity in, 213; and "noise," 184: extrinsic (analyzer) areas, 17, 33, 40, 57, 62, 70, 94, 129, 138, 182; as input-dependent, 213; and posterior intrinsic, compared, 43, 66-7, 77, 116, 229, 233; realization of combinative potential, 215; responses of, and midbrain reticular formation, 238: frontal granular, propagation of seizures arising in, 242: frontal intrinsic (association), 42, 59, 64, 69, 77, 218; and core emergency systems, 131, 141 fn., 151, 176; holding functions of, 138, 164; and nonspecific input, 163-4; and organization of behavior, 141, 163 ff.; and psychotic regression, 189; and

reticulocortical input, 116, 249: function of bands of large pyramids in, 56, 64, 83, 88, 93, 139-40, 212-15: functional organization, cat somatosensory, 208: generalized eulaminate, 51, 52, 56, 57-8, 60, 71, 77-8, 83, 87, 139, 214; frontal and posterior, compared, 164: internal lamina (V-VI), 40, 46, 48; effector functions of, 218; memory-functions of, 59, 61, 64, 184, 216; metabolic rates and variance of unit activity in, 213; and sleep, 253: intrinsic (association) areas, 70-94; problem of informational supply, 71-2: mesial, 60; motor representation in (monkey), 176: motor cortex (area 4), 108, 248; auditory projections to, 248; projections to gracile and cuneate nuclei, 101: plexiform (tangential) layer, 36, 50, 54, 58, 60, 62, 63, 69, 87, 89, 113, 216; communicating functions of, 75, 182, 184, 219; as mechanism establishing temporary connections, 190; regression of horizontal cells in, 190; structure, 111; as terminal link in reticular system, 111, 190: posterior intrinsic (association) areas, 17, 44, 48, 59, 62, 64, 65, 69-94, 117, 129, 131, 138, 172; and attending reactions, 175-6; and behavioral sequences, 168-9; and extrinsic, compared, 43, 116, 229; and frontal intrinsic, compared, 42, 59; and intelligence, 140, 142, 252; and midbrain reticular formation, 158, 163; and subcortical reward systems, 115, 176: rhinencephalic influence in frontal, 135-6: as seat of "consciousness," 217: second motor area, 93, 248: second sensory area, 93, 248: second visual area, 230 fn.: as sorter of invariances, 31, 32-3: "strip" regions, 32, 69, 71 fn., 73, 116, 118 fn., 147, 176, 223, 254; and conditioned responses, 187: structure of major subdivisions, 54 ff.: supracallosal cortex, motor representation in (monkey), 176: vertex, 165; desynchronization at, and caudate stimulation, 248: vertical columns in, 55, 82, 113; mode-specificity in, 76, 78, 88, 93; Mountcastle (specific) type, 33, 35, 37, 44, 60, 88, 238; Scheibel (nonspecific) type, 33, 44, 46, 69, 222; in striate cortex, 226 ff.
Cerebral synaptic inhibitors, 17
Chimpanzee, innate fear of snakes in, 252
Cholinesterase, 115: and serotonin, 181
Cingulate (*gyrus cinguli*), 120, 131: anterior (area 24), 144; and "freezing," 147; as part of reward system effector apparatus, 148: anterior cingulectomy and paranoid psychoses, 148, 160: area 23, pp. 176, 256: area 23-24 ablation, 147: and behavior, 169 fn.: and frontal cortex, 151: functions of, 146: and hippocampus, 147, 175, 241: motor representation in (monkey), 176: neocortical spindling elicitable from mid-, 256-7: posterior, 147: pregenual, effect of lesions to, 147: projections of anterior thalamic nuclei to, 149: seizure-proneness, 246: "strip" regions in, 176: and vocalization, 144
Cingulum, and cingulate spindling in neocortex, 257: distribution, 220
Cistudo (box tortoise), brain of, 124
Cochlea, 92
Cochlear nuclei, neuron counts (monkey), 225
Colliculi, differentiation of, 206
Commissural fibers, cerebral cortex, 69, 75
Conditionability, and deconditionability, of higher and lower evolutionary forms, 135, 205: of decorticate mammals, 25, 100
Conditioning, 26, 27, 48-50, 65, 165,

188: avoidance- and mental-emotional disorders in man, 148, 259: extinction of, 185, 214; mechanisms, 209-10: Freud's view of, 210: and neocortex, 210: olfactory, 137, 242: rostral migration of "centers" of, 106: trace-formation at midbrain and other neuraxial levels during, 134, 155, 210
Conflict, 200-1
Consolidation (of CR's), 137 fn., 155, 207: and hippocampus, 170
Contrecoup, 19: facilitatory, as relieving primary inhibition, 115, 130
Core-systems, 32, 50-53, 60, 63, 65, 72, 73, 75, 79, 81, 86, 93, 129: as competing with neocortex for control of the thalamus, 189: and dreams, 251-2: dynamogenic, and frontal cortex, 151: influence upon "intrinsic" activities of neocortex, 136: neuronal populations, 211: release of, in frustration, 248-9: and tendency of mind to work in contraries, 162
Cornu ammonis, 220
Corpus callosum, 36: origin of fibers, 62 and fn., 69 and fn., 219
Corpus striatum, 111, 120, 133, 135, 244
Cortico-thalamocortical relay, 71, 252: and nonspecific system, 166: role in memory-formation, 32
Crescendo stimulation, 127
Cuneate nucleus, 100, 116
Curiosity, 51
Cyclostomes, 238
Cytoarchitecture, of neocortex, 54 ff.: relation to function, 67, 104-5

D

Dendritic networks, 36, 56, 61, 62, 63, 89: as analogue systems, 162 fn.: as chemoreceptor, 178: as "collecting" apparatus, 214: "flooding" of, 184, 258
Denervation sensitization, 107, 229: in neurally isolated cortex, 105 fn.

Depersonalization, and stimulation of the amygdala, 144, 241
Depression, involutional, 115: and emergency system, 148-9
Desynchronization, hippocampal, 169: neocortical, and caudate spindling, 254; mediated by acetylcholine, eserine, or pilocarpine, 180; in rhombencephalic sleep, 253
Diagonal band of Broca, 120, 121
Didelphis (Virginia opossum), brain of, 124
Diencephalon, 111, 128
Di-isopropylfluorophosphate (DFP), 212
Ding an sich, neurophysiological reasons for unknowability of, 92
Discrimination, perceptual, 141: visual, and bilateral inferotemporal resection, 220
Distance receptors, 78 fn.
Divergence of input, auditory system, 225: and functional flexibility of the CNS, 230: in neocortex, 228
Dopamine, in basal ganglia, 180
Dorsal longitudinal fasciculus of Schütz, 98, 154-5: origins of, 123, 134
Dorsal pallium, three divisions of, in reptiles, 133
Dorsomedial grey, 111
Dorsomedial nucleus (thal.), 58, 60, 151, 164, 175, 206, 241, 250: fibers from frontal eyefields and orbital cortex, 219
Dreams, central nervous mechanisms underlying, 250-53: of children, 252: displacement and condensation in, 251: as paralleling subcortical answering effect trains, 251: symbolism, 251
Drives, cyclical recurrence of, and spinal induction mechanisms compared, 171: as diminished by actions, 156: as distinct from motives and emotions, 7: genesis of, 132, 171: intensification of, and emotion, 159, 249

Dytiscus (beetle), activity in isolated cord of, 237

E

EEG, and behavioral changes, 258: focal slowing in neocortical, during extinction of conditioned responses, 185-6
Effector states, as inhibiting receptor-system activities, 146
Electroshock, 115
Emergency responses, biological rationale of, 39: and normal survival responses, compared, 161, 200: and *pallium basale,* 173: and rhinencephalic effector functions, 172: as stimulus-bound, 174: as stresses, 205
Emergency system, 16, 33, 39, 45, 114, 117, 126, 129, 130, 131, 170: and acquired stupidity, 218: action of, in altering CR's, 185: and caudate-ventralis anterior, 255-6: and effector divisions of the CNS, 142: functional relations with normal survival system, 174: inhibitory action as limiting rage, 172: inhibitory action on neocortex, 197: as mediating massive mobilization, 179: and normal survival system, compared, 18: and psychic disorders, 148: release, 147 fn.: and rhythmic movements, 237: and ventral hippocampus, 245
Emotion, as arising from drives or motives thwarted, 8, 11: capacity for, as mark of evolutionary advance, 11: as distinct from drives and motives, 7: genesis of, 132: as giving rise to thought and conversely, 209: lessened by actions, 156: nature of, 132, 136: role in instinctive behavior, 4; in memory-formation, 43; in recall, 45: as source of improvisatory behavior, 9: visceral concomitants, 204
Encephalitis lethargica, 155
Encephalization of function, 26, 93, 106, 109: as increasing pre-behavioral delay, 157: and the rhinencephalon in man, 150
Endocrine feedback, as reinforcing central nervous motivational states, 17, 130, 141
Engram, theory of memory, 35
Entorhinalis, 120, 122, 176: ablation, and sensory fixation, 239: and projections of the dorsal and ventral hippocampus, 241
Epilepsy, 258
Epinephrine, 180: effect of intramuscular, on gastric contraction (cat), 203: and nor-, effects on cerebral blood turnover, 243: and nor-, effects on nerve, 180, 243: and tonic activation system, 111: and tonic immobility, 17, 197
Equipotentiality, Lashley's doctrine of cortical, 234
Ergotropic system, neurotransmitters of, 181
Eserine, 180, 212
Experimental neuroses, in sheep and goats, 199-200
Exteroceptors, evolutionary improvement as exceeding that of the interoceptors, 15
Extinction (of CR's), electrocortical events in, as mimicking thalamic deafferentation, 185: of long-standing CR's, 210: mechanisms involved in, 209-10: variable behavior phase in, 185
Extrapyramidal system, 51, 142, 153, 181

F

Fasciculus retroflexus, of Meynert, 121
Fainting, from psychological shock, relation to repression, 186
Fantasy, in relation to dreams, 251-2
Fear, 33, 115, 117, 118, 184, 205: changes in cerebral blood flow in, 203: depersonalization in, 241: "freezing" in, 238: as function of phylogenetically old divisions of CNS, 174: intensification, by in-

ternal blocking of an avoidance response, 159, 163: in man, following stimulation of the amygdala, 144: mixed autonomic signs in intense, 174: onset phase of, 145: psychological effects of intense, 141, 183: role of reward systems in, 246: and rhythmic movement, 237: states of, as stresses, 18; as physiologically threatening, 200: and "strip" regions, 254: threshold of, lowered by cingulate area 23-24 ablation, 147

Feeding responses, 153: blocking by *d*-amphetamine, scopolamine, 180: and lateral hypothalamus, 121: and *pallium basale,* 173

Ferocity, effect on, of amygdalectomy, 144; of cingulate area 23-24 ablation, 147, 148: enfeeblement of, by damage to emergency system, 172, 179

Figure-ground, 87, 225

Flechsig's terminal zones, 35, 89, 217 (*see also* Cerebral cortex, intrinsic sectors)

Forebrain, effects of blocking outflows of, to interpeduncular nucleus, 158: evolutionary expansion of, and innate behavior, 204: responses of, and midbrain reticular formation, 103

Forel's tract (tractatus fasciculorum tegmenti), 122, 134, 151

Forgetting, incompleteness of, 91: mechanisms of, in fearlike arousal, 184: and stress, 183

Fornix, 123, 241: precommissural, 121, 152: postcommissural, 122

Foveola, 93

Frontal eyefields, 206: "fast" pathway to, in man, 238: projections to dorsomedialis, 219

Frontal lobe, cingulate projections to, 151: as corresponding to core dynamogenic systems, 151: cytoarchitecture, 59: and delayed-action performance, 151: effect of stimulation on learning, and performance of the already learned, 249-50: lobotomy and topectomy, 160, 167: nonspecific input, 164: projections of dorsomedialis to, 151: rhinencephalic projections to, 164: and secondary olfactory system, 175

Fronto-occipital bundle, 220

Frustration, effects upon behavior, 9, 248-9: neurophysiological mechanisms underlying, 161, 249

Functional dominance, orders of, among structures of the CNS, 75, 119, 131, 136, 142 ff.; among receptor and effector divisions of the CNS, 158

Functional unanimity (consistency), principle of, among structures of the CNS, 81, 108, 135: mechanisms subserving, 104

G

Gamma motor system, 237

Ganser's tract, 122, 152

Gating, of nonspecific input, by hippocampus, 46, 143: reticular, in gracile and cuneate nuclei and olfactory bulb, 116, 118, 145: of sensory inputs, and frontal intrinsic cortex, 168: subcortical, of input to posterior intrinsic cortex, 43, 44, 51, 89

Gerstmann's syndrome, 139 fn., 223, 253

Gestalt psychology, and concept of progressive changes in memory, 87

Gestalten, conceptual, 225: perceptual, 87

Gestures, cortical organization of, and role of emotion in, 247

Globus pallidus, 108: caudate spindling in, 253

Golgi type II cells, 53, 55

Gracile nucleus, 100, 116: depression of evoked potentials in, by stimulation midbrain reticular formation, 248

Grammar, anticipatory and non- , in neocortical processes, 251: as embodying theorems, 47, 86

Gudden's (dorsal and ventral) tegmental nuclei, 122, 155

H

Habenula, 153: lateral and medial nn., 121: ventral, connections with dorsal thalamus in mammals, 152
Habituation (electrocortical), 112: as beginning at neocortical level, 129: to stimulation of subcortical "reward" areas, 128: sequence of events in, 160
Hallucinations, and stimulation of the amygdala, 144
Hamster, 35
Handedness, 113
Hiding reactions, and "strip" regions, 254: and ventralis anterior, 243-4
Hippocampal-cingulate system, and neocortex, compared, 175-6: and *pallium marginale,* 173: predominance of receptor functions in, 173, 179: sexual representation in, 145
Hippocampal formation, 123
Hippocampal gyrus, 243
Hippocampal pallium, and hypothalamus, 124: in *Necturus,* 123
Hippocampal seizure, paths of propagation, 241: functional decortication during, 241
Hippocampus, 39, 44, 46, 69, 79, 121, 122, 125, 152, 164, 169, 176: anterodorsal, 150, 152, 176, 245: and behavior, 169-70: and cingulate, 147, 241: dorsal, propagation of seizures, 245: and facilitation in neocortex, 151, 169, 176: as first brain-structure showing true cortex, 173: and memory-formation, 204: neocortical projections of, 156 fn.: neuronal population of (rabbit), 211: projections of ventral, 241: propagation, ventral seizures, 245: rebound feeding or avoidance, following stimulation of, 240: and receptor processes, 143: response to entorhinal stimulation, 241: rostral, and "emotionally charged" memories, 242: seizure-proneness, 246: sensitivity to anoxia, 209: stimulation of, and 17-OH-CS levels, 150, 198: spreading depression in, and neocortical arousal, 241: and temporal lobe seizures, 242: ventral, and fear-responses, 245
Histamine, 180, 181: and punishment systems, 182
Homeostasis, 18, 22, 24
Hyperorality, 172
Hypogastric nerve, facilitatory-inhibitory sequences obtainable from, 199
Hypogastric plexus, and ejaculation of semen, 19
Hypoglossal nucleus, 101
Hypoglycemia, stages in insulin-induced, in man, 119 fn.
Hypnosis, 210
Hypothalamus, 97, 98, 106, 122, 124, 153, 156, 202: anterior, role in sleep, 150, 244; midline, 244; extreme punishment from stimulation of, 127, 130: and frontal cortex, 164: lateral, and feeding reactions, 121, 126, 146, 203, 239; and reward reactions, 125, 126 fn., 235: medial, and "satiety," 121, 130, 150, 239; and punishment reactions, 130 fn., 150, 181, 235: midline, changes in stomach and duodenum following stimulation of (monkey), 203: periventricular zone, and fibers of dorsal longitudinal fasciculus of Schütz, 123: posterior, and amygdala, 241; and self-stimulation, 130; stimulation of, and changes in cerebral blood flow, 202-3; thalamic projections of, 151; and tonic activating system, 155 fn., 236, 244, 256: preoptic region, 203, 244: and rage, 155: and seizures of the amygdala, 241: and system of the mammillary peduncle, 124: transfer of functional primacy from, in evolution, 133: tuberal region,

203: and ventral hippocampus, 241: ventromedial nucleus, 160, 203; and anterior lobe, cerebellum, 244, 245

I

Ichthyopsida, dominance of hypothalamic influence in forebrain of, 124: dominance of olfaction in, 133
Id, 45, 188: not an item of direct conscious knowledge, 190 fn.
Idothea, 205
Imprinting, 214
Indeterminacy, areal gradient of, in neocortex, 77, 78, 79, 229
Induction, spinal, 171: negative, function of, 201: relation to answering effect principle, 201, 208
Inferior colliculi, neuronal population (monkey), 225
Inferior longitudinal fasciculus, 220
Information, distribution and processing of, in neocortex, 69-94, 139, 183: divergent distribution in auditory pathways, 225; in neocortex, 229: midbrain reticular formation, and economy of neocortical distribution, 91: processing, in CNS, 99; in frontal intrinsic cortex, 164; in midbrain and neocortex, compared, 99-102; in neocortex, impaired by motivational-affective states, 146: representation in neural nets, 89
Information theory, 91
Inhibition, and internuncials, 199: locally mediated, in neocortex, 36: nonspecific, in frontal cortex, 164: reticulocortical, 142, 163
Innate releasing mechanisms (IRM's), in man, 6
Insomnia, mechanisms in, 253
Instinct, apparent fundamental objectives of, 15: as not involving innate aims or ideas, 3
Instinctive actions, flow-sheet for, 5: role of emotion and memory in, 4
Instinctive gratification, nature of, 3 ff.

Insula (Island of Reil), 144: and amygdaloid seizure, 241
Intelligence, hippocampal system as constitutive of, 176: as a receptor system activity, 139: secondary olfactory and frontal intrinsic systems as regulative of, 177
Interpeduncular nucleus, 98, 121: effect of lesions to, 154 ff.: and Ganser's tract, 122: species differences in function, 154
Intersystemic relations (in CNS), 103-6, 109, 110, 136, 155: and core motivational systems, 127-9, 132, 145 ff.: role of neurohumors in, 239
Intracortical communication, major routes of, 36, 49, 71, 75, 82, 83, 182: noise-to-signal ratio in, 184 fn.
Irradiation, of information in neocortex, 78, 89, 91
Isthmus, 206

J

Juxtallocortex, 60: frontotemporal, 137

K

Kamin effect, 246
Klüver-Bucy syndrome, 139
Knowledge, distinguished from conditioning, 27
Koniocortex, 40, 51, 56-7, 67, 77, 87, 88, 211: auditory, 92
Korsakoff's syndrome, 149

L

Latency, of generic and specific recognition, compared, 64: of primary perception, diminished by reticulocortical inputs, 90: of responses of the thalamic specific relay, association, and nonspecific projection systems, 73 ff.
Language, 47
Lateral geniculate, 67 fn., 73, 74, 221: laminar distribution of visual afferents in, 92: predictability of events in, 229: retinal representa-

tion in, and striate projections of, 225-34

Lateralis posterior (thal.), 42, 57, 58, 60, 73, 74

Lemniscal section, bilateral, effects of, in the cat, 21, 25, 102, 103, 229: bilateral (medial lemniscus) and spinothalamic, in man, 119 fn.

Lemniscus, medial, 223

Life-expectancy, change in human, since Neolithic times, 214, 233

Limbic midbrain region of Nauta, 121-2, 134, 151

Limbic system, 12, 21, 26, 46, 98, 120-37: and emotion, 132: and learned behavior, 134: and neocortex, 134-37 (see also Rhinencephalon and Olfactory systems)

Logical positivism, 224

Lumbricus (annelid worm), activity in isolated cord, 237

Lysergic acid diethylamide (LSD-25), 17

M

Macaque, amygdalectomy in, 144, 179: resections, temporal cortex, 172, 179: sexual behavior in, 5

Man, analogical reflex in, 38: avoidance conditioning and psychic disorders, 148, 187-9, 246: brain of, comparative morphology, 124: civilized urban, and ambivalence, 162: effect of stimulation of the amygdala, 144: as extending effector capability by tools and machinery, 139: "fast" visual pathway in, 238: functional mental disorders seldom genuinely euphoric, 189: life-expectancy of precivilized and modern, 214, 233: nature of the psychological self, 189-90: pleasure-responses obtainable from septum in, 143: Protestant and Catholic psychological types, 162: regression of anterodorsal hippocampus, and medial and dorsal anterior thalamic nuclei in, 150: seizures of the amygdala in, 241: self-alienation, 190 fn.: thalamic-habenular connections in, 152: as uniquely subject to functional mental disorders, 11, 21, 131, 136, 160

Mammillary body, 122: dorsal and ventral hippocampal projections, 241, 245: and dynamogenic pleasure states, 149, 172: effect of stimulation of, on blood pressure, 150: role in sleep, 150, 244: and seizures of the amygdala, 241

Mammillary peduncle, nucleus of, 122, 150: system of, 98, 122, 124, 176

Mammillo-tegmental tract, 122, 153

Manic-depressive psychosis, negative cast of euphoric phases of, 259: rhinencephalic intervention in, 259

Mass action, tendency toward, in structurally primitive neural systems, 105

Massa intermedia (thal.), and caudate spindling in neocortex, 257

Mathematics, and abstract thought, 223-4

Mean square successive difference statistic, 68 fn.

Medial forebrain bundle, 170: origins, in forebrain, 121, 122, 123: motivational functions of, 99: self-stimulation in, 125

Medial geniculates, neuronal population (monkey), 225

Medulla, adrenal, 197

Medulla oblongata, 101, 111: automatic reflexes, 202

Memory, in avoidance, 10: "basal," 50, 62, 63, 64, 70, 88, 115, 163, 164, 166, 171, 183; reassociation of, in adolescence, 188; neocortical representation of, 219: as conserving improvised forms of behavior, 27: and changes in postsynaptic membrane, 213, 228 ff.: as CR's incapable of extinction, 48-9, 209-11: deficits in, and cortical damage, 36, 44: "emotionally charged," as evoking focal rhinencephalic activity, 134, 242: enzyme-induction theory of, 213: half-life of unreinforced, 208: and hippocampal resection, 169-70: "models" of learned behavior in, 185: nature of, 35-41, 165, 168, 178, 212-16, 228-34: olfactory, 248: "one take" formation of, 170: in *Philanthus triangulum*, 28: primary adaptive functions of, 9, 23, 65: repression, 183 fn.: and reticular "driving," 163: retrieval of, 43: rhinencephalic, 134-5: and RNA, 207, 208, 228: role in instinctive behavior, 4: subcortical "support" in establishment of, in neocortex, 26-8, 43: "temporary," 191-2

Memory-mechanisms, 40: neuronal, 212-16, 228-34: as similar in all parts of neocortex, 67: three types proposed by McCulloch, 28 ff.

Memories, motor, 59, 140, 165, 218

Mental disorders, and avoidance conditioning, 148, 187-9: disintegration of reality-principle processes in, 189: inhibition of pleasure-systems in, 131, 189

Mentation, 146

Metabolism, diurnal cycles, 205

Meta-informational system, in brain, abstract memories as comprising, 48-9, 85, 139: theoretical requirements of, 98

Midbrain, 28, 46, 51, 54, 69, 108, 116, 165, 167, 168, 170, 176, 182, 220: arousal systems of, 145: in habituation, 129: processing of information in, 102: self-stimulation in, 125, 128

Mind, tendency to work in "opposites," 162

Mnemonics, 47

Monoamine oxidase inhibitors, and schizophrenia, 182: and systemic accumulation of norepinephrine, 181

Monkeys, innate fear of snakes in, 252

Motivational-affective states, 32, 33, 53, 80, 81, 115, 126, 136, 165: ambivalent, 162: autonomic and endocrine feedback in, 17: answering effect principle in, 19, 24, 126: circular buildup of, and effector system activity, 156: de-differentiative effects of onset phase of, 91: intrusion, into perceptual processes, 62: "modality," 133: neocortex and, 159: and organization of actions, 247: relation to conditioning and memory-formation, 26-7, 43, 44, 79, 84: relation to levels of non-specific input, 74-5: and secondary and tertiary olfactory systems, 204: subcortical representation, 132

Motivational systems, subcortical, 26, 50, 153: and behavioral plans, 138: horizontal organization, 171: interaction, at onset of arousal, 200: synergic mode of action, 114: tegmental, 99: vertical organization, 170

Motives, basal, 204: distinguished from drives and emotions, 7: frontal cortex and maintenance of, 167

Motor systems, reticular priming of spinal, 108: skeletal, and cerebellum, 153

Multiple convergence mechanism, in neocortex, 75, 80-1, 87, 220 (*see also* Redundancy)

Myelination, as furthering function, and conversely, 220: in intrisic sectors of neocortex, 70: order of, in mammalian CNS, 220

N

Necturus (mud puppy), brain of, 123-4

Neocerebellum, 108

Neocortex, 26, 27, 28, 44, 125, 167, 170, 232 fn.: anatomic and functional relations with rhinencephalon, 134-7, 152: as automatically reinforcing core-activities, 115: as cholinergic, 118 fn., 239: as competing with core for control of the thalamus, 183, 189, 256: dependence of conditioning upon, 100, 154-5, 159, 204: effects of caudate stimulation on, 142: effects of frustration on "intrinsic" activities of, 161: "escaping tendency" of, 51-3, 110, 172: as exerting control over the midbrain RF, 116 fn., 129, 152, 166: extrapolative processes in, 166: factors protecting delicacy of function, 110: functions of bands of large pyramids in, 56, 58, 212-15: hippocampus and maintenance of facilitatory climate in, 143: impairment of posterior sector activity by motivational-affective states, 146: influence of amygdala and hippocampus upon, compared, 151: inhibitory effect of subcortical emergency system on, 197: "intrinsic" activity of, 46-7, 49, 50, 52-3, 81, 86, 110, 114, 118, 119 fn., 139: "irradiation" of information in, 78, 89, 91, 163, 229: laminar distribution of nonspecific fibers in, 216: as localizing its own functions, 77: as mediating habituation, 129: memory-functions of, compared to those of midbrain RF and rhinencephalon, 135: parasensory areas, 57: parts of, as "a-thalamic," 217: as phasically acting system, 105, 109: primordium of, 143: projections to medial habenular nuclei, 121, 152; to septum, 152: in the rat, 234-5: as receiving no information from tonic activating system, 118: receptor functions of, and intelligence, 139: relations between receptor and effector divisions of, 156, 163, 167: reticular "driving," 163: sensitivity to anoxia, 209: several-stage processing of information in, 139: shielding of, from midbrain outputs, 114: similarity in topographic organization, to hippocampal-cingulate system, 175-6: as sorter of invariances, 55: specific inputs as temporally prior to nonspecific, 116: structure, as compared to that of midbrain RF, 99; and *modus operandi*, 54-94: transaction-rates in, 55, 231, 238: variance of unit activity in, during sleep and waking, 198: vertical mode of action, 36

Neopallium, 21, 22, 51, 75, 81, 88, 98: "escaping" tendency, 172: as modulator of rhinencephalic activity, 135: receptor functions of, and intelligence, 139, 179: relations with midbrain RF, 106, 109, 114: similarity in plan of organization, to hippocampal-cingulate system, 175-6

Neurohumors, 178-82: effect of each as dependent on relative concentrations of several, 181: mechanism of release at synapse, 178

Neurons, all-or-none activity, and memory-functions, 36-7: "biasability," 228 ff.: convergence of inputs, and divergence of outputs, in neocortical, 213: "functional inertia" in, 214-15: functions of perikaryon, 212: non-learning, 92: relation between graded and all-or-none activity, 212; of properties to size, 214

Neurotics, automatism and hopelessness in, 201: dominance of pleasure principle in, 188: impaired development of memory-systems in, 188: stratagems of, 188-9, 201

Nonspecific cortex (reptilian), 50

Nonspecific input (neocortical), 42, 51, 54, 60, 65, 67, 74-5, 79, 85, 90, 114 fn., 166, 183: de-differentiative effects of, 163, 185, 229: and extrinsic sector activity, 183: and frontal system, 164: as impairing neocortical function, 118, 161: high levels of, and cortical inhibition, 182: hippocampal gating of, 40, 143, 169: and intrinsic sector activity, 184: as patterned by cortico-thalamic feedback, 86, 239: and posterior intrinsic sector activity, 197: three-part spectrum of, 162

Nonspecific system, tonic and phasic

280 / THE PHYSICAL FOUNDATIONS OF THE PSYCHE

divisions, 111-14: functional competition between, 113: of midbrain, as ergotropic, and of thalamus, as trophotropic, 114
Normal survival system, 16, 45, 114, 126: comparative morphology, 143: and emergency system, compared, 18, 143: and hippocampus, 245: and mammillary body, 149-50: and *pallium basale,* 173: relationship to emergency system, 174, 197: and receptor divisions of the CNS, 142
Norepinephrine, and epinephrine, effect on nerve, compared, 180, 243; effect on cerebral blood turnover, 243: and ganglionic transmission, 180: as reward system neurotransmitter, 180: systemic accumulation and release of, 181
"No-solution problem," 161, 197
Novel events, perturbing effect of, 39

O

"Obstinate progression," and interpeduncular lesions, in cats, 154
Occipital lobe, results of massive subtotal damage, in man, 71-2, 221
Odors, aversive reactions to, intensity and persistence of, 137, 242; tendency to become generalized, 242
Oedipus complex, 6, 195-6
Olfacto-habenulo-interpeduncular system, 121, 152-60: in *Amblystoma,* 152: as bringing reticulomotor system under rhinencephalic and neocortical control, 152, 179: in mammals, 152: and mammillo-tegmental system, compared, 153: plan of, 153: and rhinencephalic motivational systems, 171
Olfactory bulb, 93, 120, 215: granular layer, 215: mitral cells, 92, 215: "partitioning" in, 215: reticular gating in, 116, 215: tufted cells, 92, 215: virtual generators of slow potentials in, 215
Olfactory lobe, 123

Olfactory phobic responses, persistence of, 137, 242
Olfactory system (primary, secondary, and tertiary, of Pribram and Kruger), 10, 46 fn., 106, 120-37: medial parolfactory area, 121: and motivational-affective states, 204: slight variation of, in mammalian evolution, 123, 133: *secondary,* 132, 168, 176; effector functions, 143 ff., 179; extensions of, in neocortex, 149, 175; functional relation to tertiary system, 145 ff.; high- and low-energy divisions, 244; nonolfactory functions of, 136-7, 204; primordium, 144, 173; as regulative of thought, 177: *tertiary,* 153, 155, 232 fn.; as constitutive of thought, 176; effector and receptor divisions, 176; functions of, 143 ff.; primordium of, 144, 173; and receptor processes, 173, 179; relation to secondary system, 145
Olfactory tract, intermediate, 121: lateral, 120: medial, 121
Olfactory tubercle, 120, 121
Optic radiation, 220, 236
Optic tract, 121, 236: basal, 157, 221, 238
Orbital cortex, 140, 144, 149, 152: area 13, pp. 145, 146, 244: area 14, p. 244: and ferocity, 148: electrocoagulation of midventral quadrant, in depressives, 148, 160: projections to dorsomedialis, 219: and temporal pole, 220
Orgasm, 19, 127, 146
Orienting reflex, in "simple" schizophrenia, 198: as subcortical release phenomenon, 33-4: tonic and phasic forms, 112, 207
Ovulation, from stimulation of the medial amygdala, 144, 240

P

Pallium basale, 123: functions of, 173
Pallium marginale, 123: functions of, 173

Paracentral lobule, 149
Paracentralis (thal.), 112
Parakoniocortex, 40, 51, 56-7, 77, 83, 87, 252: "collecting" functions of, 88
Parasympathetic system, connections with sympathetic, 202: hypothalamic representation, 203: and onset of arousal, 141-2: and "reward," 16, 108: and sexual or rage states, 18, 127
Parsimony, principle of, as shown in functions of the autonomic and compound olfactory systems, 204-5
Partitioning, 57, 62, 72, 75, 83, 88, 117, 141, 183, 184, 221: "extrapolative," 72 fn., 87 fn. (*see also* Attention)
Pecking order status, and amygdalectomy, 144
Penis, erection, and anterior cingulate stimulation, 147: snake symbolism, 252
Perception, acuity of primary, and subcortical activity, 62: assortment of, prior to conscious awareness, 64: of novelties, 38: sequels to primary, 73: sequence of events in, and in thought, compared, 222-3
Periaqueductal grey, 122, 123: effect of lesions to, 155: and nonspecific activation, 155 fn., 256
Periextrinsic cortex, 44 fn., 76, 91, 229, 252: and "complex" retinal fields, 227
Peristriate cortex, 77
Periventricular grey, 105: and encephalitis lethargica, 155: and nonspecific activation, 155 fn.
Peromyscus (deermouse), 205
Phasic output (of neural subsystems), functions of, 103-4: as equivalent to information transmitted, 105
Phenacetylurea, 159
Phosphocreatine, laminar distribution in rat neocortex, 63, 68, 90, 213, 216
Pilocarpine, 180

Plans, 251
Pleasure principle, 6-7, 46, 167: dominance, in neurosis, 188: and dreams, 251: as mediating activity from the bottom of neocortex up, 49: processes as figuring in verbal thinking, 85-6
Pleasure-states, composite nature of, 127: and rhinencephalic receptor functions, 172-3 (*see also* Reward)
Pons, 106, 108: emergence of, in mammals, 206
Posterior commissure, 112
Posterior horn, cortical and subcortical projections to, 101: nucleus proprius of, 101
Postinhibitory rebound, 24, 77, 145, 197, 200: of rage-response, following cerebellar stimulation, 202: in spinal motor reflexes, 201
Postsynaptic membrane, 178, 180: changes in, and memory, 213 ff., 228
Postsynaptic potentials, 178
Postural reflexes, 107
Prägnanz, 87
Precuneus, 220
Prepyriform cortex, 60, 120: rhythmic activity in, in attention, 198
Pretectum, 112
Primary processes, *see* Pleasure principle
Projection (Freudian), 30
Propriospinal neurons, distribution of cortical and subcortical fibers to, 101
Psychic blindness, and parastriate damage, 223
Psychoanalysis, 210-11
Psychomotor seizure, 159: following stimulation of the amygdala, 240: and unilateral removal, temporal pole, 243
Psychotics, breakdown of reality-principle processes in, 189: paranoid, and rage-rebound, 149
Ptarmigan, 34
Pulvinar, 31, 42, 58, 60, 61, 77, 217, 219-21
Punishment, states of, as related to

subcortical emergency systems, 16, 114-15, 128, 155
Punishment systems, 117: as adrenergic, 108
Putamen, 108: and neocortical seizures, 242
Pyramidal outflow, to gracile and cuneate nuclei, 100: as superimposed on reticulomotor, 108
Pyramidal system, 109, 158
Pyramidal tract, projections to midbrain RF, 100-1
Pyriform cortex, primordium, in *Amblystoma,* 124

R

Rage, 20, 33, 115, 127, 148, 163: and amygdalectomy, 144: mixed autonomic signs in, 174: onset phase, 145: and perifornical region, hypothalamus, 155: psychological effects of intense, 141, 146: rhinencephalic mechanisms in, 245: and rhythmic movements, 237
Rat, neocortex of, 234-5
Rational conscious "I" (self), 53, 89, 184, 188: disintegration in psychoses, 189: nature of, and sense of inner division, 189-90
Rationalization, 27, 45-6, 167: and dream-work, 250
Reality-principle processes, 7, 19, 23, 26, 27, 28, 46, 52, 53, 72, 85, 86, 89, 164, 165-7, 247, 251: breakdown of, and psychosis, 189: disruption of, by motivational-affective states, 150: driving of, by subcortical emergency system, 149: as mediated by abstract memories, 66: as mediated from the top of neocortex down, 49, 54, 84 fn.: underdevelopment of, and psychic disorders, 148, and fn.
Recognition, two-stage perceptual ("generic" and "specific"), 29-31, 64, 73, 74: generic, 39: specific, 72, 81, 157, 184
Recruitment, 111, 113, 118, 182, 197, 258

Redundancy, as compensating for unreliability of components of nervenets, 90, 212: in distribution of lateral geniculate fibers in striate vertical columns, 230: as favoring indeterminacy in the central processing of information, 229: in frontal system, 164: in neocortex, 75, 80-1, 87: on periphery, 92
Reflexes, conditioned, "consolidation" of, 137 fn.; nature of, 166; resistance of olfactory to extinction, 137: unconditioned, latency of spinal, 157 fn.; visual, 157
Repression, and avoidance, 10: and caudate nucleus, 255: and dreams, 250, 252: and extinction, 185: mechanism of, 183 ff.: "return of the repressed," 186; in psychoanalysis, 210; in suicide or self-mutilation, 189: and self-esteem, 209: subcortical deadlock in, 186-7
Regarding (attending) reaction, 118 fn., 141 fn.: in alerting, 174: in *Amblystoma,* 238: caudate and VA in, 174 fn., 255
Reinforcement, internal, or circular, 39, 155, 170
Reptiles, brain, 133: nonolfactory cortex, 143, 176
Reserpine, and release of bound norepinephrine, 181
Reticular (ascending) activating system, 97, 236: adrenergic and cholinergic subdivisions, 239: dependence of neocortex upon, for tonic maintenance, 105: as distinct from thalamic AS, 111, 114, 115: dorsal and ventral components, 111, 122, 238: and hippocampus, 176: and tonic immobility, 196
Reticular "closure," 26, 134: and extinction, 242
Reticular formation, medullary, adrenergic and cholinergic divisions, 236: *n. reticularis gigantocellularis,* 122 fn. (*see also* tegmentum, medullary)

Reticular formation, mesencephalic, 10, 25, 26, 69, 79, 91, 97-119, 134, 156, 182, 232 fn.: adrenergic and cholinergic divisions, 236: as basal motor system, 158: and caudate-VA system, compared, 255: and central integration, 103, 119: and compound olfactory system, 106, 136: extrathalamic cortical projections, 50: "fast" visual path to, 238: fine-structure, 99, 157: formation of temporary connections in, 190: and habituation, 129: and hippocampus, 169: inhibitory effect on neocortex, 142: latency of responses, as compared to specific system, 221: motor representation in, 107: and neopallium, 106, 109, 206: and olfacto-habenulo-interpeduncular system, 152, 179: pyramidal projections to, 101: responses to peripheral stimulation, 100, 157: "reward" and "punishment" systems in, 99, 107-8, 128, 131: rostrally and caudally directed outputs, 107, 142 fn.: somatotopic organization in, 100: stimulation of, and arrest, temporal lobe unit activity, 117; and caudate spindling, neocortex, 254; and latency, sense-reception, neocortex, 116: tonic and phasic components, rostral output, 114, 116, 118: trace-formation in, 135 (see also tegmentum, midbrain)

Reticular formation, pontine, adrenergic and cholinergic divisions, 236: ascending facilitatory (dorsal) and inhibitory (ventral) divisions, 236, 239, 253: ventral and caudate-VA as ascending inhibitory system, 256

Reticular nucleus (thal.), cortical projections, 218, 222

Reticulocortical input, and cortical "driving," 184: as disruptive neocortical activity, 114: extrathalamic, 50: inhibitory, 142, 184, 199: and memory-formation, 32: and "noise," 183: and striate cortical responses to light, 238: supportive and controlling action, 103

Reticulospinal projections, 108, 109: arising in *n. reticularis gigantocellularis,* 122 fn.

Retina, ganglion cells, 92: mode of representation in, lateral geniculate and striate cortex, 225-34: predictability of neuronal events in, 229: "predictive" responses of, 72 fn.

Reuniens (thal.), 112

Reverberatory (thalamocortical) circuits, 29, 35, 39, 40, 69: cortico-subcortical, 79: evidence for, 219

Reward, states of, as related to subcortical normal survival systems, 16, 27, 50, 114-15, 127-8, 155: terminal, and effectiveness of CR's, 160, 186

Reward systems, 126, 129, 130: as cholinergic, 108: in "freezing" reactions, 246: high- and low-energy subdivisions, 244: inhibition of, in human mental disorders, 131: and norepinephrine, 180: and rhythmic movements, 236-7, 240: thalamic reticularis as component of, 114

Rhinencephalon, 12, 28, 46 fn., 51, 116, 131, 156, 165, 170: absence of mosaic of topographical representation in, 132: anatomical and functional relations, with neocortex, 134-7: comparative morphology and primitive functions, 143 ff., 173-4: dual nature of responses obtained from, 132-3: and extinction of CR's, 161: and frontal cortex, 164, 167: generalized (non-olfactory) functions of, 136-7: and the id, 190 fn.: and innate responses, 134: memory-functions of, 135, 247-8: motivational-affective functions of, 142, 172 ff.: as neocortical dependency, 136: resections of, and mental illness, 160: reward and punishment in, 125-8: as second-string brain in mammals, 160: self-stimulation in, 125: stability of form throughout

mammalian evolution, 211: subordinate role in higher mammals, 135
Rhombic brain, 202, 203
Rhomboidens (thal.), 112
Rhythmic movements, 107: and anticholinergic drugs, 237: and cholinergic midbrain system, 145: and core reward systems, 236-7, 240
Righting reactions, 107
RNA (ribonucleic acid), and memory-formation, 207, 208, 213, 228

S

Salamander, relative development of effector and receptor functions in, 139, 142
Satiety, and medial hypothalamus, 121, 181
Schizophrenia, inextinguishability of orienting reflex in "simple," 198: neuronal changes in neocortex in, 258: septal dysfunction in, 182, 257: taraxein hypothesis, 257
Scopolamine, 180
Scorpion (*Scorpio maurus*), 22
Scotties, impairment of behavior by early sensory restriction, 34, 119, 207
Secondary processes, *see* Reality principle
Seizures, cortico-subcortical paths followed by, 208, 242: hippocampal, and caudate spindling, precruciate cortex, 254: proneness to, of various rhinencephalic structures, 246: subcortical, routes of propagation, 241
Selachian fish, 123, 173
Self-image, and suicide, 188-9
Self-stimulation, factors determining, 125-9: as maximal in areas showing convergence of reward and punishment systems, 128, 130: modified procedure, and resulting changes in size of reward and punishment areas, 130: rates, in anterior hypothalamus, 125; in mammillary body, 125; in medial forebrain bundle, 125; in posterior hypothalamus, 125; in preoptic region, 125; in rhinencephalic cortex, 125; in septal region, 128
Sensory deprivation, 34, 36, 207: subcortical release in, 213
Sensory fixation, and entorhinal ablation, 239: hyperorality accompanying, 239: and perifornical region, 117, 238
Septum, 61, 69, 79, 80, 111, 116, 120, 121, 170; as area of convergence, reward and punishment systems, 128, 143: caudate spindling in, 253: dysfunction, and schizophrenia, 182, 257: and interpeduncular system, 152 ff.: islands of Calleja in, 216: primordium, in *Amblystoma*, 124: projections to hippocampus, 143: projections to medial nn. of, 123: and seizures of the amygdala, 241, 245: and seizures of the dorsal and ventral hippocampus, 245: seizure-proneness, 246: *n. septalis dorsalis*, 152, 245: stimulation of, as deferring and enhancing responses to noxious stimuli, 240: and "strip" regions, 254: tegmental projections of, 121-22
Serotonin, 17, 180, 181: as reducing cholinesterase activity, 181
Sexual excitement, 127: bradycardia at onset of, in man, 141: onset phase of, 145, 163: psychological effects of intense, 141, 146: and rhythmic movements, 237
Sexual representation, in *pallium basale*, 173: in rhinencephalon (man), 177: in septal-hippocampal complex, 143
Sleep, 253: rhombencephalic, 104, 162, 253, 256: telencephalic, 104
Speech, 60: linear and non-linear processes in, 153
Spinal system, innate rhythmic slow-potential activity in, 237
Split-brain preparations, 69, 101-2, 239: interhemispheric transfer of visual learning in, 205-6, 220
Spreading depression (of Leão), hippocampal, 241

Stellate cells, 55
Stimulus generalization, 33, 64, 141, 187
Strata sagittalia, 220
Stresses, emergency responses as, 205: fear-states as, 18
Stria medullaris, 121
Striate cortex, 73: avian, 205, 211: common axis-orientations of "simple" fields in, 228: *modus operandi,* 225-34: predictability of neuronal events in, 229: response of units to "mild" reticular stimulation, 238: "simple" and "complex" retinal fields in, 225 ff.: vertical columns, 226
Striatum, *see* Corpus striatum
Strio-amygdaloid complex, 120 fn., 179
Subcallosal gyrus, as terminus, medial olfactory tract, and origin, medial forebrain bundle, 121
Subiculum, 220
Sublimation, critique of Freudian concept of, 176-7, 250
Substantia gelatinosa, 111
Substantia nigra, 107
Subthalamus, 98: and seizures of the amygdala, 241
Suicide, 189
Superior cervical ganglion, 17
Superior colliculus, 101
Suprasylvian gyrus (cat), 73
Survival responses, biological rationale of, 175
Sylvian fissure, 247
Sympathetic system, 127, 197: connections with parasympathetic, 202: and fear-states, 18, 144: hypothalamic representation, 203: preganglionic fibers of, to adrenal medulla (man) 197: and "punishment," 16, 108 (*see also* Autonomic system, Superior cervical ganglion)
Synapses, axodendritic, in cortical layer I, 216; in midbrain RF, 157: axosomatic, 56; nonspecific, in layer VI, 166: cholinergic and adrenergic in reticular formation, 107: limiting information capacity of, 35: synaptic cleft, 178: synaptic transmission, 212: synaptic vesicles, 178, 212

T

Tachycardia, in primary fear responses, 197
Tadpole, activity in isolated cord of, 237
Taraxein, 257
Tectum, 25, 153, 159
Tegmentum, medullary, adrenergic and cholinergic divisions of, 236: distribution of fibers of, to lower cord, 101, 109
Tegmentum, midbrain, 101, 105: arousal from lateral, 125, 154: enhancement of trigeminal evoked potentials, following destruction of, 248: lesions to ventral, as producing tremor, 107: medial and lateral regions, and waking, 155: projections from interpeduncular nucleus, 122, 152: projections from mammillary body, 122: and seizures of the amygdala, 241: stimulation of, and hippocampal theta activity, 249: ventral and dorsomedial as reward and punishment divisions (rat), 99, 125, 154, 236
Temporary connections, in neocortex, 190, 229
Temporal lobe, 44, 77: anterior, 131, 140, 144; and seizures, amygdala, 241: bilateral inferotemporal resection, and visual discrimination, 220: blocking of unit activity in, by midbrain stimulation, 117: "experiential" responses from stimulation of, 208: inferior gyrus, 71 fn., 172; lack of commissural fibers, 113, 222: lateral region, results of stimulation, 99: lesions, and behavior, 138: middle gyrus, 71 fn., 172, 222: perforant pathway, 152, 169: pitch-discrimination, following bilateral removal, 206: propagation of seizures from,

242: superior gyrus, 172; lack of commissural fibers, 113, 222: temporal pole, 80, 144, 172, 243; and anterodorsal hippocampus, 176; and orbit, 220: topographic representation of affect in, 79-80

Tetrahymena geleii S, 212

Thalamic reticularis, 54, 69, 108, 118, 156, 161, 163, 164, 165, 175 fn., 182, 183, 190: action upon midbrain RF, 112, 115: as cholinergic, 112, 114, 118 fn.: cortical projections, intralaminar nn., 248: as dependency of neocortex, 113-4: labile mode of projection, 77; and "useful noise," 258: neocortical feedback to, 86, 116, 118 fn., 175 fn., 239: as part of reward system, 114: projections from ventral tegmental area of Tsai, 123

Thalamus (dorsal), 73, 76, 90, 98, 111, 129, 133, 153, 168, 182: and amygdaloid seizure, 241: anterior nuclei, anteroventralis and cingulate area 23, p. 244; and frontal system, 164; regression of medial and dorsal in primates, 149, 150: mesial, and cingulate spindling in neocortex, 257: nonspecific projection system of, 17, 26, 41 fn., 58, 62, 65, 78, 79, 80, 118, 182, 206; de-differentiative action, 91; laminar distribution of cortical fibers, 216, 219; ventral component of, 111: posterior, 159: reticular nucleus of ventral, 110, 111: "shell" and "core" subdivisions, 151, 206: tonotopic organization in, 206: specific projection system of, 32, 51, 60, 61, 64, 65, 71, 77, 78, 80, 91, 117, 151, 238

Theta activity, hippocampal, 61, 121, 123: and caudate spindling, precruciate cortex, 254: and tegmental stimulation, 249

Thought, 89: and abstract memories, 70, 86 ff.: as anti-entropic, 90: as disorganized by high levels of nonspecific input, 90, 117: effect of fear on, 183: and frontal intrinsic cortex, 168: as function of outer laminae, neocortex, 63, 166-7: mechanism of obsessional, 167: and plexiform layer, 190: as producing emotion, and conversely, 209: and secondary and tertiary olfactory systems, 176-7, 250: sequence of events in, in neocortex, 222

"Thing" memories, 29-31, 40, 41, 42 ff., 53, 55, 58, 64, 65, 66, 70-94, 117, 129, 223, 230: and CR's, 160, 210: generalized components of, 92: interlinked by abstract memories, 49, 251: loci of representation less predictable than those of "type" memories, 79: and orienting reflex, 34: and Scoville-Milner operation, 170: and sensory deprivation, 34: and stimulus generalization, 33: structure of, 35, 44, 216: and "type" memories, compared, 31, 32: two modes of constellation and retrieval, 45 ff., 79

Threat display, as resembling sexual, in birds and scorpions, 22

Tonic immobility, 17, 115, 196, 200

Tonic output, of neural systems, functions of, 103-4

Tract of Clark and Boggon, 151, 164, 241

Transcortical reflex, 35, 70, 206

Transmarginal inhibition, 185 fn.

Trigeminal nerve, 248

Trophotropic system, 114: neurohumors of, 181 (*see also* Reward systems)

"Type" memories, 29-31, 55, 57, 64, 65, 66, 70-94, 119 fn., 168: as composed of mosaics of vertical columns, 37, 39-41, 42, 44, 51: and data of Hubel and Wiesel, 231: "elaborated type" memories, 83, 88; in CR's, 187; in dreams, 252; in effector outflows, 223; and perceptual gestalten, 87; in thought, 222: as intervening between sensory input and system mediating conscious awareness,

217: and orienting reflex, 34: reformation of visual, after occipital damage (man), 221: and "thing" memories compared, 31, 32: and sensory deprivation, 34: and stimulus generalization, 33, 141, 187: structure of, 35

U

Uncinate fasciculus, 220
Unconscious, logic of the, 27
Uncus, 170, 243
Universals, 233

V

Vacuum reactions, 15 fn.
Vagus, sympathetic fibers to (monkey), 202
Variance (of unit activity), 55, 59: and cortical depth, 63: predicted areal and laminar differences in, in neocortex, 90
Ventral tegmental area of Tsai, 123
Ventralis anterior (thal.), 111, 222: and avoidance, 243-4: and caudate spindling, 254: and conditioned behavior (cats) 254-5: inhibitory functions, 176 fn., 239, 248: and regarding reaction, 174 fn.
Ventralis lateralis (thal.), 58, 108
Ventro-oralis posterior (thal.), 108
Vision, "fast" subcortical path, in man, 238: mechanisms underlying, 225-34: perception of angles, 227

W

Wasp (*Philanthus triangulum*), 28
Wit, 146
Words, defects, as medium of thought 85-6: as "thing" memories, 85
Writing, 60

Z

Zeigarnik effect, 209
Zona incerta (hypothal.), 111, 238
Zona intermedia (spinal homologue, lateral tegmentum), 101, 105